VICEROYS

VICEROYS

The Creation of the British

CHRISTOPHER LEE

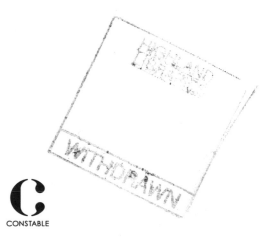

C

CONSTABLE

First published in Great Britain in 2018 by Constable

1 3 5 7 9 10 8 6 4 2

A CIP catalogue record for this book
is available from the British Library.

ISBN (hardback): 978-1-47212-475-3
ISBN (trade paperback): 978-1-47212-474-6

Typeset in Electra LT by Hewer Text UK Ltd, Edinburgh
Printed and bound in Great Britain by Clays Ltd, Elcograf S.p.A.

Papers used by Constable are from well-managed
forests and other responsible sources.

Constable
An imprint of
Little, Brown Book Group
Carmelite House
50 Victoria Embankment
London EC4Y 0DZ

An Hachette UK Company
www.hachette.co.uk

www.littlebrown.co.uk

To Aggie
Vicereine who fed an elephant

CONTENTS

VICEROYS

1856–1862	The Viscount Canning
1862–1863	The Earl of Elgin
1863–1863 (Acting)	Sir Robert Napier
1863–1863 (Acting)	Sir William Denison
1864–1869	Sir John Lawrence
1869–1872	The Earl of Mayo
1872–1872 (Acting)	Sir John Strachey
1872–1872 (Acting)	The Lord Napier
1872–1876	The Lord Northbrook
1876–1880	The Lord Lytton
1880–1884	The Marquess of Ripon
1884–1888	The Earl of Dufferin
1888–1894	The Marquess of Lansdowne
1894–1899	The Earl of Elgin
1899–1905	The Lord Curzon
1905–1911	The Earl of Minto
1911–1916	The Lord Hardinge
1916–1921	The Lord Chelmsford
1921–1926	The Earl of Reading
1926–1931	The Lord Irwin
1931–1936	The Earl of Willingdon

INTRODUCTION

There was never an empire like the British Empire, according to the senior history tutor at school, even while the Empire (always an upper-case E on the blackboard) was being dismantled. The Spanish under the Habsburgs and then under the Bourbons by the 1700s was the largest empire in the world. It was the Spanish and not the British Empire about which it was said that the sun never sets. It began in the early sixteenth century and started its decline in the nineteenth century, particularly after the Spanish American war of independence. The British Empire kept going.

The Spanish Empire spread from the Americas, north and south, Asia, the Pacific and the Caribbean. It returned its last colonies to their African people in 1976. The Catholic Monarchy was called the first European state. A dozen languages were spoken and understood and the second most understood language in the world, Spanish, survived. The other modern empires had none of the scope nor history of the British and the Spanish.[1]

There were three common aspects of the British and
Spaniards: first, when their empire building began both had
long unbroken histories of monarchy. Athelstan was recognised as King of not just the English, but King of England in
926. Charles 1 in 1516 became the first Spanish monarch.
They had a constant identity and did not slide through ever-
moving borders under more powerful cultures and ambitions.
Secondly, both nations had coastlines. Spain was part of the
Iberian Peninsula and Britain was an island state; thus both
were easier to defend compared with the inland European
states. Most importantly, both had constant access to the way
of the rest of the world, even the unknown – the sea. You
cannot have an empire unless you have a coastline. After the
nineteenth century, did countries build empires in their own
continents – unless you count the Warsaw Pact? A landlocked
nation cannot guarantee to reach its empire to supply it, bring
back its spoils or defend it.

It was no coincidence that the most brilliant royal school of
navigation that would make that access possible was the other
Iberian monarch, Infante Dom Henrique, o Navegador,
Prince Henry the Navigator of Portugal.[2] Henry was further
south; therefore the rest of the world was closer. He knew for
sure that Africa was there and it was bigger than others thought.
He wanted to search for African gold and the legendary Prester
John. Whatever his ambitions, Prince John created the lines
and angles that made possible the great tracks that gave us the
Age of Discovery. All that was needed were the means to follow
them.

The British were slow to build the ships that had the distance
and strength to follow rough waters; when they did a vessel was
no more than the size of a small suburban back garden.
Columbus's largest and most famous ship, the *Santa Maria,*

was no more than fifty feet – the typical size of a private yacht on a mooring at Cowes today. Drake's *Golden Hind*, in which he circumnavigated the globe,[3] was barely one hundred feet. Once the ships were built and the basic navigation was good enough, the British followed the Dutch south then east into the Indian Ocean. They went in search of pepper and silk. They went to buy; they stayed to trade, then live. Thus the British Empire was conceived. It was a conception of opportunity, not of determination. The British went first to where the Dutch were, the East Indies, then to India where the Portuguese were, along with the silks that they could trade anywhere. They stayed because the Mughal needed them to protect himself from the Portuguese; the longer they stayed the more money they made and the more they needed the paraphernalia to protect their interests. Thus the uneasy commercial pregnancy produced an almost healthy birth. The British wanted to stay and to expand in India and they fought the Portuguese and particularly the French so to do. But this was the act of a small offshore island people attempting to create an empire, to become *Novi Romani*. The British in the Caribbean fought to defend their interests against, for example, late-eighteenth-century France. In India, there were battles that sent the French packing, but even then there was an understanding that when the two countries were at war, their trading entities in India should not be.

The coming about of the British Empire to outlive even the much admired Spanish possessions, the direction and influence it gave on British contemporary history and the sheer Kiplingesque theatre of it all have bewitched schoolchildren for generations

At the centrepiece of my personal curiosity has been the viceroys. I once taught that nineteenth-century India was what the British did with aristocrats who neither were not quite Whigs nor hunted south of the Thames. It was a feeble, spur-of-the-moment aside in contemporary history supervision because today the social distinction of hunting north but certainly not south of the Thames is no longer understood by those who hunt for an Upper Second. Here then one of the first distinctions when discussing the rights and wrongs of British colonial history. Never begin the debate from our own times. They were caretakers until a truly great but split nation was ready to go her own way and the British accepted that it did not want to be there, could not govern and had never really wanted to after the Sepoy Rebellion. Victoria liked India and learned Urdu and wrote in Hindustani to her Indian munshi, her clerk, Abdul Karim – which said it all.

The importance of understanding the raj, that period of history from post-Mutiny to 1947, is that it began very differently in the early 1600s. The British never went to the east, never mind India, to conquer the subcontinent. Apart from the motive of trade, the British were not a world power; there was no such nation anywhere. Certainly, the British were, in modern speak, punching above their weight, but they had no marauding galleons that put nations to fright, nor armies that trampled across even the nearest continent. They were offshore traders who might have been very different if the Normans had not arrived. The British were also quick learners, as are any competent corsairs. If the Norman Conquest had failed, the whole north-east of England would have survived and the Saxon development of trade into north Europe would have expanded – partly as a consequence of having to avoid William in his continental ambitions. Moreover, the deployment of a protective port-by-port fleet along the English Channel would have led to an earlier trade in the Iberian Peninsula and the employment of privateers into the Saxon fleet with knowledge of the African coast as far south as the Bay of Benin.

The Mughals were not looking for three or four west European nations to settle in, aggressively, to trade or steal. The Mughals had long lived with the traditional threat from the interiors of Asia, whence they had themselves come. Also, India was the subcontinent under threat. The British did not land and take over. Mughal India was fractured. It had princes who protected themselves from insiders rather than outsiders and it manufactured and traded separately. One consequence of the way India was laid out into princely states when the British arrived was the failure to see how they could ever trade as one developing nation. India did not approach that state until well into the nineteenth century. Through the English East India Company, the British gradual reign in India – and the slipping away of the Mughal Empire – coincided with the Civil War in England and the emergence of a political system rather than rule by cohorts of similar persuasion. When the East India Company was testing its full strength, a form of government and parliament in London had developed and was strong enough to produce recognised legislation to somewhat restrict the way the Company traded. The East India Company grew in company with the British system of parliamentary and then political democracy. They were rarely out of step.

The raj was the only moment of complete empire for the British and it is the only time, lasting not even a century, that the history of the British century has been brought to wider audiences. The twenty viceroys each carried glamorous cloaks. However, there is another aspect that must have some credence: as this story uncovered the times from 1858 to 1947, it has also revealed the identity of the British as seen by people elsewhere in the world and still, without them realising, the British themselves. Modern British identity was moulded during the raj, never earlier and certainly not later.

With the blessing of an astonishingly patient editor, Andreas Campomar, and an agent who would have been a fine viceroy (although certainly not a Curzon), Christopher Sinclair-Stevenson, I was allowed to see if I was right about the viceroys, none of whom, incidentally, ever hunted south of the Thames. Heartfelt thanks for enviable proof-reading by Jacqui Lewis.

CHAPTER I

IN THE BEGINNING

The story of the British viceroys of India and thus the raj begins in 1858 during the Indian Mutiny and ends in 1947 with the partition of the subcontinent into two countries; with mainly Muslims in newly created Pakistan and mainly Hindus in India, who before the year was out would be at war with each other.

The longer story – of the British in India – comes in three stages: from the early 1600s to the first governor of the presidency of Fort William (Bengal), Warren Hastings in 1774; from Hastings to 1828 and Lord William Bentinck, the first governor general of India, to the Sepoy Rebellion in 1857; from Canning, the first viceroy, to Mountbatten, the last British viceroy. Raj means rule and the only period when India was *directly* ruled by the British was 1858 to 1947; therefore that period is the British raj.

The first question is why did the British go to India at all? The second question is why did it take so long to get there?

The first answer is that they failed to establish themselves in the Java spices and silk trade but were given permission by the

Mughal Emperor to trade in India. They were late getting there because they were facing the other way: slave trading from the Gulf of Benin to the Caribbean; pirateering bullion from Spanish galleons out of Central America and curiously, considering the maritime reputation of the British, they feared piracy themselves, had limited long-haul shipbuilding expertise and were not entirely sure how to get to the East Indies by sea.

How could they not be sure? Atlantic crossings were simple navigation: across on the trade winds and back via the Gulf Stream. But the voyage that opened the east to north Europeans was much harder and no one had tried it until Vasco da Gama found a way around the Cape of Good Hope into the Indian Ocean in 1497; even then the charts were kept as secret as an alchemist's dream. There were few secrets about the prizes to be made.

Spices and gay cloths had come overland for centuries. The British had bought and traded them in the markets of the Levant and the ports and cities of western Europe, Antwerp and Venice. They had done so since the tenth century, so the East Indies and spices were no mystery. The voyage to the East Indies, however, was almost entirely in uncharted waters for the British, who had limited navigation instruments and experience sailing in square-riggers in the prevailing monsoons of the Indian Ocean. Moreover, there was little certainty about what was to be found along the African eastern seaboard. Where could they put in for weather, repairs or worse? Little wonder that it was not until the end of the sixteenth century that a British merchant venture could be funded, and find sailing masters and vessels and crews. Even then, it was only after the destruction of the Spanish Armada in 1588 that investors and captains would accept the risk of being attacked by Spanish corsairs and most of all could convince the monarch, Elizabeth

I, to sign a proclamation that effectively said that the small fleet sailed on her behalf and therefore the sailors had sole rights to her protection. It was the sixteenth-century mercantile version of a royal monopoly voyage. It would run for more than two centuries.

The commodore of the flotilla carried letters patent from Queen Elizabeth I to say that whomsoever came across these brave merchants should know that they represented the wishes and commercial pleasure of the great Queen of England. Most of the eastern traders had never heard of the great Queen, although the mainly Dutch and Portuguese traders in the East Indies had.

'ELIZABETH, by the Grace of God, Queen of England, France, and Ireland, Defender of the Faith & co. To all our officers, ministers, and subjects, and to all other people, as well within this our realm of England as elsewhere, under our obedience and jurisdiction, or otherwise, unto whom these our Letters Patents shall be seen, showed, or read, greeting. Whereas our most dear and loving Cousin, George, Earl of Cumberland, and our well-beloved subjects . . . and others . . . they, at their own adventures, costs, and charges, as well for the honour of this our realm of England, as for the increase of our navigation, and advancement of trade of merchandize, within our said realms and the dominions of the same, might adventure and set forth one or more voyages, with convenient number of ships and pinnaces, by way of traffic and merchandize to the East Indies, in the countries and parts of Asia and Africa and to as many of the islands, ports and cities, towns and places, thereabouts, as where trade and traffic may by all likelihood be discovered, established or had; divers of which countries, and. many of the islands, cities and ports, thereof, have

long since been discovered by others of our subjects, albeit not
frequented in trade of merchandize.'[1]

A royal proclamation, directed at home to those who would
also try to crash the new trade and should not, was not enough
to assure the success of the English venture, but the English
believed that they would be able to trade because there was
enough for everyone and because the English assumed something of a right to access in the world, a world most of which
had lain undiscovered for the Elizabethan, in spite of tales and
the celebrity of circumnavigators such as Sir Francis Drake
(1540–1596). The importance of the moment was that even
though the British did not have supremacy at sea they had a
new treaty of sorts with the Spanish that promised fleets would
be left alone – for the moment. Captains were encouraged to
take the risk and the men had few options; the riches were
tempting enough and the sailing masters only sailed for riches.
Sixteenth-century masters rarely sailed for adventure. They
sailed for wealth – that instinct of any empire-building including Britain's. There were and would continue to be fortunes in
spices and later exotic teas and pepper, even more so than the
other bedrock of the empire, sugar. So their navigators called
them the Spice Islands and the Sugar Islands.

The financial power of pepper was enough for it to be a
form of currency. Its earliest importance can be sensed by the
fact that the second oldest livery company in the City of
London is The Grocers, who evolved from the Guild of
Pepperers and were incorporated in the twelfth century. The
Pepperers dealt in huge – gross – quantities. Gross became the
common trading term and gross became Grocers. Spices and
pepper had been traded in London for centuries. In the 1400s,
the nutmeg, pepper, cloves and mace spice trade alone coming

through the Venetian market was recorded in millions of pounds weight. By then western Europe was established as the biggest mixed-nation market because more people could justify spending (as opposed to simply having the money) on the imports from the Far East.

Gold and silver imports from the Americas had much influence on wealth patterns; the desire to buy more from what the East Indies had to offer grew and the trading companies were able to organise purchasing and transportation on an increasingly efficient scale. By the 1500s the eastern markets were never to shrink. There was an expanding wealthy class in western Europe and to pamper this wider society traders were better organised, investors were spreading their interests and better, bigger, faster and safer ships increased the demand and supply of eastern goods. A historical illusion of the British reflects the homegrown idea that from mediaeval times, the British ruled the world and fought almost everyone else to a standstill to prove their strength, collecting in peace negotiations even more colonial holdings. The East alone puts British glorious domination in doubt.

The Dutch dominated the spice trade to Europe. The British still speak about the English East India Company as an example of great tradition and power and the enthusiasm is well founded but the Dutch should not be footnotes to English triumphs. The United East India Company, Vereenigde Oost-Indishe Compagnie (VOC), was trading with a twenty-one-year charter in 1602 and was the world's first stock company and the largest corporation ever. As an example of the size of the Dutch institution and investment the VOC traded in 4,785 vessels during the seventeenth and eighteenth centuries whereas the English East India Company discharged just 2,690.

Elizabeth never saw the successful return to England of the first of her well-laden ships. Nor did she know that a century earlier, long before she was born, the Portuguese had opened their first factories in Goa. (Factories from *factorium* and in the sixteenth century factories meant offices of factors, that is, agents). The British had from the west pushed into the Far East in 1596 – sixteen years after Drake's circumnavigation. Drake had sailed his five ships west in 1577 to plunder Spanish bullion ships in the Spanish Main but could not get back because the Spanish fleet were waiting for him. He went south around the isthmus of South America, then north to California (and claimed it for the Queen on his way), then further north in search of the Northwest Passage, then west to Japan, then west north of Australia and to the Spice Islands

Drake continued across the Indian Ocean (he may have attacked a Portuguese ship and 'rescued' the invaluable Indian Ocean charts), missing the subcontinent, and rounding the Cape of Good Hope and North to anchor off Saltash. Drake, the greatest ocean sailor in British maritime history, might have inspired East Indies ventures. Few could do what he did and survive. The search in the 1590s for the Indies under the enormously experienced Benjamin Wood failed. He and his entire flotilla were lost at sea. Even Drake lost four of his five ships. Sailors were going into little-known waters even though the Spanish, Portuguese and Dutch had already found their similar ways east. It was a voluminous chart table in an Iberian vessel attacked by an English ship that gave the Elizabethans the chartwork needed to cross the Indian Ocean into the East Indies. The first task of mercantile explorers was to petition the monarch for her permission to sail for the Indian Ocean because they needed the royal patronage as a means of intro- duction and confirmation of their *bona fide* even if the Queen had no real knowledge of the princes and kings they would meet.

A royal proclamation was a document that would attract financial backing, for it effectively said that the holder had exclusive rights to the trading. Under these conditions and with this authority three vessels sailed for the Arabian Sea in 1591 and one of the ships, the *Edward Bonaventure*, went on as far as the Malay Peninsula before returning to Torbay in 1594.

On 31 December 1600 Elizabeth issued a new proclamation together with a fifteen-year charter granted to the Earl of Cumberland and 215 others to trade under the name *Governor and Company of Merchants of London Trading With The East Indies*. This was effectively permission to hold a monopoly on British trading east of Suez and west of the Straits of Magellan.

Enough was known of the Indian Ocean's prevailing weather conditions so important to square riggers, where outward bound stores and safe havens for repairs were to be found and, most importantly, reliable charts. Under Sir James Lancaster, the Company put to sea bound for the East Indies. Lancaster, not without terrible mishaps, returned to England in the year his patron died. Her successor, James I, sensibly had no hesitation in continuing support for the Company without instituting any difficult legislation that restricted the voyaging and commercial success. Within six years he had licensed other consortia but made it known that the *Governor and Company of Merchants of London Trading With The East Indies* was the Crown's preference and that, unless there was a three-year period without profits, then the Company had royal patronage for ever and a day; so it would be for close on four hundred years to come. The crucial question for investors was not so much whether there would be profits. Few could have doubted that from reports and the first returned cargo. The bigger question was how to sustain such levels of discovery and trading. After Lancaster, there could be no let-up in the voyages.

The plight of Henry Middleton, who was given command of the second voyage with his pennant in Lancaster's former ship, *Red Dragon*, was an early warning to others that nothing in these ventures should be taken for granted. The voyages were far from home and in often treacherous waters, although a ship reliant on often unreliable weather reporting and treacherous manning by even British locals did not have to sail 7,000 miles to run into seemingly insurmountable difficulties. The old sailors' adage that at sea only the weather was predictable and even that was variable came true.

Middleton's squadron sailed from the Thames on 25 March 1604. He had not logged a hundred miles when he found that the ship was undermanned – an easy enough mistake only discovered when the watch was changed. After an eight-hour sail a further headcount was taken and Middleton was told that the ship now had twenty-eight more men than needed and so did each of the other ships. It was a regular enough swindle (also some of the bosun's mates who counted ship companies could not count) aboard sailing ships, enormously driven by manpower as they were. When they stood off Cape Verde three weeks later for stores, one of the merchants went missing. There was more to come. Scurvy ran through *Red Dragon* and Middleton was forced into Table Bay to put eighty sailors ashore, where locals attacked them. The reduced fleet reached the Maluku Islands in February and Middleton found himself and his crew involved in a war between the Dutch and Tidore tribesmen and then a local conflict between the Portuguese and the Dutch. It was a bloody affair and involved more than cutlass and pistol. Large ordnance was pitched and fired with devastating effect as Dutch and Ternate locals fought Portuguese and Tidorean, who in turn sacked and pillaged the local fort. It was a typical trading war for cloves. The raging fire destroyed the fort and inevitably the stores of cloves. Middleton and the survivors on *Red Dragon* were seeing evidence enough that spices could be traded in the sack houses of the Levant and western Europe, but the origins of the cargo were to explain for decades the burden of laying hands on the abundance in this seed corn of the British Empire.

The Dutch would hold their own against the English intrusion for a full century because, in spite of all the English had learned about getting into the new trade, they did not have much with which to trade. They knew what they wanted to buy. Bantam in Java was the international market of south-east Asia and had most finely decorated woven silks and fine cottons, which the Europeans and English wanted. But to trade meant having much to barter. The English arrived with their very European-climate broadcloths. They hoped to barter for fine silks and cotton calico. Even the English silver attracted little attention.

CHAPTER II

THE RETREAT TO INDIA

When James Lancaster sailed for Java in February 1601 in his ships of the Company of Merchants of London Trading with the East Indies he had imagined that heavy wool was just what was needed in the East Indies. More immediately, the British did manage to set up agents and warehouses in spite of opposition from individual Dutch agents and traders armed with private armies. The most infamous confrontation remains the Amboina Massacre of 1623. It was at this point that the British decided to redirect their trading effort in the East Indies. They did not leave the area we would call Jakarta. Instead they began the slow trading diplomacy in India and the adventure that would lead to the viceroys. A little caution is worthwhile. Firstly, the British did establish a factory in Bantam that was certainly there for some decades and, secondly, they were soon one of the principal traders in the China Sea and the Straits. The Dutch from the spice area expelled the British in 1623. They returned to Bantam in 1628. They traded uneventfully up to 1640, when the Dutch did send them packing, but this coincided with the beginnings of substantial English trade in Madras. Put together, the events in the East Indies and the British diplomacy and trade in India were coincidental enough; the British simply moved on and with limited resources put most effort into India where the opportunities were recognised as greater than in the Spice Islands.

Sir James Lancaster's first recognised East India Company voyage was armed with a Royal Commission and a set-up fund of more than £14 million in 2017 currency. In short, the consequences of a failed voyage would not be contemplated. Resorting to common skulduggery was a better option than withdrawing to England with empty holds. Skulduggery prevailed. Lancaster hijacked a Portuguese vessel laden with silks and calico and precious metals. He swapped the stolen cargo for pepper at Aceh and spices at Bantam. Even though he established an agency at Bantam his fleet of four, full to the tweendecks, sailed for England. The British were not to rely on piracy or any version of it. Piracy was never a rich man's ambition and Indian textiles were a far superior currency to anything they had yet found.

The Mughal rulers of northern and central India were hardly insignificant princes set in crude times and places. Mughal India was the focal point of sixteenth- and early-seventeenth-century civilisation and when the fledgling East India Company sent, in 1608, one of its experienced and Turkic-speaking captains, William Hawkins, to seek an audience with the Mughal Emperor, there was much diplomacy to be agreed before the English could feel they could invest in a subcontinent ancient enough to have had an empire centuries before the British arrived.

India had a civilisation older than western Europe. Sometimes known to Europeans as the Indus civilisation, that

is, either based on or to the east of the Indus River, was a soci-
ety that had developed by 2500 BC. By 1750 BC that society had
corrupted and scattered. Even 500 years before the birth of
Christ, Aryan peoples had established separate kingdoms in
the Ganges delta. The Mauryan Empire that grew under
Chandra Gupta[1] was split into small kingdoms. By AD 600, the
Arabic invasions of the Northwest Frontier had begun.
Uncertainties and ensuing conflicts continued for a millen-
nium until much of India was brought under the rule of the
Mughal during the first half of the sixteenth century when
Babur the Great, who traced his line from Genghis Khan, had
conquered Delhi in 1527. At the time of the coming of the
East India Company it was Babur's grandson, Akbar the Great,
who controlled most of India from its centre to its northern
borders.[2]

The message from the Company was simple: it wanted to
set up in India. The hopes were as high as anyone could judge
in such an alien society with a leadership too taken with cruelly
or indifferently demonstrated power so that no one, certainly
not the British, could be sure that here was where the future
lay. If it did not work, what would happen? The British would
have, on a much smaller scale, sat uneasily in Bantam or may
even have returned to Europe and looked harder at America.
The empire may not have been in the British mind, but on
reflection it might so easily have never happened. Certainly
the British at this point were second-rate traders. Nothing
more. True, the Emperor got on with Hawkins but how could
he have ever agreed to anything with a country that did not
have a proper ambassador in India? In this early-seventeenth-
century period there was no diplomatic service. An agreeable
and hard-drinking sailor from a trading company who had
fallen on hard times was not the man to pull off a major

diplomatic triumph with the ruler whose kind had all but conquered their known world.

It was not until seven years later that the then King, James I (Elizabeth had died in 1603) appointed the man who would be the first British envoy to an Indian court. Even then, when the Mughal made King James's man, Sir Thomas Roe (1581–1644) petition the Emperor Sher Afgan Ali Quli Khan Jahangir to open an agency at Surat, the Mughal Emperor made Roe wait outside for months before even greeting him. Roe, in a letter to the British ambassador to Constantinople (Istanbul, where later Roe himself would be ambassador), was hardly pleased with his lot, camped in Mandu as he was, waiting on an Emperor he was fast coming to loathe.

'Death and I have been house fellows and are grown familiar . . . I am full of India, even to fastidious . . . Our settling here is no other than by commands to the ports and town which we desire; nor yet to all, and those revocable at pleasure and subject to daily alterations. Neither will this overgrown elephant (the emperor) descend to article or bind himself reciprocally to any prince upon terms of equality; but only by way of favour, admit our stay so long as it either likes him or those that govern him . . .'[1]

Roe came from a county family (Norfolk) and a line of powerful financiers (his grandfather and then his uncle were Lord Mayors of London and he, Thomas, was a senior investor in the Royal Council of Virginia and had sailed in 1610 in search of El Dorado and its legendary capital Manoa). He was also entrusted with the most delicate and private embassies of James's court and so, when the King decided he had to send someone to India, Roe was one of the few he trusted who had survived the experience of hazardous travel through the jungles of Central America!

In early February 1615 Roe set sail from Tilbury to India. The weather was so grim that his ship did not reach the Lizard until March. It took Roe a month to sail the English Channel, not unusual in a square rigged ship against a headwind. His ship anchored off Cape Town for two weeks and then put to sea for India and made Surat on 18 September, nine months after sailing from the Thames Estuary. The Emperor Jahangir was having dealings with the Portuguese (mostly he was at minor war with them), who insisted that, in return for peace, the British should be banned from the Mughal's country. To counter the arguments, here was another impediment to British trading efforts; neither Roe nor any of his staff spoke Jahangir's court language, Persian. Roe spoke Latin and could use that for bargaining with the Portuguese, but nothing more. This year, 1616, was a crucial point in the nursery of British ambitions in India. Not one of the British in the land spoke the only language spoken at court. The Portuguese were of some help but had their own interests to look after and the Dutch were about to launch into India. Roe had only one tactic: bribery. His single piece of palm greasing was very British and very unusual. Roe gave the Mughal a state coach. The Mughal was delighted. Paintings, bejewelled swords, hunting dogs and whiskey followed the coaches.

The Mughal was in Ajmer with a camp of perhaps 200,000. Each had to be satisfied. The bribery took time. So did the procedures and protocols. When Jahangir struck camp and headed for the hills and jungles, Roe, with his own staff all in his red and green colours camping beneath the flag of St George, had to follow in as much style as possible while being careful not to upstage the ruler. When Roe sailed for England in February 1619 he did so with Jahangir's good wishes. The Mughal would not give a formal treaty to the Englishman but there was a letter of welcome for the far-off monarch, James I. Roe, the first ambassador, had shown what might be possible – with the right Mughal and a well made coach. The footings of the British Empire were dug with the designs not of the monarch but of the English East India Company, with a court of directors (24) and a governor with rooms in London. From the early 1600s until the 1850s the British traded with and then ran India through a commercial enterprise

The Mughal Emperors may not have been much impressed with the English. Simply, once the British had the authority of the Mughal Emperor and comptroller of the imperial house behind them, they could extend any formal agreement without it having to be renegotiated. Payment here and there would usually be the way to add to a concession. They bragged that they could take what they wished and struck deals that suited them with local and regional potentates who could always find some authority to agree should it be financially worthwhile. The British brought their own armies to protect their styles of commercial wars. Those armies were far from invincible and, in somewhere with climate and conditions as inhospitable to even south Europeans, causes other than battle wounds took a huge toll.

Soldiers were not usually living in ideal and clean conditions and they often took little care of themselves. A common wound would be vulnerable to disease and there were few medical attentions. Consequently, it was often the case that more died from what might have been easily treated conditions than on the battlefield. The Portuguese appeared particularly vulnerable and they died in their thousands during the battles for territory and the freedom to trade as they wished.

While the style and often evil reputation of the Portuguese in India made it harder for the English to get agreement with Mughals wary of any European country, it was also clear that the superior military capabilities, especially at sea, of the English could be used to defend the Indian princes. And so it was to be, while at the same time both the 'good' and the 'bad' Portuguese were recognised by the English as having broken the way into India and breached the positions of invincibility of the Mughals.

The English did well from the military and commercial ice breaking accomplished by the Portuguese at a time when the English were learning the trade of colonial creep just as Portuguese colonialism was in decline. There was, too, a growing suspicion that the European allies of the English, the Dutch, were far from friends and having done for them further east would do the same in India. More formally, the English were in good concert with the Dutch. On the front line of new colonialism the proprietors and directors of the Company were quite certain none was to be trusted. The obvious retreat to opportunity and prosperity for the British came when it was clear they could not succeed in the East Indies against the Dutch on the scale that was necessary to turn the East India venture into a success rather than, at the very best, a break-even project.

The Dutch had strength across the region and the monopoly in the Straits of Malacca. It is worth remembering that the contest was not between Dutch and English. The local traders did more than take sides. They were there to trade. They would fight on the Dutch side because the trade link was established. The confrontations were often skirmishes but the wars were real enough. Between 1652 and 1674 and 1781 and 1810 there were four Anglo-Dutch Wars, which were all about who controlled trade. The English would continue to trade in the

East Indies but in the most sensible manner. They would establish themselves in India where they could get goods, especially fine silks that made trading sense with the East Indies spice dealers. If there was something in the order of a 'breakthrough' it was when Jahangir authorised the English warehouses, factories and permissions to trade from Surat on the western seaboard of India. Why would Jahangir do that for the English? Firstly, because the English could make sure the maharaja came by European goods that he otherwise found difficult to secure and secondly, and perhaps most importantly, the English could protect Jahangir, particularly from the Portuguese. Jahangir wrote to James I

'I have give my general command to all those kingdoms and ports of my dominions to receive all the merchants of the English nation as the subjects of my friend; that in what place soever they chose to live they may have free liberty without any restraint and at what port soever they shall arrive that neither the Portugal nor any other shall dare to molest their quiet and in what city soever they shall have residence I have commanded all my governors and captains to give them freedom answerable to their own desires to sell, buy, and to transport to their own country at their pleasure. For confirmation of our love and friendship I desire your Majesty to command your merchants to bring in their ships of all sorts of rarities and rich goods fit for my palace . . .'[2]

By any standard that was an acknowledgement of free pratique. It was a foothold in an India in which thousands of English men and women would one day be born. It would become the new home of a new generation of the British, the imperial invader and the expatriate.

The first invaders came from the Persian Gulf and did so at the earliest times of Islam – the year of *hijra* (emigration) and the start of the Muslim calendar is 622. The arrival of Muslims included those who were there to attack raiders from India who frequently plundered Arab wealth. However, the Arabs did not cross the natural frontier, the Indus.

The Indian kingdoms, especially the three that made up the frontier of al-Hind, were dominant in the seventh century while the princes of Kabul guarded access into and from India for more than a century until the late 800s AD. Seemingly the lands and peoples of India have always been at conflict. The seventh, eighth- and ninth-century invasions, mere skirmishes that became battles that became wars that became conquests, were over the same grounds and in the same phrases and language as many in the late twentieth century and the twenty-first century, based on ancient histories, anxieties and centuries old suspicions.

Eighth-century rulers in Kabul were not so differently motivated than those in more recent times. The Islamists who moved across what was then Multan settled easily among the Sunnis in much the same way as they might today. The Saffaridi who overran Kabul in 871 AD had very twentieth-century motives of occupation and exploitation of territory and peoples, as was illustrated by the Muslim Delhi Sultanate that ruled much of India through five dynasties (Marmluk, Khilji, Tughlaq, Sayid and Lodi) for three centuries. In the tenth century, at about the time that Edgar was consolidating the gains of Athelstan as King of England and not just of the English, the Central Asian and Persian Muslim raiding armies plundered northern India. These were not territorial wars. The raiders sought slaves and treasure. They achieved both. The territorial Muslim expansion did not take hold until the twelfth century, following the

Sunni expansion of Sultan Muizz al-Din Mohammed in the 1170s. The consequence was the establishment of the Delhi Sultanate before the end of that century. The spell of the five dynasties would survive slaughter and desecration, until Babur, the Turkic prince descendant of Tamerlane and Genghis Khan, attacked Punjab from his stronghold at Kabul and went on from there to defeat first Ibrahim Lodi at Panipat in 1526, then in 1527 Rana Sanga of Mewar and then the Afghans of Uttar Pradesh and Bihar in 1529.

Babur was dead the following year but left his successors control of much of northern India from the Indus to Bihar in the west and to the Himalayas and south to Gwailor, not a hundred miles south of Agra. The dynasty rarely had the luxury of relaxing control and indeed Babur's surrendered to the Afghans. It was Akbar (1542–1605) who recovered the empire in 1556 and is seen as the finest of all the Mughal Emperors partly because he established a system of administration that was as fair and considerate as possible to Hindus as well as his Muslim followers. As the British sailed for India with Elizabeth I's proclamation, Akbar reigned.

By the time of the English submissions for trading rights and the establishment of agencies, Akbar's son Jahangir was in power; it was his son, Shah Jahan, who built the Taj Mahal at Agra and the Great Mosque at Delhi. If there was what is commonly seen as a step-change in the Mughal rule, then it came with Shah Jahan's successor. Whereas Mughal rule worked with some success because of the acceptance of Hinduism as well as Islam (the religion of the rulers), it failed in the next generation when Aurangzeb became Emperor (1658–1707).

Certainly, Aurangzeb expanded the empire, but he usurped the Hindu population in important positions, banned their separate schooling practices and persecuted the Sikhs and Rajputs. When he died in 1707, Aurangzeb left the Mughal Empire in India in rebellion and throughout the long reign (1719–1748) of Muhammad Shah (1702–1748) factional divisions could not be calmed and the invasion and the occupation of much of northern India by the Marathas, the yeoman farmers and warriors whose modern origins may be found in the north lands of the 1st century AD, left the Mughal Empire little authority and strongly settled only in the region of Delhi. The last of the Mughals, Bahadur Shah II, became Emperor during the year of Victoria's accession to the throne, 1837. He survived with no real authority, although respected as a man of considerable cultural understanding, and was reasonably content to see out his time in Delhi as a client prince of the British in India. Towards the end of his life, sepoys from Meerut overran Delhi and forced him to declare that he was the leader of what generally would be remembered as the Sepoy Rebellion – the Indian Mutiny. The rebellion was over in 1858 and Emperor Bahadur Shah II was sent into exile in Burma, Myanmar. He died four years later. His going was the end of the Mughal Empire in India.

A little more than two centuries after the British arrival in Surat, they brought about the end of the rule of the Mughals. Even without the Sepoy Rebellion, Bahadur Shah and his like would have gone. His going could be the point to ask what would have happened to India if the British had never arrived?

John William Kaye, in an observation in his study of the East India Company system, wondered if the Indians would have been 'more or less happy and prosperous if they had been left to the government of their old Mahomedan [sic] conquerors and rulers'.[3]

The British did plunder the riches of India but not by conquering an indigenous monarchy. They overcame and usurped the authority of the Mughals. As Kaye saw it, both the British and Mughals were aliens. Looking at the way Mughal Emperors treated non-Muslims after Jahangir and Shah Jahan, especially using Aurangzeb as an example, the British have the verdict on points. In the early 1600s and right up to the twentieth century the case was simpler. The British had failed in the East Indies and were now setting out for fortunes in India. The central bank and ambition of this cause was the East India Company.

The Company had the trading and territorial expansion opportunities to grow quicker than it did. Missing were the initiatives among the often unsure and insecure staff and the sheer hard work of working in a strange environment where no conventional trading practices resolved difficulties that were thrown up by new colonists falling back on repression to overcome people and conditions that were seen as opposition to the Company rather than as both sides being quite uncertain how to trade or work together. Here was the basis for the brute force of all that would go wrong at the time as well as colonial in examination centuries later.

The directors of John Company lived with the asset of uncertainty. There was even the aspect of the security of the offices, the factory, the storage and transfer of trading goods and all this in an alien environment, despite the willingness of the Mughal Emperor to encourage the English in return for riches such as were from Europe, and protection. The

Company had to provide its own security and here were the origins of the famous India Army, although the protection of interests in these early years was in the hands of ragtag bunches of mercenaries barely more trustworthy than the local thieves and insurgents who might threaten the English traders.

These are not at all impressions of plumed doffed British colonial history. The monarch of a small island people had no reputation to flaunt that would bewitch a Mughal ruler and his viziers. They were not overwhelmed by people who came with petitions for their safety and good hearing signed by a woman about whom they knew little. The English ambassadors, with Elizabeth I's signed petition, were seen as envoys from poor and obscure fishing islands off the coast of north-west Europe. How could they be of any consequence? They were kept waiting in the anterooms; why would the Indians of the great Mughal think otherwise, until of course the small people from small islands produced a state coach and more as presents for the Mughal. Equally the Indian princes would rely on the British for their thrones, right up to 1947. Immediately in the seventeenth century the ragbag regiments of the East India Company would take on the role of protector.

Realism and opportunity won the hour and did so partly through the intelligence and diplomacy of one of the most remarkable women in Mughal ruling history, Nur Jahan (1577–1645), Jahangir's Empress and his number-one consort. Nur Jahan was Jahangir's twentieth and favourite wife and the most powerful woman in the seventeenth-century Mughal Empire. Nur Jahan, born of Persian nobility in the city of Kandahar (today in Afghanistan), is the only Mughal Empress to feature on the crown side of the empire's silver coinage. There, too, is a passing irony. Elizabeth I is remembered still for her Tilbury speech when she proclaimed that she had the body of a woman but the heart of a man. Nur Jahan, a sturdy huntress, was remembered by a poet as

'Though Nur Jahan be in form a woman, In the ranks of men she's a tiger slayer . . .'

Nur Jahan displayed few weaknesses and the envoys of the Company would learn from their dealings with her that Mughal and later thrones in India were often no different from those in Europe – behind each one, another power operated the wires of authority. So the English learned to wait, antici- pate and show appropriate thanks where it was most due; this approach led to the expansion of the relationship between the English and the ruling Emperors. The first trading post had been set up by 1619. Fifteen years later, the Emperor agreed the same terms as had worked well in Surat for the English to move into Bengal in 1634. Five years on, in 1639, John Company's burgee flew above the post in Madras, in Bombay by 1688 and Calcutta two years later.

Bombay and its islands were the most important acquisition for the English East India Company. The Company recog- nised the strategic as well as the commercial value of coast and estuary control in places like Bombay harbour; moreover, the increasing pressure that the Dutch were placing on the Company made it clear to the Crown that some way had to be found to get English hands on the western seaboard. The solu- tion came in 1661 with the restoration of Charles II[4] to his throne and his marriage to Catherine, the daughter of King John IV of Portugal. Part of Catherine's dowry was a group of the islands of Bombay. It was hard to see what the King's estate could reasonably do to manage the islands and most of all protect them. The answer was with John Company, an independent trading organisation, owned by the British government.

In 1668 the Bombay islands were leased to the East India Company at an annual rent of £10. Empires were rarely so cheap and never such a bargain. The way and breadth of the Company and the expanding period of the British commercial interests of the seventeenth century and into the first part of the eighteenth century inevitably changed the way the Company was minded by government, which was in itself radically changing from a court party to the beginnings of party politics; soon, government would develop economic and foreign policies for their values rather than the personality rivalries that had existed for centuries. India was shifting in its power politics, the Company had become a colonial invader with its own army and an active interest in how the princes governed and the government in London exercised a controlling interest in the Company to keep it in line with an emerging and sophisticated foreign policy far more complex than simply dealing with a perceived threat from Roman Catholic France and Spain.

The British interests were strongest in Bengal. It was the most profitable area, yet it was northern India that was most vulnerable to attack because assaults came from the land. For example, the Persians sacked Delhi and the Afghans, led famously by Ahmad Shah Abdali, swarmed over the border and plundered even further south. Amid all this, the Mughal princes and governors were setting up their own states and regional interests. With the virtual collapse of the Mughal Empire, the individual states each had to be attended to by the Company, according to the power politics of the princes. So, the emerging principalities of Bengal, Hyderabad, Oudh, the Maratha Confederation and Mysore, together with the Rajput princes and the Sikhs in Punjab, each had to be watched by the British politicians and traders. Each prince was bribed when necessary and fought when all else failed. Here was one reason why the East India Company expanded its private army of sepoys.

Sepoys were native soldiers and the name itself comes from the Persian for warrior. It was in this period of the mid-1700s that the contrast in styles of the French and the British were most apparent and would eventually lead to confrontation, not entirely because of the conflict of interests in India, but because of the wars between the two countries thousands of miles away. The French hired and drilled Indian sepoys, albeit not always loyal, long before the British. This advantage threatened the British foothold in India.

The Mughal Emperor Abdul Muzaffar Muhi-ud-Din Aurangzeb, The Universe Seizer, died at the age of 89 in March 1707. Aurangzeb was the sixth of the Mughal Emperors of India and ruled more than 100 million people in more than three million square miles. The British would come to rule more than four times that number of people and square miles. Within two decades of the Mughal's death, the pattern of rule and influence in India changed.[5]

Aurangzeb ruled by fear often enforced by strict moral codes (not unlike those in twenty-first-century Islam when inspired by socio-economic scales). His single-mindedness appeared to be a profitable policy, although his severity towards many of his peoples provided few long-term dividends for India. The Mahratta in the south were in open rebellion led by Shivaji Bhonsle (1630–1680), whose military successes (the battles of Pratapgarh, Pavan Khind, Chakan, Kolhapur and Nesari are still recited) and the movement for independence in India inspired long after his death. Towards his end, few would

support Aurangzeb; the Hindu uprising in the Hindu Jats
rebellion against religious taxes led by Gokul Singh (executed
in 1670) marked an example of opposition that was far more
than tribal and peoples' differences.

The military power with which Aurangzeb's Mughals had
ruled had waned in India. Towards his end, Aurangzeb was a
fugitive even from his own sons, although he outlived many of
them. Much of his adult life had been spent conquering the
Dakkhin Plateau covering most of the central and the southern parts of the subcontinent and the origins of many great
dynasties and states including the Maratha Empire, extending
at one late stage to one third of the subcontinent.

The complexity of Mughal rule in this eighteeth-century
period challenged the supposedly efficient European authority. The British and the French stood by for war seemingly in
every decade of the century. It was a century of increased profits from an ever-expanding Company who, after just a hundred
years, ruled like a twenty-first-century global trading corporation. The Company was more than a trading company. It was
also a conquering army. Its military enemies were the French
and the princes, who were just as likely to join a battle on
whichever side had the upper hand.

The British did not have a simple task of rule especially as
the French had, in the eighteenth century, remaining territorial ambitions but the Company, apart from its land and naval
superiority, had one advantage over French commercial interests. The British tended to make deals with whichever prince
controlled whichever region they were interested in. The
French system was to trade with the centre of power. When
that centre moved in ever-increasing concentric political
circles, French influence was stretched. Instinctively the
French and British traders agreed on one particular policy, if

at all possible, to stay out of each other's wars. Even when France and Britain went to war, neither company wanted conflicts to disrupt trading, nor did they wish to lose any chance of taking the advantage of that war. It was a sensible idea but someone had to lose the faux truce. This commercially inspired neutrality was abandoned to sensible opportunism in 1746 when a British naval squadron put into Calcutta for repairs. With the sea to the south free, the French assaulted and captured Madras, the British headquarters in southern India. When the peace agreement was made two years later the conflict in India continued. There was a crudeness in the way of trading and commanding in eighteenth-century India that was not so different from what was practised elsewhere in the globe but now might be seen as a purely British way of exploiting the opportunities in India and behaving badly towards the people. The charge of colonialism – or worse, imperialism – is too hard to live down.

The major success was in the Company's main area of interest, Bengal. Bengal was, in the mid-eighteenth century, a confrontation waiting to happen between local rulers and the British. Its tradition as the richest state with the most condensed population made it a natural arena for the Company's commercial expertise. But the local rulers had moved on from the days of benign negotiation and now wanted far more from the British, who seemed to be getting too much for themselves.

So, it was inevitable that, in 1756, the twenty-one-year-old Nawab of Bengal, Siraj ud Daula, (sometimes ud-Daula) sent his troops to assault the two Company headquarters, one at Calcutta, the other at Kasimbaza. This event, on 20 June 1756, came to be known as the Black Hole of Calcutta. Siraj ud Daula went the way of many of his predecessors; he was murdered. Company officials did very well financially and the enterprise did even better in trading terms. When the new nawab, Mir Jaffr, felt aggrieved enough to object to Company practices, the British got rid of him. They replaced him with his son-in-law, Mir Kasim. He showed his gratitude by giving the Company Burdwan, Chittagong and mid Mapur. When in 1764 Mir Kasim also felt hard done by, the Company got rid of him as well. It would be very difficult to describe British expansion in India as an exercise in quiet government. The eighteenth century was one of old orders changing. This was not a time of sheathed swords, nor damp charges and squibs. From North America, to France and the rest of Europe and then to Asia and in particular India, nations were herded into new states. In India, a thousand princes still reigned. A small island people had come to reign over them and had sent young men with a little education, a little breeding and huge ambition to be what they could never be in their little islands. It was, too, a century of ambition. The English East India Company was a natural adventure for a young man to be what he wanted to be rather than what he was. So it was for Robert Clive, one day Clive of India.

CHAPTER III

CLIVE, HASTINGS, IMPEACHMENT

A Company man might have neither military training nor instinct but conflict was so easily at hand that a run with the army could be the way to notice, distinction and riches. That was the origin of the story of Robert Clive. Clive (1725–1774) was all about India. One of thirteen children, he was not born in hard times but such a large family presented its difficulties. Clive moved a lot, lived with relations and was sent to a variety of schools, none of which was splendid nor distinguished although one – Mr Stiling's School in Hertfordshire – taught bookkeeping. Clive showed little learning but considerable aggression and was rescued from dire straits by being sent and articled in 1743 to the Madras offices of the Company; the other two Company offices were in the presidencies of Bombay and, supremely, Calcutta. Typical of Clive's itinerancy, the ship was diverted to Brazil and took fifteen months to reach India and he was impoverished and depressed. He attempted suicide. His pistol did not work. His frustration and gloom haunted him and made him bad company.

It was a trying time for Clive and his closest colleagues, who weathered the brunt of his mental states. This pattern was disrupted in 1746 when the French attacked and took Madras. Clive escaped, joined the Company army and distinguished himself. Under the command of Major-General Stringer Lawrence, Clive defended the French attack on Cuddalore and by the spring of 1749 it was Lieutenant Clive who rode with Lawrence, who thought Clive was a born soldier.

The conflict with France lulled and Clive put away his military livery and returned to his desk, by this time a much larger one as he was faced with the task of logistics for the troops. The commissions were considerable. Fortunately for Clive's bank balance war was only taking a rest and in 1751, Captain Clive was back in the saddle with 800 men and his reputation to seal, which he did by capturing Arcot and for fifty-three days that year defending it against a combined French and Indian army. Six years later, in 1757, he sealed his epithet, Clive of India, at Plassey.

Most of the British who served, then at Clive's times and right to the end in Mountbatten's era, lived at a finer level than they would have elsewhere – certainly in England. Many of the British who went to India were from lower and lower-middle class backgrounds and by their colonial positions assumed an untested authority over the people of India. These new colonialists took their lead from their jobs, those above them and the levels of authority over the local employees and community. The colonial lower classes might also have found themselves treated as lower caste by the senior colonials as people who would, in the United Kingdom, have been treated as people with little breeding and no right to position. In doing so, the British assumed a new identity – that of the British aristocracy without the charm and responsibilities and therefore the image of arrogance that arrives with patronage over those who have nothing by those who have left behind nothing. By Clive's time, certainly by the time of the first of the governors general had become the new Mughals and, as with that other generation of princes, the British did well from old practices. Clive's victories, concessions and protection were thus consolidated in territorial as well as commercial terms. The new nawab was Mir Jafar. The way of India at the time was that the victors were tipped heavily in financial and political terms by the new nawab. Clive had made a lot of money after the siege of Arcot. Now, following the battle of Plassey, Clive received a gratuity from the nawab of more than £230,000, plus tenancy rents that would give him £27,000 a year. If the backhanders and presents seemed outrageous they really were not, although in 1773 Clive had to explain himself to the House of Commons, where he had been accused of corruptly enriching himself. He responded:

'. . . I stand amazed at my own moderation . . .'

Parliament and its government could chuckle at Clive's wit but beneath the joke was increasing concern that there was too much corruption; some skimming commissions and interest rates were ever acknowledged as inevitable and it was the way of the world, not just India. The 1773 Regulating Act immediately gave the British government partial jurisdiction over India through the East India Company, which ruled as an agent of the Mughal Emperor of India.

The centre of British-Company rule was Bengal. The British through the Act appointed for the first time a governor general and supreme council of Bengal to be elected by the East India Company's court of directors. All positions, including governor-general, would be for five-year terms. The governor-general was the forerunner of the viceroy, the first of whom, Lord Canning, would be appointed in 1858 under the Government of India Act. In 1833, the Charter Act retitled the head of British India as governor-general of India. Warren Hastings was the first governor-general of the presidency of Fort William in Bengal (not first governor-general of India.)

When he arrived in office Hastings understood the opportunities for generous personal funding although he did not fully realise them until his second term of office. Little wonder that when it became his turn to be accused of riches beyond his expectations, Warren Hastings did not find a sympathetic audience that might quietly chuckle at his witty riposte. Once accused, Hastings was always going to be pressed for answers.

The Sir Joshua Reynolds portrait of Warren Hastings in the National Portrait Gallery in London shows a slim, balding and daintily dressed fellow better suited to a late-eighteenth-century salon than the Bar of the House of Commons, at which he would be impeached and all but ruined for lining his deep coffers with the commissions and corruptly gathered pay-offs as virtual ruler of India. He was all of these yet spitefully accused. He fought long and hard and eventually cleared himself and his considerable debts. Hastings, like many of his generation, went to India in poor and difficult circumstances. His family came from a line of country gentlemen from Daylesford in Worcestershire. The family had lost Daylesford and Hastings rightly believed that his impeachment meant he could never find the funds to restore the home that had been in the family for 500 years. Hastings vowed that once his name was cleared (he was one of the few confident enough to believe it would be) he would buy back his family land. It was a dark picture of a young man, one of disappointment. Yet his shortened education at Westminster had taught him all about quick wit, bravery in games, cultural confidence from languages, historical awareness and what might work or what might fail.

Like Clive's relatives, influence was cashed in to get Hastings to India and the Company. He arrived in the Company's capital of Calcutta in 1750. Calcutta, even by this time, was the 'New York' of British India. It was the commercial centre of Bengal and home to the people who created change and exhibited everything that was happening within the Company and the considerable other commercial ventures of India. The Emperor's palace was in Delhi. India's counting house was Calcutta. Hastings did not have an easy time. He became an ally of the governor of Bengal, the senior Company man in India. Bad decisions, or at least the interpretations of negotiations with the prince, the Nawab of Bengal Mir Kasim (d.1777), who had been installed by the British when they replaced his father Mir Jafar, who turned out to be double-dealing with the Dutch East India Company. Hastings believed that for all his faults, including some double-dealing, Mir Jafar was badly treated by the British, even though in his later years, Mir Jafar had been losing control and making poor decisions and taking additional 'commissions.' When the British installed Mir Kasim, Hastings objected. He was ignored particularly by some of the British who did financially well by supporting Mir Kasim. Mir Kasim modernised his Bengal army. Mir Kasim's capture of the British in Calcutta was one of the turning points in the British attitude towards him. The British went to war with Mir Kasim and he was defeated at the Battle of Buxar in October 1764. Significantly, not only was Mir Kasim defeated, but two other princes, Shah Alam, who made a separate truce with the British, and Shah Shuja-ud-Daula, who ran and blew up the only escape route for his own followers. Mir Kasim's defeat gave the British the complete run of the Ganges Valley, the North East India and as a leader he was the last nawab who could muster the forces to contain the British. Instead, the British humiliated him.

They took everything Mir Kasim had and drove him out of Buxar on a lame elephant. His clothing was sold to pay for his funeral. Hastings had already been accused of taking money from Mir Kasim. Nothing was proved and no one tried hard to change that. Hastings returned to London the following year, 1765, and lived in some style, pushing his case as a valuable advisor by promoting ideas including an Oxford chair in Asian languages and his belief that Bengal, the seat of British India, was now British and the princes would like to be protected and therefore ruled from London. In 1769, Hastings returned to India and en route fell in love with the wife of Baron Carl von Imhoff, a junior officer in the Madras army, who lived in Hastings's house in Madras when her husband went to Bengal. They later married. It was a successful second marriage for them both; Hastings became a more cheerful fellow and was promoted to governor of Bengal in 1772. He now had authority, or assumed it for himself into an area rarely touched in London.

Following a 1765 review in the Company of how to control influences, especially in Bengal, there was, in Hastings's time as governor, an irregular position of authority granted to a Muslim, Mohammad Reza Khan. Hastings sacked him and assumed authority formerly held by the princes. When asked, Hastings simply talked about all sovereignty in Bengal being British. In other words, Bengal and thus British India's stronghold were British. The British were not in Bengal courtesy of the Indians. The Company, he anticipated, would eventually have no direct purpose because the British government would subsume all its powers over India. When it did, the British Crown would govern India. The British did not want that now because they did not have the political structure to see how it would work.

There was no bureaucracy that could, from London, impose the style and sentiment of Britain through the council in India. Hastings was thinking ahead about a Bengal that was potentially as powerful as some European states with which Britain had been to war or fallen into alliance. This would be seen as twenty million people with twenty million sets of problems or opportunities and, potentially, twenty million revenue sources. Hastings would stay in Bengal for a further thirteen years to test his hypothesis. Hastings left India in 1785 and the greater part of his ambition, revenue collecting, was unsuccessful. The sale of salt and opium was an aid to the economy.

In 1784 William Pitt the Younger introduced what became Pitt's India Act, which was not repealed until an amendment to the 1916 Government of India Act:

'An Act for the better Regulation and Management of the Affairs of the East India Company and of the British Possessions in India, and for establishing a Court of Judicature for the more speedy and effectual Trial of Persons accused of Offences committed in the East Indies . . . etc.'

Pitt's India Act was a reform of the 1773 Act and the powers to enable the British government and the Company to together rule Madras, Bombay and Bengal. The Act made clear that Britain's role in India was now clearly political and commercial and that the two functions, while separate, inevitably crossed. Therefore, the ruling system had to be clearly defined and the terms of reference for each office and appointment spelt out so that neither role clashed but each would have procedures to follow when one concerned the other. This was a difficult path to follow and taken at a time when the British were still not used to large government even in their domestic affairs. They were dealing with the consequences of losing the major and most hopeful part of their first empire, America. They were at or close to war in Europe, while feeling the way to the first functions of Cabinet government and also being aware of the restless and ambitious imaginations in France that would shortly bring about the French Revolution, which would in turn force many in nearby Britain to question their own cultural, political and social prejudices.

The instinct was not so much entrenchment as simple pulling together resources and defining authority. The 1784 Act did just this.

The British East India Company was heading in the doubtful direction of 'owning' India and thus becoming the commercial, military and political moguls of the eighteenthth century. It could not be done. On paper the Company may have looked as if it could rule India. In reality, it could not. Anything so large and potentially even richer and more profitable would only usurp the status quo of a safe investment and ultimately become the focus of an even wider and more powerful military conflict for Britain than the French wars of Clive et al. had ever declared. Simply, the British government most certainly could not let India go.

The 1784 India Act would stabilise and, as far as the colonists were concerned, legitimise the British imperial presence in India. Thus the first stage was to make the Company directly accountable to the British government. Nothing could be changed without the British government's sanction. While the Company had day-to-day running of Indian possessions, the proper authority was now with a board of control of six, including a secretary of state as president of the board of control, the chancellor and four privy councillors – a board that would report to the Crown. This was government control. A court of directors – the most financially powerful group in what now would be called The City – would run the Company.

The restructure and further control of the Company amounted to greater observation of what was going on in India under London's authority. This was the 1770s. There was a primitive form of communications. Instructions and reports took months to change hands. Few had the experience of monitoring such an organisation and trying to do so efficiently from thousands of miles away was an impossibly risky task. Interpretation was easier than exact compliance; the process was open to mistakes and corruption both financially and legislatively. The irregularities were in part corrected but the regulations that commanded reform produced further irregularities. Yet despite government control and a regular examination of the way the role of governor-general could function as the on-the-spot steward of India, the system of despotism, corruption and individual speculation and creative government continued whether or not the Company was governed from London. Even Pitt's Act, as thoughtful as its draughtsmanship was, could not legislate for one aspect of the British venture in India since the beginning.

The commercial exploitation of the subcontinent, the rule and uses of its peoples and the very size and complexity of these two continuing dilemmas meant that the British rule from 1612 to the very end was too big to be anything but subjective colonialism with all its frailties, even though legislation demanded more control and change in the way the Company operated. The first decision recognised the huge, even impossible task a governor had to manage Bengal, balance the wishes, demands and disappointments of the princes, be prepared to defend the territory and to act in every way like the lord of the biggest manor imaginable.

When Hastings was given more autonomy officials in all parts of Bengal bombarded his new council with complaints about his policies. The council listened and in many cases believed the cases to be true or proper subjects for investigation.

The wider accusations of corruption would always find guilty examples. Hastings had dismissed very senior Indian officials, many of whom now accused him of being corrupt. Hastings was vulnerable and knew so and so did his enemies. The image of Hastings, self-made by commissions in India, was not hidden. It was fine for Clive to joke about his fortune, but not Hastings. His enemies were within his council, his own supposedly trusted men and in the great and good of the day in London.

The glitter on Hastings's career was to be tarnished by the political consequences of a duel he fought in 1779 with the ruling council member Sir Philip Francis, who became an MP, and with an impeachment in the House of Commons brought about by Edmund Burke, Charles James Fox and Richard Brinsley Sheridan. The charges included being involved in a colonial judicial murder, corruption and 'misde-meanors'. The impeachment took seven years, virtually bankrupted Hastings and came to nothing. He was acquitted and given a good enough pension by the Company – about £250,000 a year in present-day value – by early twenty-first century conversions.

Hastings, following Clive, shaped the future of India and its people for a century to come. He attempted, and in part succeeded, to make it so that his followers would agree that the Company had to understand and respect the culture and ways of the people who were part of the exploitation of the subcontinent. There is no doubt that India was stripped of many assets and there is no doubt that individuals made their fortunes by joining the universal system of taking commissions and bonuses by which most trade ran smoothly. This practice applied to both the newly arrived clerk and the governor-general. So with Hastings.

The story of Hastings's impeachment is told elsewhere; it is enough to say he was found not guilty, received a pension and restored the long-lost family estate. However, those who went after Hastings's reputation were not minor or entirely spiteful characters. Edmund Burke, as just one example, believed the even bigger indictment than the fortune Hastings gathered was the stripping of Indian assets. The King, George III, approved of Hastings, but there were few public figures to speak for him. They did not wish to be associated with the case yet the longer it was heard the more it would favour Hastings. People would become tired of the hearing; the prosecution would appear vindictive rather than solemn. Hastings was acquitted.

There was a further neglected aspect: the affair started in 1787 and was not finished until 1795. It coincided with some events of the French Revolution. Hastings made his case with claims about how he had held together empire. The matter was hearing less about profit turning and corruption and more about preserving empire, assets and, importantly, identity. It was a good defence.

CHAPTER IV

CORNWALLIS AND SHORE

Prime Minister William Pitt (1759–1806) set himself the task of producing a government policy on India that would have to be followed by the Company civil servants. This in effect meant that 100 years before India was formally the major part of the empire, and Victoria that subcontinent's Empress, the Crown, through Pitt, established hard and fast rules for the way in which Britain's interests would be observed – even though it did not directly govern the territory. The East India Company no longer had a free hand.

The Company could make what profits it wanted; it could capitalise on its influence and patronage, and have absolute control over investment and all appointments. However, the Company could not have its own, that is, exclusive, India policy. It was restricted where it had to follow London's directives. But this was the most powerful trading company ever seen. It had too the strongest hold over the most powerful people in the subcontinent and many of the same sort in England. Lord Macaulay's description of the company bribing all who could 'help or hurt' at court is a classic description of the gentle corruption slipping from hand to hand among the willing if sticky fingers of London patronage.

'Ministers, mistresses, priests, were kept in good humour by presents of shawls and silks, birds' nests and attar of roses, busles and diamonds and bags of guineas.'

In a darker yet grander way, the Company bribed and bank-rolled rulers, princes, sultans and viscounts, bankers and governments their individuals,. Even when heading to a dip and its own bankruptcy and living up to its critics as a blood-stained monopoly that was largely unnecessary for the business of India, the largest trading company ever known, and that changed the way the world did business, at the time of Pitt's India Act was run by only 150 or so clerks and directors from a modest London office. The profits were in the original commodities: spices, silks, teas. But the more the Company came to control in the eighteenth century it also gathered in an even more lucrative crop – taxes and revenues. In doing so, the Company became imperial administrators with the often complicated bureaucracy that came with a very large – more than 200,000 men – standing army. By 1833 the government in London had revoked the Company's licence to trade in India.

The government safeguarded its interests by insisting that the important positions of governors should mainly come from its own list. This meant a government man was always at the top and therefore could make sure that the Crown's interests and wishes were observed. In London a Board of Control was established that in all but name became a colonial office. But even with an official government department and clear guide-lines set out for the Company, Pitt always assumed that the

Company would look after its own interests first and foremost. It, the government, made every effort to understand the ways of the territory, far more so than it had in North America. Ironically, General Cornwallis, the man who had surrendered Yorktown in virtually the deciding act of war in America,was sent to India in 1786. He became the first governor-general who was not a 'local man' – a product of neither the civil service nor the Company.

He inherited the legacies of Clive and the reforming Warren Hastings. Building on existing policy, Cornwallis began making the link between the political needs of London and the natural function of a trading organisation. The India Act had made a clear division between the commercial role of the Company and the need for a professional government of the territory. Civil servants were poorly paid under an assumption that they would make their private small fortunes through corruption and adventure. Cornwallis gradually replaced the Indians at senior levels in the India civil service with British administrators. The meticulous and assiduous Indian clerk could flourish as a caste. However, like all members of social groupings, this bureaucratic caste would find great difficulties in ever breaking through to the higher echelons. One way of succeeding in making the bureaucracy efficient and therefore the Company profits reasonable was to introduce the right conditions for stability in India. Cornwallis had gathered a process of diplomacy that worked well among the princes who were still ruling their own country.

There were changing influences and levels of authority. Some princes became more powerful. The Maratha leaders took for themselves more territory and at the same time re-established relative stability. These mini-wars and balances of power could easily go on about the East India Company without apparently affecting profits. However, the territory ruled was not the whole of the subcontinent and the Company could not and had no desire to rule over the whole of India. Firstly, there were simply not the resources to hold territory once taken. Secondly, the capability of the Company was already stretched. To try to oppose the majority of states and impose British rule would have made little commercial sense. Moreover, not all of India made political and financial sense to the Company.

Cornwallis and his successor, Sir John Shore (1751–1834), were able to maintain a policy of keeping the British interest in India confined to the activities of the trading house. The Company had always, either through corruption or open policy, managed to do business with political and financial leaders in India. It was a dream world for accountants who were sometimes accused of dreaming up rather than dreaming of. Shore would have none of this. Shore was a severe looking evangelical Christian whose longer-lasting reputation is not that of a former governor-general but as the man who founded the British and Foreign Bible Society.

Many governors and governors-general demonstrated only a formal religious persuasion, but Shore, who had been a sea captain and a Latin scholar, found joy in his faith. He spent time in India relying on it. He was known as a man of the faith and therefore could be trusted not to 'pickle his own onions' as the phrase of the time had it – he would be beyond taking a profit from anything that came his way. He was given de facto charge of investigations into disappearing revenues because the people above him were too busy looking after their own profit and knew he was above larceny. When famine yet again struck Bengal, many of the food supplies were diverted for the profits of Company men. He said as much and made sure nobody could cover up that diversion. On another occasion, critics suggested Shore was too close a friend of Hastings, but the insinuation never stuck. Shore was above suspicion. In 1793, he arrived as governor-general in Calcutta only to be told that the previous man, Cornwallis, was staying on because he did not fancy leaving. Why? There was rumour of war with France. Cornwallis was not an enthusiast. Shore's reputation was of a man who broke few laws and none intentionally. He was given instructions from London and they seemed perfectly adequate to him and allowed him to stick to his principle that what is morally wrong cannot be politically right. Thus was written the habit of the non-interventionist; this was during a period when the governor was tested week by week to intervene between differing factions and princes. He did not much care to do that and was criticised for behaving that way. Yet he was quietly right for much of the time and famously so when he was about to be recalled, only for the Company to find that Shore's decision on how to deflect a plot was better informed than the more militaristic demands of others.

When Shore left, this quiet son of the manse observed what few in London had recognised: British power had become sovereignty from having been mere dependency. He was right. India and the Company were running out of time.

The realism of profits and fewer losses appeared in the books of the man who followed Shore between 1797 and 1805 as governor-general. He was Richard Colley Wellesley the First Marquess Wellesley (1760–1842). His more famous brother Arthur Wellesley was the first Duke of Wellington and less so as lord lieutenant of Ireland, confronted as he was by the hopes of so many for Catholic emancipation. The difference between Wellesley and Shore was surely a demonstration that looking for a stereotypical governor-general is a fruitless task, other than a reference to the aristocracy, particularly after 1858. Shore came from a modest background. Wellesley did not. Wellesley did not like Shore, whom he considered of low birth and timid. Wellesley was not timid.

Wellesley displayed an aristocratic tendency, not surprising in one who was a viscount at birth and at twenty-one had the earldom of Mornington thrust upon him on the death of his father Garret Wesley who, following the example of his own father, had got through most of the family money, forcing the young Wellesley to sell the Irish interests including property and the estate. Pitt had arranged an English peerage for him in the year he was sent to India. So, he was also Baron Wellesley. That is not a role to be ignored in the personality of a governor-general at any time, never mind at a period that had witnessed a governor's impeachment. It is never possible to be certain that a politician has the support of his or her peers. Politicians rarely change sides but frequently abandon allegiances, especially if ignored in the handout of political and financial spoils. Wellesley, or Mornington as he was more formally known at that time, fell into the class that by their very power (not always influence) meant others in their way or style took a view on them. Wellesley was seen as a political insider who exercised every advantage that came his way, and might be remembered as an exuberant imperialist; it was a title that needed no defending at the start of the nineteenth century when the mood of what was right or even acceptable cannot be compared with what might be the standard 200 years on. For example, his younger brother Arthur Wellesley's first campaign in India was the final Mysore War. It was tactical and theatre warfare at its most set-piece and so was the looting that followed.

After taking the palace of Tipu Sultan, Arthur Wellesley came by a musical tiger, which he handed over to his brother

the governor-general. It was thought amusing. The idea that it
might represent the fall of the sahib class in India was a prepos-
terous artistic jujube to be shown off at parties rather than a
gruesome object to lurk in the corner of a forever damp morning room. It was not a cheerful model tiger. The tiger held a
screaming East India Company servant in one claw – not the
governor-general.

There was too a reminder that in this period, high office in
India was not a career expectation. Candidates and successful
governors were first and foremost London politicians, not colonial servants. After serving a term, most would return to London
to find another big posting or retirement. Few stayed on other
than those who had nothing and would have even less if they
returned to England. Wellesley was at the top end. After India
he would be expecting something bigger. He had been a treas-
ury lord in Pitt's administration and a supporter of Wilberforce
in the anti-slavery movement. These appointments were trails to
even the highest offices and Wellesley may not have displayed
contempt for the East India Company administrators, but he
had the air of regarding them as lesser mortals. After all, they
were commerce and trade. This is not a minor point of snob-
bery. For example, at this very time, Pitt's financial advisor,
Robert Smith, had been raised to the peerage by Pitt only to find
himself ostracised in the House of Lords. He was a banker,
indeed a very important banker. But to the English aristocracy
his new-found peerage would not disguise the fact that banking
was trade and he never quite established himself among the
peers – maybe he knew too much about their finances.[1]

Wellesley was without a good fortune but thanks to his
friends he was not without good fortune. In 1784 he had
become one of the two Members of Parliament for the rotten
borough of Bere Alston in Devon. (The other was Viscount

Fielding. The seat disappeared in the 1832 Reform Act). Nine years later Wellesley, still an MP and of course without a stipend, had the very good fortune to be appointed to the India Board of Control. It was during this period that the running of India and the relationship and terms of reference between the East India Company and the government was being rewritten and would remain so until the first viceroy in 1858. It was thus an important moment in Wellesley's career, still governed within the Regulating Act of 1773. It was not good law; it was too soon made.

The Regulating Act laid out regulating terms for the Company but did not provide any solution to the 'too-big' state of the East India Company, the most important trading entity the British had ever created and the most powerful in the world. Moreover, the Company was in debt because its structure made management difficult and it could not pay its monopoly tax to the government and to the Bank of England because its until then hugely profitable tea exports to America had collapsed. The tea was there, some seven million kilograms of it rotting in bond and depots; but the market had collapsed because the Dutch were usurping the British trading position by supplying the transatlantic market through illicit channels.The state of taxation and supply in America was about to produce a change in British colonial history.

Tea drinkers in America did not mind the source of their tea. Lord North the Earl of Guildford (1732–1792), the prime minister, was perhaps too easily accused of losing the American colonies – the Intolerable Acts unwisely followed the so-called Boston Tea Party in 1773 and the American War of Independence would start at Lexington two years later. In this atmosphere, North was caught between the powerful anti-Regulation lobby that included influential Company

shareholders and because there was no other way of controlling such a huge global asset. The Regulating Act in theory
stopped Company employees from bribing or receiving bribes
and it restricted directors to four-year terms – not long enough
to amass fortunes by questionable means. In the long term,
more importantly, the Act appointed the governor of Bengal as
governor-general of Bengal while putting Madras and Bombay
under the governor-general's command. Here was the origin
of the single territorial control of the Company in India. This
was not the command of the whole of India but the command
over the Company's territories.

Among other provisions was the appointment of the British
Court and thus the British legal process at Fort William,
Calcutta. The Regulation Act changed the form of British
control over the doings of the East India Company, but it did
not do it well because the government had only partial control
and,in the manner of long-distance control that was a natural
state of global business in the eighteenth century, the government did not have the machinery or perhaps the expertise to
assume what would later be absolute control. It took another
decade and clearer minds to put right some of these
shortcomings.

To manage and legislate for the near absolute control of
foreign territory must be put in the context of the weakness of
the government, back home. In spite of the apparent genius
of Pitt and his ilk, we might remember the failures of the
national leadership who were managing the war against France
at exactly the same time that the management of India was
being questioned. Moreover, the political condition of the
British at home was far from an example to those seeking solutions to colonial weaknesses. A time of uncertain political
reform in India took place against a backdrop of domestic

crises that started in 1798 with the Irish Rebellion, then continued with the war with Napoleon, Catholic emancipation, slavery laws and then the Reform Act. All these events occurred through changing British governments, a new and unsettled monarch, the reshaping of political parties and stronger-willed and more authoritative leaders than at any time. Such upheaval meant that the opening twenty years or so of the nineteenth century were the fastest moving and most politically turbulent of any century for the British; during all this, they were trying to reform India and guess where British rule in Madras, Bombay and Calcutta went next.

Each governor witnessed this frailty although, given the times, never thought it odd and may have indeed only understood it in retrospect. This was the case with Wellesley, who went to India for eight years, during which time the Company flourished, increasing its profits by some 200 per cent. Too impressive? There was sometimes a little imaginative accounting and conflicts of interests. In the Spring 1833 edition of the *Asiatic Journal* the dilemma of one, Charles Grant, tells an unusual tale:

'The late Charles Grant, Esq., was for a long time the commercial resident at Malda, where, in addition to a liberal salary, he received a considerable commission on all the articles purchased by him for the Company. On making up his accounts, at the end of two or three successive years, he found that the sum, which became due to him was very great, and that he was in fact making a large fortune very rapidly. Being a man of the most scrupulous integrity, he sent all his books down to the governor general in Calcutta (Cornwallis) and begged that they might be very carefully examined, as he was making money so fast, that he suspected he was not coming by it honestly, though he could discover no error in his accounts. The Governor returned the books to him unexamined, and begged him to be quite at ease on the subject; adding that he wished all the servants of the Honourable Company were equally scrupulous.'²

Scrupulous servants were not unknown. The governor-general whose sentiment he quoted was Lord William Bentinck. He was the first governor-general of all India, a lodging that continued until the coming of viceroys in 1858. Bentinck was there from 1828 until 1835. When a list of all the British governors of India, even up to 1947, is posted, Bentinck would probably come out as the one who cared most for India and her people and had the chance to make life for them better. He was the third son of the man who succeeded Pitt the Younger as prime minister in 1806, William Bentinck, who apart from twice being prime minister is remembered as having every title in British nobility from baron to duke and being great-great-great-grandfather to Elizabeth II. It was inevitable that the younger Bentinck would rule and at the age of nine he became Clerk of the Pipe; the nominal keep of the pipe rolls in which English laws inscripted on vellum were rolled and archived. He joined the Coldstream Guards at sixteen and at thirty one was a major general and governor of Madras, only to be sacked two years later after the troops mutinied when Bentinck ordered that they could not wear their traditional dress and had to wear army uniforms. A half century later, the insistence by the British that soldiers wear British uniforms was one of the causes of dissatisfaction among sepoys that caused the 1857 Mutiny.

By 1811, Bentinck was a lieutenant general, had seen service in the Peninsular War and was commanding British troops in

Sicily. He was recalled once again, this time for giving away territory to the wrong side. Bentinck took cover on the backbenches of the House of Commons before being sent as governor general to Madras with the aim of making that presidency of the East India Company profitable. This he seemed to do. He also made English the court language rather than Persian and established a British education for westernised Indians in order to get the next generation working with the British in India. This was the 1830s. Still, a future governor would have said that this was the good age of government by despotism. When he had gone, apart from a rumour that he planned to sell the Taj Mahal, Bentinck was remembered as a fine governor general who first thought for the good of the people he governed. Not all viceroys followed his example but then no viceroy ever followed the example of any other viceroy. Each governor general was an individual and not a timeserver. They arrived sometimes having served in India in some lesser role, for example as a governor of one of the presidencies; there they had very principled views of what was wrong in their times. More importantly, when governors general arrived there was, inevitably in an advancing society with threatening neighbours or internal differences in the subcontinent, a military crisis needing attention or even, because of conflict, other issues within India unresolved. There was little chance of a new governor general arriving to settle down for five years without much to do. If the First Lady was bored it was because of her own personality and because there were rarely things to be done whereas His Excellency could work from dawn to well beyond dusk and still find the day's work not done.

The days of fortunes to be made still existed but new bookkeeping and restructuring meant that the workings of the governor faced greater scrutiny and the commercial interests outside the Company were vigorous. The Company was losing its powers, the monopolies pared and vigilance from London tighter. Furthermore, British ambitions in the opening 1800s were not to govern India but to run more efficiently their interests and so dominate the hundreds of major princes and even more minor nawabs. Annexation and division in India meant skirmish and battle would continue. Conflict would decide the power politics of the states and principalities. This was true from the Carnatic region in the south-east to Bengal in the north. Under the Board of Control and the Company interests, Bengal expanded, taking in other princedoms. The Company nudged the Nawab of Oudh into handing over virtual control, for not much of a pension. By 1803, Delhi itself was in the hands of the British. The old nawab, Shah Alam, was paid off with a pension of £100,000 a year. For his dignity he was called the King of Delhi. His residence was the famous Red Fort. The wars may have been a series of campaign skirmishes and cavalry assaults but they would decide the way the Company army and then the British army in India saw themselves. They were regional, had separate identities and had their own duties to defend. The major campaigns meant the movement of large formations. This was often unpopular and showed the limitations of colonial armies and the need to enlist the princes.

During the first couple of decades of the nineteenth century the British fought the second Maratha War. The result was a further consolidation of British interests and, most importantly, the merging of Gujarat with the presidency of Bombay. From it, the Company also controlled Agra, Delhi and Meerut. Here was an addition to the North-West Province. By the time of Wellesley's going, India had been administratively rearranged – or at least in theory, as Lord Minto soon understood when he arrived to succeed Wellesley.

Gilbert Elliot-Murray-Kynynmound (1751–1814), the Lord Minto and later the first Earl Minto, became governor general in 1805. (Exactly 100 years later his descendant, the 4th Earl of Minto, was appointed governor general and viceroy). He was considered a sophisticated candidate for India with the style of a mild-mannered judicious governor who would have felt comfortable in a well-founded church quietly governing middle-class England. For now his hope was to quietly appease his masters who had sent him to India with instructions to maintain good humour and thus good apolitical order – more Cornwallisian than Wellesleyean – and to keep an eye on the liberal use of penknives among the clerks and the like. Instead the 56-year-old Minto landed at Madras to face large-scale mutiny and some 600 prisoners liable to be executed.

Mutiny rarely fits easily with an all-guilty verdict, especially as the ultimate punishment is death. What then was Minto to do? Dismiss the mutineers from Company service with no opportunity of return and leave an unspoken threat over them? They needed to understand that one of the options, apart from execution, had been deportation. To ban a Hindu from his country was an agonising punishment, although one unlikely to be successfully implemented. The fear of deportation loomed large half a century later when the British were attacked in the Indian, or Sepoy Mutiny. One of the reasons in 1857 for that rebellion was the very real likelihood that the Bengal sepoys would be deployed into Afghanistan and that was abroad, overseas, to them and a dreadful prospect.

Minto appeared lenient (as Canning would be seen after the Mutiny) but it was the right decision, especially as the slaughter or deportation of 600 men would have created a great martyrdom and everlasting angst on a par with the Amritsar massacre.

The period of Minto's governorship was not a time of lucrative trading and tax collecting. He arrived in India just two years after the Battle of Trafalgar (1805) and so Napoleon's navy had been reduced to a coastal and occasional small international flotilla; certainly, it was without a large-scale fleet that effectively threatened the maritime supremacy of the British. That did not mean Napoleon had given up getting to the Far East including British India. The roads to India were hard to defend. The geography for deploying troops in forward positions was impossible without treaties and pacts with the Persians et al. and Britain could not rely on the neutrality of the peoples between the Bosporus and the Indus.

The policy of the Company in London was that it should never make special agreements with princes and chiefs. The reason was obvious: get an agreement with a prince and all the prince's enemies were then your enemy.

There were hundreds of castles in almost every province and each had a chieftain and chances were that each chieftain was at some warfare with another. Moreover, each castle commanded an area that could be a taxpaying district and, as ever, experience suggested that not all the chieftains could be trusted; they too were subjected to similar and often constant threats from vagabond leaders who were unlikely to follow an agreement with the British signed by the prince they were in the process of robbing. Minto's reasoning was carefully argued but its resolution meant he had to have good forces of his own, reliable commanders who could spread a considerable amount of fright among the princes and chieftains. Minto saw the problem of chiefs and princes in one province, Bundelkund, fighting among themselves as an inevitable loss of influence over the chiefs and therefore the authority and dignity of the British, including the government in London.

Minto sent out a decree that no one should be mistaken; the new governor general was to enforce his authority and all disputes, instead of being settled by the sword, would be referred to the British district commissioners. That should have been the end of it, except that the skilful marauding bandits felt no need to toe any governor's line.

In the case of Bundelkund, it took nearly four years to get close to Minto's solution but, seemingly inevitably, the harshest enemy of the province lurked among the Company's tax collectors, who drained so many that the province fell into nothing but resentment and the poverty that made certain it would be never forgotten.

When Napoleon appeared to be a threat as far as India and when this hazard coincided with changing legislation on the authority of the Company, the directors of the Company were more sensitive to the impossible politics of India and understood the need to take constitutional decisions in London rather than allow the governor to make adjustments. For example, there was no single head of state and no overall governing body. A single province could produce hundreds of princes and princelings, each one of whom tended to plot from each sunrise and so had to be understood and in most cases avoided.

The governor general's word could be law but not necessarily obeyed and enforcement took far more than a display of pomposity. The directors in London would have cared to stick to the rule of non-collaboration with princes and similar. That would work if the idea was simply the running of British interests without continuous streams of suspicions. However, there was for the directors a threat to be faced head on and therefore more dramatically: Napoleon had an ambition to move further to the east, in spite of his naval defeats at the Battle of Aboukir Bay in 1798 and particularly at Trafalgar in 1805 (which his own admiral commanding the Franco-Spanish fleet at Trafalgar, Villeneuve, had predicted).

Discussions of the Franco-Russian Treaty and Franco-Prussian Treaties of Tilsit (July 1807) centred upon the consequences of Napoleon's victory at Friedland, the decimation of Prussian territories and consequent drawing of boundaries for the Duchy of Warsaw and Kingdom of Westphalia – all and each part of Napoleon's command of central Europe. (All reverted after his defeat in 1815). The Tilsit meetings and discussions had a diplomatic and military codicil that, while unconfirmed, alarmed the directors of the East India Company. France had unspecific but generally approved promises of Russian help in her fight against colonial Britain and therefore in particular, Britain in India. Britain, thus far comfortable that Aboukir Bay and Trafalgar had given them reason to think Napoleon would find it difficult to move east given the logistical conundrum for any general moving an army big enough to invade, now had to break the house rules on diplomacy. A line was drawn along the old silk roads that took in Afghanistan, Lahore and went through Persia. The British needed what would now be called defence agreements that reassured the Company that the princes of this route would help repel a French advance. Of course, no agreement would ever do that.

The tradition of watching to see who was winning a fight and then sign up on that side was not about to be abandoned. Moreover, why should regional princes cooperate with the British, especially as they rarely cooperated with each other? For example, the Sikhs were forever at each others' territories. The most celebrated of them all, Runjet Singh (1780–1808), had since 1803 commanded Punjab through which an imagined French advance would have to reach if they ever decided to invade, which they never did; however, the enormous cost and time taken to plan against an attack took every waking moment in Calcutta and London. There were of course still threats from within India, especially the real suspicion of what next with the Mahrattas.

Talks and hopes raised by the British and largely repelled by the Sikhs were no longer important when put in the context of a non-French threat. However, the Sikhs plus the success of the British in the latest skirmishes and battles with the Mahrattas had Minto apparently through strength telling the Sikhs to restore all land they had taken. What Minto, being quite pompous, did not know was that the Sikh leader he had written to, Runjet Singh, never got Minto's letter of demands. Bored, Runjet Singh had gone home from a skirmish to his palace in Amritsar for hours of 'mirth and pleasure'. Minto's demands went unopened so he sent in the army. It was set-piece diplomacy enforced by military might that no one wanted to exercise. In 1809 a truce and then a treaty were agreed. It was a painful confrontation by the urbane and middle-aged Minto and the irascible prince in his mid-twenties running on the adrenalin of success and mirth. The elaborate embassy sent to Afghanistan had no better success; a more complicated story was similarly futile largely because almost every side managed to get into a frenzy of military activity and consequent loss of territory over a threat that did not exist. The movement of the army was everything to the Company. It did not defend India as a territory; it guarded the Company as a trader and tax collector just as it had since the beginning when it camped as a mixture of odd fellows and mercenaries. By the late eighteenth century the Company was big enough and regulated sufficiently that without its army it would have collapsed. It was bigger than the British army itself and fought beyond the battlements of Calcutta; thus the Company army would parade the British to empire.

In the 1820s they were at war with Burma and a decade later with Afghanistan. A decade on from that, and the wars included Sind (now Sind Province in Pakistan) and the Sikhs in Punjab. Moreover, between 1814 and 1816 there had been the Gurkha war, immediately followed by the third Maratha war. Between 1845 and 1849 there were two Sikh wars and from these mixed wars and troops came one of the most famous of the British regiments. The Gurkhas in the early nineteenth century gradually encroached into British interests in the Bengal provinces. It was decided in 1814 that these Gurkha movements threatened British interests.

The Gurkhas were not confining themselves to a gradual migration of their peoples. They were sending raiding parties. The problem for the British was that the dividing and subdividing of the territory included the provision of certain border rights and extensions for the Gurkhas. Moreover, the British began to see the mini invasions as more than an expected spread of Nepalese interests and a direct challenge to British authority. So in 1814, under General Sir David Ochterlony, the British mounted an expeditionary force into Nepal.[3] It took two years to crush the Gurkha opposition. It was a rugged terrain and far from the set-piece military campaigns on the plains and fields of European conflict. Curiously, it was this confrontation that began a partnership between the British army and what became its Brigade of Gurkhas.

They were there the following year when Pindari tribesmen reinforced by disaffected Maratha troops once more beset the British. Officially the Maratha leaders supported British rule. If the two British armies wanted to beat the Pindaris, then they had to do so without worsening relations with the Maratha. They, if they chose, could put ten times the number of men the British had into battle. War with the Maratha was inevitable. On 21 December 1817 in the battle of Mahidpur, 3,000 Maratha soldiers were killed. The British took nearly 800 casualties, killed or wounded.

The senior commander of the British forces was General Lord Francis Rawdon-Hastings.[4] He was an experienced soldier who had fought in the American War of Independence and should be remembered as the man who bought Singapore for the British in 1819, if it were not for the image of Sir Stamford Raffles.

The princes defeated, they had now to look to the British government for money and position in order to maintain any authority over their own people. It is here that Rawdon-Hastings's diary produces the perfect description of the British rule in India. It can be likened to that of the way of a strict public-school housemaster. The recalcitrant boy will be beaten. That same boy will be then encouraged to play games and even be invited to tea parties so long as the games are played by the housemaster's rules and his social courtesies observed:

'The dispersed plunderers having now no head under whom they could reunite, will look out for other modes of subsistence; and it is to be hoped that a tranquility will prevail in central India which we may improve to noble purposes. The introduction of instruction into those countries, where the want of information and of principle is universal, is an object becoming the British Government. It is very practicable. Detachments of youths, who have been rendered competent at the Lancastrian schools in Bengal under the missionaries, should be dispatched under proper leaders to disseminate that method of teaching. Its progress would soon enable numbers to read and comprehend books of moral inculcation in the Hindustani language.

Lady Hastings caused a compilation of apologues, and of maxims relative to social duties, to be printed for the use of her school at Barrackpore. The boys studied it, to all appearance profitably, but many individuals of high caste in the neighbourhood used to apply for the perusal of copies. It has all the attraction of a novelty, while the simplicity of what it recommends is likely to make impression on minds to which any reflection on the topics was ever before suggested.'[5]

War during the first half of the nineteenth century provoked sharp lessons for the Company and the British: that wars of the subcontinent were repeats of previous conflicts and the base reasons for them could not be resolved, and, the British would never be able to deploy the numbers of trained troops they needed even for containment. Even in the twenty-first century there are reminders of Britain's involvement in the Afghanistan War with a coalition of willing nations led by the United States came with British battle honours already 150 and more years tattered.

The first Sikh war (1845–1846) and the first Afghan war (1839–1842) were linked. In the summer of 1838 a treaty was signed over Afghanistan, which the British, in the form of the East India Company, either believed or hoped would stop Persian and Russian incursion in Afghanistan. The British had large interests in the kingdom. They certainly believed that there was a constant threat from Punjab in the east and/or Persia in the west. There was also constant fear by the British that the Russians would control Afghanistan and therefore threaten India. (A fear raised in the British Foreign Office in

December 1979 with the Russian intervention into Afghanistan to put down what they saw as a threat to the Soviet Central Republics and what could have followed).

There were two claimants to the Afghan throne. One, Dost Muhammad, was supported by the Russians. The second, supported by the British, was Shah Shuja. Here was the source of the first Afghan war. The British army of the Indus, under Sir John Keane, took Kandahar.[6] Shah Shuja was crowned. By the end of July 1839 Dost Muhammad had abandoned Kabul and had taken refuge in the north. The warring Afghanistan and the tribal defaults have not much changed in 200 years. A garrison of 8,000 East India Company troops remained at Kabul to preserve the authority of Shah Shuja. An uneasy truce lasted until 1841. The son of Dost Muhammad, Akbar Khan, roused sufficient troops and people to mutiny against this all but British rule.

The British ambassador to the court in Kabul was Sir William Hay Macnaghten.[7] He was effectively the British ruler. He had no regard for the tribesmen and warlords of Dost Muhammad. However, it was his task to make sure that the apparent truce would survive. If any proof were needed that Macnaghten was right in mistrusting the Afghan leaders it came two days before Christmas in 1841. He had a meeting arranged with Akbar Khan. It was supposed to be a meeting to discuss differences. Akbar Khan's senses of diplomacy were limited. The discussion did not continue for long. Akbar Khan murdered Macnaghten. Apart from the outrage, the British position was now precarious. Akbar Khan's stock was high. He had himself killed the British envoy. Among his people, therefore, he had nothing to prove. A couple of weeks later, in early January 1842, the British garrison at Kabul was forced to surrender. Akbar Khan promised the British that they would be able to withdraw from Afghanistan in all safety. Who would have trusted this Afghan murderer? Major General William Elphinstone was the commander who surrendered the garrison. He died almost immediately.

Some 16,500 British wives, children, troops and Indian troops filed out of the Kabul garrison, surely with little faith in Akbar Khan's promise of safe conduct to India. The Afghans massacred most of them on the Khyber Pass road on 13 January 1842. A very few were taken prisoner and thrown into prison at Kabul. All that was left of the British presence in Afghanistan was the garrison at Kandahar and that at Jalalabad, both under siege. General Sir George Pollock was the man designated to rescue the three pockets of British survivors and their followers at Jalalabad, Kandahar and Kabul.[8]

Pollock had joined the East India Company's army at the age of seventeen. He fought at the siege of Bhartpur two years later and in the Gurkha war of 1814 to 1816. Ten years later he was fighting in the first of the Burmese wars. He was a natural choice, perhaps the only one, to lead the rescue attempt to Jalalabad. Akbar Khan's tribesmen began the siege of Jalalabad in March 1842. Pollock did not manage to raise the siege until 16 April. Pollock then pressed on to Kabul. There were just ninety-five prisoners left. He made them safe and then destroyed the grand citadel. Pollock returned in triumph, but in a sombre mood. The story of Pollock's planning is well recorded elsewhere. (See, in particular, *The First Afghan War and its Causes* published in 1879 by Sir Henry Marion Durand. Durand later became governor general of Punjab).[9] By December 1842 the British, the East India Company, could no longer justify the cost and the danger of being in Afghanistan. They pulled out just twelve months after the murder of Macnaghten. The successful Akbar Khan brought his father

Dost Muhammad to Kabul in triumph. Here was a lasting lesson of the feebleness of any outside force or ideology to rule over the Afghans. It was a lesson, seemingly, unlearned by the British and all who followed, including the Russians and Americans, into the twentieth and the beginning of the twenty-first century.

The wars of Victoria's soldiers continued. Peace seemed so far off when the smallest skirmish led to terrible reprisals. The withdrawal from Afghanistan had hardly been completed when the British entered upon the Sikh Wars (1845–1849).

The Sikhs came from Punjab. Here was a centre of loyalty to the British. Their leader at the beginning of the nineteenth century was Ranjit Singh. Ranjit Singh, partly with the help of the French, had structured the Sikh army along European lines. The competence of the Sikh army was partly responsible for the ridding of Afghans from the province of Punjab. However, Ranjit Singh had not achieved his ambition: the establishment of a Sikh state. He did overpower Kashmir and Teshawar. He really wanted the territory across the Sutlej River, the important waterway that runs, roughly, from the area of Amritsar down to Bahawalpur where shortly, after it joins the Chenab River, is now in Pakistan. In 1839 he died and with him went the Sikh support for the British. The British had annexed Sind Province and there was much speculation over whether they would do the same in Punjab. There was hardly any secret about the Sikh unrest nor their intentions and so when, on 11 December 1845, 20,000 Sikhs crossed the Sutlej, the British army was there. Within a week the two forces engaged at Ferozepore. There was some confusion among the British.

Sir Hugh Gough, who commanded the army, had to take orders from the governor general, Sir Henry Hardinge, a soldier governor who joined Gough's staff. Hardinge wanted reinforcements. What might have been a quick victory for the British turned into a slog, but it was enough to eventually have the Sikhs driven back beyond the River Sutlej. The following year, 1846, the two armies met again. This was the wretched stuff of military legend with the 16th Lancers charging full tilt at the Sikh positions. The Sikhs withdrew. A fortnight later Gough's army all but slaughtered the Sikhs. The first war was done and a truce of sorts was signed on 11 March at Lahore. However, the Sikhs, a warrior caste, believed they could still overwhelm the British.

The Punjab protectorate under Sir Henry Lawrence had two years' breathing space to prepare for what seemed an inevitable uprising. There were, in 1848, skirmishes. Gough had prepared his army, but perhaps not for the casualties he was about to receive at the battle of Chillianwallah on 13 January 1849. The Sikh artillery attacked Gough, not yet reinforced from forces on their way from Multan. He sent in his infantry. Fighting continued from mid-afternoon to late evening. By then the British had taken the Sikh lines, but at an awful cost. On the British side alone, more than 2,300 soldiers were killed. Gough may have won the battle, but he had lost his command. He was told he was to be replaced by Charles Napier.[10]

Napier was an experienced officer, having fought in Ireland and conspicuously in the Peninsular Wars under Wellington. It was Napier who defeated the emirs at the battle of Meeanee in Sind in 1843 and, when in control of the province, is said to have sent his report to London, 'Peccavi' [I have sinned]. His command in the Sikh Wars was shortlived. He left India in 1851 and died in England two years later. Yet another first-class soldier saddled with the reputation of military symbolism who would never bring about long-term periods of peace for which so many perished for no great reason in colonial and increasingly imperial India. The Company army was the symbol of that British imperialism long before total power over a society – which is a common definition of imperialism – was laid firm as it would be after the 1850s when direct rule was established with the viceroy as the monarch's representative. Imperialism was not the pejorative term for the British way as it can sometimes be in the twenty-first century.

British rule was not so despotic than the one it replaced. In some cases, Company and later direct rule was fairer. The army's role was crucial in making this at all possible. The Company army was the constable of India. Like all military institutions, the company of men were broadly picked. The footsoldiers of the army were largely Indians but not career soldiers. Europeans, often not well-trained nor altogether reliable non-commissioned officers, also took their places in mercenary ranks. So a large part of the army could be and would be hired for the battle and then let go. By the Victorian period, the structure was more established and with permanent orders of battle and full-time soldiers. By the start of the nineteenth century the regiments were largely sepoys, some 80,000, thus Indians protecting British interests in India, British interests that were protected by a poorly organised Company army even post-Clive. There were more than 200,000 by the time of the Mutiny. Towards the end of the eighteenth century the Company reorganised, with the army run from a newly structured hub that would be seen, in twenty-first-century military terms, as a command or general headquarters. Central command in Georgian military terms meant one obvious change: a general headquarters breeds red tabs, that is, officers not on the front line – in modern terms much maligned (from the trenches) as staff officers. Those staff

officers got the lucrative and prestigious commands that oper-
ational officers had expected.

The determining strength of an army is often in the military
sinews and loyalties of its NCOs. The sergeants and corporals
under the command of a middle-ranking company commander,
say of captain rank, are the people who translate orders and
doctrine from above and knock together the ordinary soldiers
so that the game plan gets as close as it might ever do to working on the battlefield. This was the only doctrine known to
army structure and, doubtful as it was, it was imagined that it
could not much be improved on. In the Company army this
was an even duller prospect.

The officer class came from two groups: the Company officers and the Crown. They had but one thing in common: social
and family circumstances; they were likely to be the poorer
members of both. In the Victorian British cavalry and infantry
an officer had to buy his commission or have someone, usually
family, who would. It was a common enough practice that
started under Charles II in the 1660s and that would continue
until the army reforms in 1871. Other regiments including
engineers and the Company were considered ordinary and
the officers professionally admired but rarely socially acceptable. It was a fact that the infantry and cavalry officers had
expensive social lives. A soldier not affording the social needs
of the Mess would have had a difficult time and, because of
the period, probably would have had few connections with
brother officers from grander backgrounds. At the start of
Victoria's reign to become a lieutenant in the Foot Guards
would cost about £2,000 in Victorian pounds and £1,200 in
the cavalry. To purchase a colonel's commission (the highest
for sale) would be £9,000 in the Foot Guards, £6,000 in the
cavalry. Senior officers in the 'better' regiments were

aristocrats and they would decide who might be suitable to buy one of the purchase vacancies, as they were known. If this social standard may seem hardly different from the norm of all professional life (modern solicitors buying into law firms etc.) there is one aspect that should be considered.

A British regimental officer in the Company was senior, even at the same rank, to a Company officer. There was therefore an easily indentified unsettled view among the East India Company officers, or could be. Protest that became public was not at all unknown. That being so, the consequence was that the sepoys witnessed the dissatisfaction and we should bear this in mind when wondering why the sepoys rebelled in 1857.

The late-eighteenth-century reorganisation was reasonable in its ambition for officers. Just as the Company was famous for taking young men as clerks and giving them a career full of opportunities – Clive and Hastings were good examples – so young men sought army cadetships and were taught to command, to speak languages of India and to anticipate promotions. The newly structured army meant that a young ensign might train, cross train and learn through instruction and invaluable anecdote how to handle platoon, squadron and even what would now be company levels of men (150 or so). From quite a young age, he would also learn how to plan for time away from headquarters with all its logistics and facilities, to see what supplies were needed, how they would be carried, what conditions they could be kept in during delays or as the result of skirmish or even battle. All this formed the basis of the professional young officer who would learn to command the lives of his men and therefore the Company.

For all this an ensign would be paid reasonably well, promised leave and in the very long term expect even some sort of pension and equally, to be valued, paid and decorated for his efforts. All this at the start of the 1800s. But what of the other ranks?

High-caste Hindu soldiers were recruited from the streets of Bengal (where the Mutiny started) and similar-caste Rajputs from the province of Oudh. For most it was a good employ- ment for a single reason: they were generally paid on time, whereas civilian employment too often failed to pay consist- ently and in the long term there was a bonus unique in India for Indians: long-serving sepoys would receive pensions. Was the army popular? It is difficult to guage the popularity of the army with any data that would be acceptable today.

Until the five or six years before the Mutiny there is one point in favour of the army: its best recruiting officers appear to have been Indians. Given that a bounty was promised for every recruiter that information may not be suitable. What is harder to dispute is the fact that numbers joining satisfied recruiting needs, especially in Bengal where the Mutiny began.[11] The army had one disadvantage for the British.

Dissatisfaction within a nation or large civil group needs a place or institution to call attention to its grievance. Later in the nineteenth century, the place for public expressions of disquiet in Britain was the increasing number of trade unions. There was no such institutional venting solution in India. Indeed, there were few institutions at all to which the public had access. There was however the army. The disquiet that could vent through the ranks was not necessarily the disquiet of all the troops, many of whom had reasonable lives. But armies have widespread families and therefore act as relay stations of disquiet.

Whatever the conditions provided by the army, the soldiers themselves faced pressures from families, rumours, guilt and suspicion. Ironically, having trained an army to act as a unified force, the disturbed elements in the army (never the whole force) were trained to rebel simply by accepting the seemingly obvious truth of rumour and grievance. This became easier to imagine as the Company and the British economy became more successful, and with it the self-assurance verging on arrogance of the budding masters of the raj. The process was gradual. The testing grounds of mutiny were often small and cared for easily by the authorities. Nor were they only apparent in 1857. For example, one fear described as one of the reasons for rebellion, certainly protest, was the Indian discontent about serving outside India.

When divisions of the Bengal Army were in 1824 – three decades before the Sepoy Rebellion – due for deployment to Burma they refused to go. Firstly, the Burmese War (1824–1826) had an abnormally high death rate for Indian troops, who were generally deployed to the front. Moreover, the accounting system demanded that a regiment had to contribute to the cost of deployment. The cost of buying beasts to haul weaponry and supplies was considered prohibitive and to finance the venture, the accountants raided the overseas allowances of the troops, or so it was said they would. There was a small rebellion, some soldiers were killed in a skirmish among their own and a dozen others were found guilty of rebellion and executed. There were many wars and the allowance and disallowance of bounties for fighting in overseas deployments including Sind and the two Sikh Wars became increasingly contentious. These events did not stretch the British way of dealing with upstarts and minor rebellions. Ringleaders were trapped and, when suitable, made an example of.

The disquiet in the army when it occurred – and it was not a constant – was not always about allowances. For example, some troops took right and proper objection to being dressed as parade ground British soldiers. Dress and undress uniforms did not represent the people they were, particularly when the dressing order included shaving off beards. They were not toy soldiers and did not act like them. It seems in the twenty-first century hardly likely that such a major matter could be so insensitively handled, yet it was. By itself this would not bring about rebellion but it would cause insubordination. In the context of colonialism, insubordination was hardly below rebellion because it represented a cultural rejection of the authority of rule by the supposedly subdued. It has nothing to do with imperialism. It is entirely about the insecurity of occupation. It was as if the 150 years of rule was afraid of India and implicitly understood that it was right that it should be so.

This was a logical conclusion that accepted that there was a textbook for colonial rule and that the British had a mindset that supposed they could govern India as if it were the Home Counties of England. Above everything, Britain could make up the rules of law and government with little reference either to precedent or to questions of possible maladministration. So it was with the time of Dalhousie, the last governor general not to be a viceroy, the last governor general before direct rule, maybe the best of them all and certainly the most controversial. He liked trains.

CHAPTER V

DALHOUSIE AND LAND GRABBING

James Andrew Broun-Ramsay, the first Marquess Dalhousie and later known as the Earl of Dalhousie (1812–1860), brought the railway to India and laid the track of modern India. Some still think him the finest governor general (1848–1856) of the Victorian century. Others have it that Dalhousie's colonial genius did the East India Company little financial favour and certainly contributed to the cause of the Sepoy Rebellion; he was, they say, too arrogant to consider the consequences of his decisions and policies. At Oxford he regarded himself among the elite of society: Gladstone, Canning and Elgin were at Christ Church together. On reflection he thought his ambition must be to add to the 'happiness of my countrymen'.[1] Politically, he felt too much in lesser hands, was not good for finer hands and regarded the Reform Bill with suspicion. Dalhousie was not insignificant.

Dalhousie's father was one of Wellington's more imaginative generals, George Ramsay the ninth Earl of Dalhousie (1770–1838), also from 1816–1820 governor general of British

North America (Canada) and, later, commander-in-chief of India, who saw his role in India as demanding military assessment and political distance. He was first and foremost a soldier, but no commander could possibly set himself above politics. His son was strictly a politician but one who clearly imagined he could go his own way through that treacherous maze. Through his father's early death Dalhousie, now the tenth earl, went to the House of Lords as a Peelite but devoted most of his efforts to Scotland, seeing not much chance of political advancement in the upper house. He could have gone to India with a governorship of Madras, but bided his time. He was deputy president of the Board of Trade when Gladstone was its president and Dalhousie was thrown the brief to look at the consequences of the new element of the Industrial Revolution – the railways. He was the ideal man for the job. Dalhousie was a workaholic. He would go to work with the sun and never leave until it did. His ability to effortlessly scrutinise documents that otherwise found their way into a file to be filed forever was a warning to others to know their briefs and anticipate questions.

With the same dedication to his desk routine, Dalhousie picked and chose what he might do next. He was not vain enough to accept job offers. He waited without his masters, thinking enough encouragement had come his way with little response – by which they meant response to their suggestions. His political independence was not unique but rare during the debates over the Corn Laws when he supported Sir Robert Peel through his own reasoning rather than following a single line during the campaign. Dalhousie's opinion of himself was not out of place but there was another reason for him doing only that which gave him passion. In 1836, Dalhousie married Lady Susan Hay, a daughter of the Earl of Tweedsdale. They had two daughters but then his wife, at just thirty-five, died. Dalhousie was naturally devastated. His close friends said he never recovered. His life was then even more selective. He never took on anything unless he could drive himself with an eye to his imagined achievement. When he turned down a seat in Stanley's Cabinet and an opportunity to follow his passion as president of the Board of Railways it was because he, not quite a loner, failed to see what he would do with the post. It was in this political atmosphere that Dalhousie, just approaching his thirty-sixth birthday, was offered Bengal, as governor general. He wondered if that was him finished politically. He was told far from it. He considered the offer and then considered too the financial state of the Dalhousies.

India had its immediate compensations. He said he would go. Here was an enormous job for a single-minded man who could see what was needed to reform the rule in India. Apart from being prime minister it was the biggest job in British government because all else would have no long term role whereas a man could set about making changes in India that would last a century. So they nearly did.

Thirty-five-year-old Dalhousie, the youngest ever governor general, was sworn in at Calcutta in January 1848. He would come to be one of the most diligent and controversial governors general. Diligence was a natural instinct. Controversy came later. His reputation for being the first at his desk and the last to leave followed Dalhousie from the Board of Trade and reflected his determination not to fall into the trap of piles of Victorian bureaucracy – the biggest single industry of the nineteenth century. The instructions to a new governor general were ever easy to understand: make more money but balance the Company with the need to be seen taking more tacit control and make provisions to defend against outside attacks. The simple order make more money but keep the local situation under control ignored the need of a governor general by this time to think through practical measures that improved the lot of the employees without giving too much away. The Company was not mean, just careful with increasingly vulnerable resources.

Henry Hardinge (1785–1856), the previous governor, was a soldier and Wellington's secretary at war (1828–1830), during which time he cut staff by a fifth. He established a long-term pension system for soldiers and generally had a reputation as an officer who never tried doing anything without first understanding what it was that he was trying to do. He was not a dashing officer; he understood everything he was going to tackle when he arrived in India and for the first year and a half found the experience more or less as he had expected. Then came his war with the Sikhs and the annexation of Punjab. The Sikhs were strong. The plan weak. Gough would have pointed out, yes but successful. Hardinge left and gave Queen Victoria a flea-ridden tiger as a leaving gift. He left a more complex trophy for his successor in Calcutta – uncertainty.

Dalhousie played well the role of the White Mughal – even his wife would rise when he entered the room. Both the pomp and the circumstances were enormous responsibilities, which he undertook gladly. His Order of the Thistle (he being a Midlothian aristocrat) hung well in his robes. Dalhousie was a hard master on himself and those about him. He really did work from dawn to dusk and he truly believed that in his time he would improve the lot of the Indian people. Dalhousie was no Midlothian aristocrat looking for a sinecure and native valet to launder his breeches after a day in the field. Dalhousie's Britain was a place, if not society, of social and political curiosity. These were the decades of change. The Municipal Reform

Act; the Chartists, the Mines Act, Chadwick's Report on Sanitary Conditions, the Factory Acts, *The Communist Manifesto*, Marx as well as *Dombey and Son* as well as *Vanity Fair*, revolutions in France, Germany, Italy and Austria. These times held little hope for peace in Europe, nor for India to be quietly governed. Dalhousie had come from an England where Palmerston had lost the Foreign Office, Russell had lost the leadership of the nation, Derby had succeeded Russell and Aberdeen had succeeded Derby – all in one year. Here was a generation of change in the mind of a young man arriving in most high office in a place that was huge to take in, no matter how many dawn to dusk horseback rides he made to try to do just that. It was, also, a place that, because of its caste and caste system, could never do more than contemplate change. But change was gathering pace: in 1854, the Crimean War started: Russia on one side and the British and French supported by Turkey and the Piedmont on the other.

If there were ever a time for quiet colonial government, this decade was just it. It would not be. It would lead, in 1857, to the biggest change in British imperial history.

Dalhousie is sometimes seen as the best of the British governors general, if ever there was a best. It was he who planned the remarkable network of railways in the subcontinent. His engineers built 2,000 miles of road, irrigated farmland (but didn't build enough canals) and strung 4,000 miles of telegraph cable across India. He opened up the Indian civil service to any British subject, whatever his (never her) class or colour. All this in nine years. He did so by knowing what he wanted to do and trusting routine to keep him on course. He was up at 6 a.m. not simply because he put in a full day but because this was a common time to start the day in a climate that would by early morning be unbearably hot with an unquenchable humidity. Once out of his bed he would read the Revised Version of the Bible, then to his official boxes, then, over breakfast at 8 a.m., the newspapers. Dalhousie was in his office by 9.30 a.m. and still there until early evening and left only for the nightly official dinners, dances and governor's events. Before bed, another chapter of his Bible.

Perhaps Dalhousie never overcame frustration with a land and people including his own kind that accepted that fortune could not be brought about simply because its logical conclusions were explained and the better good hoped for. That frustration expressed itself in authoritarianism. Imperial authoritarianism enforces rules for the good of law, order and policy. It may 'bend' rules to do so. There is some evidence that Dalhousie could be accused of doing both, particularly in the British way of taking over territory that was hardly universally popular among the princes and even some of the British.[2] His policy of taking property for the British when no *legitimate* heir seemed to exist was a cause (but hardly the only one) of dissatisfaction that brought on the Indian Mutiny. This was not, as often said, Dalhousie's idea. The Doctrine of Lapse had existed since 1841. Dalhousie enforced it thoroughly.

The Hindu custom decreed that a son had to be present at the funeral of the father. The reason: the successor proves the importance and success of the father, who will therefore not burn in hell. But what if there were to be no surviving son? It was common enough practice for a boy or young man to be quickly adopted in order to observe this Hindu rite. This meant that the son, adopted or not, would also inherit possessions, including property, perhaps even the state itself in the case of a newly recognised prince. Dalhousie saw this and disapproved and vowed to change it so that the British could inherit. He used the death of the raja of Sattara as a test case.

The raja had died without issue and a false heir had been adopted. Dalhousie said that if there was no proper heir then the title should lapse. The raja's adopted heir was not proper as far as Dalhousie was concerned and the Hindu rite and tradition should be ignored.

If the male line had lapsed, so had the inheritance and therefore Dalhousie would claim the land for the Company, that is, the British. This very imperial idea of sequestration was known as the Doctrine of Lapse. There was opposition to the governor general when he declared that there was no legal heir and therefore the property, even state, belonged to the British. Some of Dalhousie's own officials expressed their doubts about the policy. He had no doubts.

'while I would not seek to lay down any inflexible rule with respect to adoption, I hold that on all occasions where heirs natural shall fail, the territory shall be made to lapse and adoption should not be permitted, excepting in those cases in which some strong political reason may render it expedient to depart from this general rule.'[3]

When Dalhousie decided there was enough doubt over inheritance in Oudh, two colonels, John Low and William Sleeman, the latter the resident in Oudh, made their opposition clear. They were overruled along with anyone else who disapproved not so much of the principle of annexation, but of the detail. The counter-argument to Dalhousie's policy was that it was perfectly reasonable for the British Company to assume the running of Nagpur or Oudh as long as this was not seen as robbery. The politics and accountancy came together without any fuss. Simple annexation meant taking over the whole state and virtually declaring it British. That was a difficult decision. Confining the action to Company administration only would improve the lot of the people, and most importantly the Company. It would of course be an expensive operation and the Company would not be expected to bear the cost. So it was up to the accountants to show that the revenues, or part of them, could be used to offset the expense of putting the house in order. But what of the surplus revenues? Who owned those? Dalhousie could well be accused of short-sightedness, but not of ambition for the wealth of Oudh. On 18 June 1855, Dalhousie declared that the Company would not annex Oudh, but it would administer it and, of course, it would take for itself any revenues it thought reasonable. In other words, the King of Oudh was simply a puppet.

Oudh would, or so Dalhousie and the Company thought, become their own goldmine from January 1856. They had not imagined many difficulties with this concept although there were hints that the puppet might not necessarily dance. This proved to be true. The King refused to sign over his state. However, the administrator, and one of the most distinguished figures in Indian colonial history, was Major General Sir James Outram. He received instructions to issue a proclamation that Oudh was now part of British India.

The complexity of taking over a state had its high and lows. On the high side, the annexation made administration simpler and opportunity for profits more likely. The anticipated loyalty from an annexed state could not always be guaranteed but the Company could reasonably expect loyalty spoils. For example, the most important army was in Bengal. Seven out of every ten sepoys came from Oudh. At the time of the Indian Mutiny, there were 277,000 soldiers in the armies of the three presidencies – Bengal, Bombay and Madras. Depending on regiments, that was 80 per cent of Indians. By itself this preponderance of sepoys was not a threat to British rule. There had been little to suggest that the vast majority were anything but totally obedient and loyal. The enforcement of Lapsed Doctrine by Dalhousie added an element of uncertainty into the minds of those like Sleeman and Low who were perhaps closer to the moods of those they ruled. It would have been wise for Dalhousie to ask London to send more British troops to even up any imbalances that could develop at times of unrest. In London this was understood, but in 1857 Britain had only the year before concluded a peace agreement to the Crimean War. Between 1854 and 1856 there had been no flexibility in the British order of battle to allow Dalhousie extra troops, or even replace those taken from India to fight in the Crimea. The balance of sepoy power, or consequence of it, could not be changed for the foreseeable future.

As a policy, and it was not Dalhousie's invention, annexation done properly improved the stability of the parts of India coming into British grip. Dalhousie's view remained simple:

'taking advantage of every just opportunity which presents itself for consolidating the territories which already belong to us, by taking possession of States which may lapse in the midst of them; for getting rid of those petty intervening principalities which may be a means of annoyance, but which can never, I venture to think, be a source of strength'

A source of strength could not be found in rhetoric. By the late 1850s, there was a precarious balance between trading and governing. Trading was relatively straightforward and it was increasing, but doing so made administration and governing by the Company harder and certainly uncertain in some areas. The Company now ruled more than 60 per cent of India. The other territory was in the hands of the princes, but they relied heavily on direction from their British Company advisors. Company men commanded even the armies of the princes. Constitutional change was really more in line with the better management and profit of the Company, which by the mid-nineteenth century was in its dying days. The strongest of the provinces, Bengal, was by the 1850s under the governance not of the governor general but a lieutenant governor; this did not appear much of a change, but it was part of the reshaping of India that would make government more efficient and there-fore reduce, although not eliminate, the governance of a largely taxed and protected possession of waste.

Dalhousie's determination to modernise India was carried with endeavour. He introduced the basis of what would become the most famous railroad in the world; he started a postal service that was an example of bureaucracy and system succeeding over all expectation. His reforms covered forest-ation, planting, care for downtrodden castes and even the protection of India's monuments in a fashion not seen again until Curzon became viceroy. If there is need of Dalhousie's own monument, it is to be seen in the India Archive. Dalhousie rewrote the rulebook of imperial government. He understood that at the very last it would be necessary to read and accept why change had been made and by what authority it had to be maintained. In this Dalhousie was unique in Britain's Victorian rule of India. But there were two keys to his success: the army and the princes.

The army was the single token of authority whereby reforms could be insisted upon. The Company army existed to police India rather than protect it from invasion. It underwent its final modernisation before direct rule from Britain. The army's reconstruction, particularly in methods of officer recruiting and promotion, did not do much to dispel the anxieties and doubts of the sepoys, who were still suspicious of so-called modernisation that would or could mean a brigade being sent abroad (even Afghanistan was considered abroad). There was, too, a full rumour in the Company army that the British planned to 'modernise' the soul as well as the rank structure. Missionaries were being sent from England with the purpose of converting soldiers to Christianity. Evangelism was a threat to an established society. An army is the fullest example of an established society.

By the mid-1850s, with Britain at war in the Crimea and still uncertain of the reaction to the changes it was making in India, the subcontinent was in a curious state of subservient seething. Moreover, Dalhousie, like other governors general, had to ruthlessly rule his own people as well as India. For example, Dalhousie had proposed radical changes that had proved too expensive for the Company and government in London and so were cancelled, an act that bruised his authority. Moreover, when Sir Charles Napier commanding the army announced allowances for sepoys, Dalhousie was forced to countermand Napier's decision partly on cost and partly because Napier had not consulted the governor. Napier lost the argument and sailed for England, never to return.

The second key to Dalhousie's achievements is easily mislaid. The key with the army was the princes. Despite accusations that the British ruled by coercion, it could have never achieved what it did without the support of the princes. The British could lean on the princes and at one time there were certainly hundreds of them, but the British also protected the princes, often from each other. The princes and the British turned out to be partners in the emergence of the post-Mutiny Raj. Yet for all the changes for the good, for all the advances in doctrine and efficiency, one element at this stage seems missing from Dalhousie's own examination of India: he did not see the Mutiny coming. He failed to see any sign that soldiers and sepoys would oppose their officers. If Dalhousie is to be loaded with any of the blame for what happened in 1857, then the irony is that he wasn't there when the discontent boiled over into rebellion.

Dalhousie left India for the same reason others had and would: ill health. India was not stuck in some caste that could remain for yet another's lifetime. He had gone half again the time of other governors. He never slouched, he never turned work away. He even refused to sign blank letter forms and insisted on reading everything, however petty, that went out in his name. His wife died on her way back to England to rest. He never recovered and stayed long enough to hand his wand to Canning on 29 February 1856. Canning's wife would also die in India and he himself would perish from his own exhaustion in the subcontinent. Dalhousie was replaced by a man the same age who had been with him at Christ Church College, Oxford: Charles Canning.[4]

CHAPTER VI

WHY THE SEPOYS REBELLED

The Indian Mutiny, or Sepoy Rebellion, began in May 1857 in the Bengal army of the East India Company. Some civilians in northern and central India supported it.

Initially, the mutineers overwhelmed Meerut, then Delhi and by the next month had reached the Ganges Valley. Many of the Europeans captured were massacred. Importantly, Punjab did not join the Mutiny. If it had, then British India may have fallen. The British did not have in Britain the reinforcements for the army needed for the wider conflict. The Punjab case showed the internal conflicts among the Sikhs more than it did any imaginary loyalty to the British. Sikhs understood that a rebellion would restore Muslim leaders who would put down Sikhs. Here is an example that reminds us that differences in mid-Victorian India were not the general population on one side and the British on the other. Conflict in India was often centuries old. How Indians behaved towards each other and why they did so long pre-dated the arrival of the British and certainly the short-lived raj. Sikh and Muslim was a perfect example of instinctive fears of two major communities. There was thus no incentive to support the uprising. Delhi was recaptured in September 1857 and Lucknow in March 1858. The civilian support did not last long.

The significant consequence of the Sepoy Rebellion was the 1858 India Act that gave the East India Company territory (British India) and the Company army to the Crown. India would thenceforth be ruled directly by the British and a viceroy would act as monarch. So India remained until 1947. Canning was the first viceroy.

Before he left for India, Charles Canning appears to have been the one person on record to suggest a crisis of considerable standing was about to happen. A single sentence to the court of directors before he sailed for India suggests that Canning had anticipated something as big as the Mutiny.

'I wish for a peaceful term of office. But I cannot forget that in the sky of India, serene as it is, a small cloud may arise, no larger than a man's hand, but which, growing larger and larger, may at last threaten to burst and overwhelm us with ruin.'[1]

He arrived in Calcutta late in February 1856 to be welcomed by the departing Dalhousie and a note to resolve the continuing and even continuous dilemma of Oudh. Outram was ill and had returned, two months after Canning's arrival, to Britain. Canning was not at all well himself and relied very much on local advice in the form of the short-tempered and very sackable Coverly Jackson, a revenue officer, who replaced Outram. Jackson spent more time quarrelling than administrating and was and is a reminder that often the viceroy's officers were opinionated, conscious as they were that they had experience whereas the viceroy was very much the new man.

More importantly, Canning had arrived at the very time of the official annexation of Oudh and the failing health of the King of Oudh, Wajid Ali. So Britain had a new governor general (not installed as viceroy until 1758), an advisor, Jackson, who was strong on gout and prejudice and who was not the right diplomat to even begin a smooth transition from regal to British rule, coping as he had to with a disgruntled King and equally dissatisfied local populations.

Canning now made one of the best decisions of his short time in India. He sacked Jackson and replaced him with the knowledgeable Sir Henry Lawrence.[2] Lawrence was to die in the Mutiny the following year. His younger brother, John Lawrence, would be equally famous in India and become governor general. First, though, there was a mutiny to deal with and one that could have brought down British rule.

The British ruled as tempered Mughals and the military symbolised the impossibility of escaping from that rule. It was not a situation unique to the British occupation of India. The army represented authority and British authority and a minority of the army was British but the biggest part of the army was the very people it policed. They easily represented a wider spread of mood in India than some may have imagined.

In the Bengal army there were more than 80,000 men within seventy-four infantry regiments. Fifty-four of those seventy-four regiments either mutinied or did so in part. At the time of the uprising only three infantry regiments were considered loyal to the British. Thus, the infantry of the Bengal army became the focal point of the Mutiny. The Madras army of fifty-two native regiments refused orders to serve in Bengal in the summer of 1857, but never mutinied. The Bombay army consisted of twenty-nine infantry regiments of Indian soldiers. There was open dissent, but not full-scale mutiny in three of those regiments. All this suggests the Mutiny came largely in Bengal. Why? Part of the answer is in its tradition of recruiting.

Bengal was the home of the full Indian battalions. Clive had formed them exactly 100 years earlier. Almost exclusively, the British recruited yeoman stock whom they judged made good soldiers and it was an obvious source of manpower. They were used to living off the land, they had an easier disposition and were likely to feel comfortable with reasonable instruction and order. This meant that the recruiting sergeants had to travel widely. There were not enough agricultural soldiers in the main Bengal recruiting areas – Dinapore and Burhanpur.[3] More recruits were pressed from north India. The non-Bengalis were high-caste soldiers, many of them Brahmins and Rajputs.

The British view was that the higher the caste then the greater the loyalty expected; this concept existed during Mughal India.

During British rule, the modern caste system was developed whereby Indians were split by the British into racial and social groups that could be recognised even to the point that only an administrative class would get administration jobs. The general rule in British India was that only those from middle and upper castes could expect to get the senior administrative jobs. On reflection, the British were happy with this system partly because it was similar to the recruiting system used in Britain.

Messing with the caste system – much earlier than even the Mughals – created difficulties. The introduction of a higher caste system in the Bengal army, not by Indians but by the British, was the seed from which insurrection grew. The British sense of order and ambition for the loyalty of soldiers actually emphasised differences that hitherto had been more or less ignored by the Indians themselves. The high-caste Hindus by the 1850s probably controlled more than 50 per cent of recruitment into the Bengal native infantry regiments. There were natural anxieties and annoyances among some of those regiments, which, even today, are typical in barrack rooms. For example, modern soldiers are very aware of the advantages of overseas allowances. In the mid-nineteenth century some of the Bengal battalions were angry when their 'overseas allowances' were withdrawn. In 1856, Canning instructed that all East India Company soldiers would be liable for general service and therefore obliged to serve outside the areas of Company control, that is, non-British India, and even overseas. This instruction appeared in the General Service Enlistment Order.

It seems likely that the greatest concern came from the old serving sepoys who thought that their traditional role and the conditions of service agreed on enlistment were being set aside. The worst condition of service abroad was no one knew where it would end. Some had superstitions or religious objections to travelling out of their homelands and especially overseas. Once the frontier had been crossed, where else would it be drawn? The most common assumption was that the British were getting rid of the distinguished Bengal army. It would be, according to the barrack room lawyers, nothing more than a general force with no distinction of caste and available for whatever task the British thought fit to give it. There was a reasonable case for suspicion, especially after Indian forces had been sent to fight in the Crimea.

The mostly British officers displayed no sympathy towards the religious and superstitious sensitivities of their sepoys. The British had a simple view: if a man wanted to be a soldier and was roughly good enough, then he signed on the dotted line and left the rest of his army life to his officers. They would even have him dressed as a British soldier. The English East India Company formed its army and dressed its soldiers as British regiments. Instead of the tribal dress and style of the traditional sepoys, they were uniformed in the European style and armed with the heavyweight weaponry of the European. This assumes importance when coupled with the uncompromisingly harsh discipline of a typically farm-born soldier force-fed on European military discipline and often with few social benefits off duty.

The sepoys were expected to maintain loyalties, enthusiasms, alertness and smartness in very basic huts built of mud and thatch, which they usually had to build for themselves. The Madras and Bombay armies were better off than the Bengalis and so there was clearly a festering sense of rebellion. Perhaps all this could have been ignored if the overseas allowances had continued and even improved upon and, more importantly, the basic rates of pay were attractive.

There was, too, an unfairness in the promotion system in Bengal. The army was logjammed by seniority when, for example, poor senior soldiers could not be replaced and so ambitious, eager and even better soldiers would find their pathway blocked. Moreover, promotion could well be out of the hands of a commanding officer. A colonel may not be able to choose the people he wanted because a senior non-commissioned officer, for example, was not going to move. He had his job cut out as he liked it, all considerations had been regularly paid up to others and there he would stay. If he left, what would he have other than a small pension? Consequently, junior soldiers felt they were not being rewarded for their capabilities. Long-serving Indian officers were equally dissatisfied with the nineteenth-century glass ceiling that prevented their rise to anything more than junior roles.

It might not be a coincidence that the mutinous regiments looked to these older and dissatisfied Indian officers for example and leadership. Dissatisfaction was exaggerated by another, common element in the Company army. Some British administrators did not accept the differences and anomalies in the ways in which the sepoys were treated, but there was one aspect that was impossible to change: unfulfilled ambitions among sepoys, the lack of understanding of what had been created within the army of castes and the inability to either think through the consequences or persuade others to do so. Furthermore, the inequalities and unprofessionalism were exacerbated by an often poor quality of British officer class. The British officers were not all Clives and the British infantry officers often faced the same frustrations as the sepoys, inasmuch as length of service decided promotion, rather than capabilities. A fine young officer might not get promoted because a lesser soldier who had served five more years got the position.

Moreover, because of centralised controls within the Company and administration, even commanding officers quite often had little authority over the regiment's discipline. A local commander might well know his sepoys and the best way to keep them on side and improve their efficiencies. Some higher command gave him little room for initiative and therefore great opportunity to witness dissent. By the middle 1850s the lack of discipline among the Bengal infantry was regarded with contempt by the other armies.

The fundamental task of a commanding officer was to hold his regiment together. Many British officers, incapable of exercising absolute control, grew even further distant from their sepoys. They, in turn, increasingly gave the impression that they would only choose to obey orders that suited them. Trust and respect between the two were not always apparent. Expressions of dissatisfaction produced harsh, bloody and sometimes fatal punishments for the dissenters. Yet conditions could be harsh enough for men to step forward with protests as, for example, in 1849, when there had been mutiny in the ranks of the regiments in Punjab. On that occasion a small group of sepoys had roused their colleagues to demand more pay. This handful of men had genuine grievances. So had the sepoys in 1857 and the conspiracy was wider spread, the grievances older and the wider agenda may have been to bring down the East India Company; the Company was hardly the authorising body in India by then, so we must assume that the dissatisfaction and ambitions against the British went beyond the army and reflected an anti-British sentiment that affected a broad cross-section of Indians.

Those with most to lose were the princes and officials. Honours, pensions and bureaucratic titles had been forfeited as a result of British policies. Central inefficiencies within the legislation of the East India Company had restricted careers and advancements despite 250 years of working and trading in India. The running of commercial houses had not gone much beyond the sixteenth-century practices of employer–employee relations. The Company, and therefore the British, still failed to either appreciate or care for the sensitivities of caste and religion. The restructuring and recruitment within the Bengal army proved this. The pensioning off of old princes without understanding the consequences for the future generation who expected to inherit reflected either British ignorance or arrogance. We should argue therefore that the Indian Mutiny was the figurehead of a movement of greater dissatisfaction among Indians.

Dissatisfaction does not fade when national identity proves inadequate to right wrongs. So it was in India in the 1850s. Some 45,000 white British soldiers, half of them in Punjab, waited in May for the inevitable uprising. Given the distance between England and India, there was no hope for immediate reinforcement. A sense of helplessness was the order of the British soldiery spread across India. The army was aware of its failures. The Company made no concessions to its weaknesses to understand the people it effectively ruled. Here again was the evidence that the Mutiny did not occur for any single reason. William Dalrymple in his unparalleled history of that moment, *The Last Mughal*,[4] should be noted when he writes:

'So removed had the British now become from their Indian subjects, and so dismissive were they of Indian opinion, that they had lost all ability to read the omens around them or to analyze their own position with any degree of accuracy.'

Arrogance and imperial self-confidence had diminished the desire to seek accurate information or gain any real knowledge of the state of the country. British India in May 1857 simmered with rebellion. The popular version of the reason for the Mutiny is not correct. The rebellion did not begin because sepoy infantry refused to chew off the ends of paper cartridges greased with animal fats. The animal cartridges had existed. The sepoys protested. But this was not the cause of the rebellion, as we see above. It is worth a few lines explaining what the cartridge story is about.

As a prelude to issuing the Indian soldiers with new rifles, cartridges arrived in India from England in 1853 (four years before the rebellion) for climate testing. The system was very simple and was the same as with an earlier muzzle-loaded weapon. The cartridge came in two parts. One contained the shot. The second part was the gunpowder that exploded and sent the shot out of the muzzle. All this was normally in a strengthened paper tube, the cartridge. The basic system is ages old and in a slightly different form is still used in shotguns.

In the 1850s the army was changing over to a new weapon. The cartridge was partly greased to make it easier to ram down the barrel. A dry cartridge, a paper one, could be universally used. The army needed to know how a greased cartridge would react to the temperature and humidity in India. The authorities in London were not impressed by any suggestion that the origins of the grease, that is, pork or beef dripping, might offend Indian religious sensitivities. During the two years of the tests there were no complaints from the sepoys. In 1856 the new Enfield rifles arrived in India. The cartridges, apart from the initial order, were to be made by the ordnance department of the Bengal army. The greasing came in three parts, the most sensitive being tallow.

Instead of thinking through the consequences of making the tallow as they did, the authorities were distracted. They now faced a consistent rumour, beginning at the start of 1857, that there was a move to convert India to Christianity. The extension of this gossip was that Christian sepoys would not mind biting into a greased cartridge in order to release the powder into the barrel. Towards the end of January came the first signs that the Indian soldiers, including officers, had asked that the greased composition should be changed. Here was no difficulty. The answer was simple: sepoys should be issued with clean cartridges and they should be allowed to grease them with whatever they wished. Moreover, any tallow would be that from goats or sheep. All should have been satisfied. However, the rumour persisted that the tallow was from pigs and cows; in ordnance records there is no written evidence that this was so. It is possible to draw modern parallels. How often government departments, especially the Department of Agriculture, have been either vague or evasive until the crisis has proved original accusations founded.

There was, in early 1857, an almost offhand agreement from the Department of Ordnance that the tallow may indeed have been prepared from substances that native soldiers might find offensive. From a perspective of more than 150 years it would seem that the offer to allow sepoys to grease their own cartridges should have resolved the matter. However, the grease question was long out of the hands of the authorities.

Might the paper, asked the sepoys, also contain some grease content? It must have been clear by February at the very latest that the cartridge and grease controversy was a vehicle to raise wider grievances. The conspirators were not going to let the opportunity slip. There were visible signs of unrest. Arsonists had attacked the homes and buildings of Europeans. The Raniganj telegraph office was burned to the ground. There was evidence of bribery among Indian officials to disrupt and exacerbate an undercurrent of unrest. The belief that the British were going to usurp the religious responsibilities of Indians and corrupt the caste system could not be countered. The unrest and movement of dissent was helped by the lack of discipline within many of the sepoy regiments; which regiments were loyal and which were not was hard to assess. By middle to late March this was becoming clearer. Open defiance was rife throughout the 19th Native Infantry and on 31 March the regiment was disbanded. However, it was by then too late to prevent the rebellion that would begin in May. Tensions increased with growing disobedience. The sepoys believed they could get away with it because of the lack of discipline.

In short, the reasons for the start of the rebellion were: the sepoys were long dissatisfied with their treatment, they did not like having to wear British uniforms, they did not want to be sent out of their area, they thought their officers arrogant, inconsiderate and not to be admired. Civilians were openly dissatisfied with the arrogance and inconsiderate attitude of British civilians from the viceroy's office down, they disapproved of corruption of their own traditions and beliefs including land-grabbing states with unproven heirs and they believed the strong rumour of the British planning to convert Indians to Christianity. Memories of the Portuguese Inquisition in India were revived to prove the consequences of any evangelical revival. The reasons for the Mutiny were wide and varied. When it came, the British were not prepared and it was brutal.

CHAPTER VII

THE MUTINY

The Mutiny began when the rebels took over Meerut and within three weeks the rebellion covered the Ganges Valley. The successful sepoys then headed for Delhi. On 11 May 1857, they were joined by the Delhi garrison and one of their first tasks was to slaughter any Christian who came to hand. Two days later a new Mughal Emperor, Bahadur Shah, was proclaimed.

On 20 May, the 9th Native Infantry, close by Agra, joined the rebellion. At the same time, the British managed to disarm the Peshawar garrison, fearing it too would mutiny. On 30 May came the uprising at the Lucknow garrison and its commander, Brigadier General Isaac Handscomb, was killed. During the first two weeks of June the mutineers carried out a series of massacres as far apart as the early centre of unrest, Oudh, central India, Rajputana, Punjab (which by and large remained loyal) and the northwest provinces.

As this was going on, Major General Sir Henry Barnard[1] grouped his forces north of Delhi, and Lieutenant General Sir

Patrick Grant arrived in Calcutta to become commander-in-chief of India following the death from cholera of General The Honourable George Anson.[2] It is quite possible that many British casualties also came to grief from disease rather than the fighting, a common factor in warfare until a third of the way through the twentieth century. By the end of June there came the notorious massacre of Europeans in Cawnpore who thought that they had been granted safe passage along the Ganges. Three days later, 30 June, the siege of Lucknow began. Later that week, now the beginning of July, Barnard also died of cholera and his place as commander of the Delhi Field Force was taken by Major General Thomas Reed.[3]

The images of the British armies in India suggest certain chaos but overall a view of a well-organised minority and uniformed rank of British defending against a large opposition of disorganised Indian sepoys. The British were indeed organised, although not always well together. They had some good officers, especially at the senior level. They had confidence: they were British, the sepoys were not. Most importantly, the general picture does not show where the British were. They were not in the right places because this was asymmetric warfare. It was not a set-piece engagement. Communications were crude and often did not reach the officers they should have. There was too a question of time. A rebellious group could achieve a great deal by operating, albeit in disorder, as scavenging separate groups. The British could not break into small sections. Command and control was everything. Without it the British were weak. Officers were trained to fight as a large unit, not as special forces. Moreover, none of it was put together with any sophistication and instantly executed.

This was the middle of the nineteenth century and the rules of engagement went with that period and in that land and at that speed. It was about this time, mid-July, that the British started to pull together their operation to put down the rebellion. On the 12th of that month, for example, Brigadier General Henry Havelock overwhelmed the rebellion of Cawnpore at Fatehpur and then, three days later, at Aong and Pandu Nadi.[4] In retaliation, Nana Sahib executed some 200 women and children. The following day Havelock advanced on Nana Sahib's positions near Cawnpore and defeated him. By the end of July there was a sense of compromise among some of the governor general's staff. On 31 July, Canning announced that any mutineer who had not committed murder would be spared execution. British newspapers condemned Canning's action as cowardice. They called it the Clemency Declaration. By the beginning of the third week in September, Delhi was back in the hands of British troops. By 25 September, Havelock and Sir James Outram had mounted the first relief of the Lucknow Residency, yet it was not until 17 November that the Residency was relieved yet again. Havelock, who stayed, was to follow many heroes in the Mutiny. He died of dysentery on 24 November 1857. Lucknow had become a symbol of British resistance but it took until 24 March 1858 for the rebellion at Lucknow to collapse and, even though there was not a single week without a battle or skirmish, major fighting went on until mid-June 1858 when the final battle for Oudh took place. Even so, there could be no official declaration of peace in Oudh until January 1859. One reason for the apparent long time to put down the Mutiny was the disposition of the Company army. Many regiments were on their ways back from fighting in Persia and that meant there were just eleven infantry regiments at full state of readiness when the Mutiny started and the irregular deployment meant key points in India were undefended. Finally, on 8 July 1859, Canning was able to declare throughout India a state of peace and what emerged as a moment of constitutional change.

The Mutiny was an act of treason against the whole of the British Empire; Canning's declaration of truce then peace precipitated the constitutional change that would create the raj and the proper definition of Empire. Eleven months earlier, the 1858 India Act that transferred the subcontinent to the British Crown and out of the hands of the East India Company had passed through the parliament at Westminster. The function of the Act was simple.

The British monarchy would take all territories of the East India Company. A post of Secretary of State for India (soon to be Secretary of State of India and Burma) would be created who would, literally, take the crimson velvet seat of the chairman of the court of directors of the East India Company as the Company surrendered its authority in Bengal and India. The Crown did not have the whole of the subcontinent; there were more than 500 small states known as native states or princely states that had not been taken by the British, some of them principalities long before the British even arrived in India. For example, Bikaner had been a state since the fifteenth century, Jaipur since the twelfth century and Kochin, a princely state since the 1100s and still expecting a full gun salute (seventeen to indicate the dignity of its ruler). These states were not to exist entirely independently outside Crown rule, nor did they wish to. The princely states became, at the least, British protectorates whereby the day- to- day running of the state was still in the control of the local chief-prince. Relations with other states and 'foreign and defence policy' were decided by the Crown. In effect, a prince would have the kudos of power but British officials and advisor would be at his elbow.

The articles of the 1858 Act were put on display at a durbar at Allahabad. The ruling of India could never be more clearly stated and immediately satisfied the princely states, which had shown unquestionable support for the Company during the Mutiny:

'Firstly and most importantly, all treaties and engagement of the East India Company with the princely states will be honoured. The rights, dignity and honour of native princes would be respected as our own.

Secondly there will be no further extension of the territories of the East India Company. No encroachment on British territories in India would be allowed and no encroachment will be done by British on territories of others.

The desire that British subjects enjoy prosperity, social advancement can be only secured by internal peace and good government

We are bound to natives of Indian territories by same obligations that bind us to other subjects

There will be admission to services/offices of the government without discrimination on race or creed

There will be an amnesty to all except those who had directly taken part in the murder of a British subject'

Thus the final assembly of the East India Company in its role as the day-to-day governor and administrator of British India took place on 1 September 1858; under the East India Stock Dividend Redemption Act it would shut its trading doors in 1874. After nearly three centuries trading, a byword of British commercial history was no more. It had come about with the search for spices. It had literally fought for footholds in what was to the English of the time a little known Asian

Orient. Its motive had been profit, never a determination to conquer and hold lands and peoples it did not understand. It had gone looking for silks and pepper and had stayed to create what became the biggest empire in modern history. It left behind in India a not always enviable reputation; yet in the times that it thrived few colonial reputations would survive twenty-first-century moral scrutiny. The Company handed over its private army of some 24,000 men – not a big army to police and defend its territories but better organised than before the Mutiny.

The Government of India Act came into force on 1 November 1858. The Crown took over from the Company. The secretary of state would be the Cabinet minister responsible in London with the advice of a fifteen-man council as advisors, although it was clear that the secretary of state considered the council but did not have to tell the members anything at all, although he would on special issues such as the stability of a region and the appointment of a new governor general. Canning as viceroy was the doorkeeper to the protocol that India was not only ruled from London but British India had its new monarch. If the princes were to be expected to show deference to the monarch in London then the governor general should have his status raised to viceroy.

Here was a distinction of the new status: the princes did not deal with the British government. The princes considered their own status and therefore dealt with the reigning monarch, not least because the viceroy was appointed by the monarch (on her government's advice) to go and rule in the sovereign's name[5]. Equality for the princes in a land where equality was not much reflected on was perfectly easy to agree.

That royal proclamation was displayed across India in November of that year along with an unconditional pardon to

all mutineers except for those who had either murdered or
sheltered murderers. There was little mercy for the latter
groups. A typical execution was to be publicly tied to cannon
mouths and blown to pieces. A simple punishment like hang-
ing was not enough for those British who saw the Mutiny as
the most hideous period in their lives. Natives had violated
white supremacy, imperialism had been raped. The perpetra-
tors would suffer in the cruellest ways; nothing less than that
would satisfy the extreme British, who wanted the governor
and government in London to order the flaying alive and
impalement of those found guilty of the atrocities against the
British women and their children in Delhi. Was this an unexpected British reaction?

The army had a history of uncompromising justice. There
was too a sense that the British, or some of them, were looking
not for justice but revenge. They had developed from early-
seventeenth-century officials kept waiting at the Mughal's door
to the stewards of the biggest empire the world had seen, with
perhaps a quarter of the world saluting their flag. The British,
not always the most cultured, the most aristocratic, the most
intelligent, had ruled by the means and often the rules of the
day for at least a century. Subjugation of large parts of India
and defeat of the Portuguese and then the French gave the
British clean scorecards to dictate to people sometimes of
superior culture, of at least ancient aristocracy and certainly an
enviable intelligence. When the Mutiny was put down not all
the British could avoid a sense of something approaching
mediaeval disbelief; the serfs had risen. Would the mood to
govern change? The Mutiny was not widespread. In the north
of India there was little support for British rule, although as
expected in a complex society the rest of the land did not
openly support the sepoys.

The options for the whole of India were not as might be expected. This was not simply a subcontinent ruled by an invader and therefore seething for the British to be thrown into the sea whence they had arrived. Firstly, many communities did quite well from the British raj. Secondly, those and other communities could not be sure what would happen if the British lost control. There was a rightly held anxiety that a restored Muslim rule would do little for the Sikhs.

There is another view that allows for the complex reasons for why people sided for or against the British and the consequences for those disparate groupings. It is unlikely that there was a masterminded national uprising. The mutinies would only take place where sepoys believed the rest of the regiment were with them. The argument in almost every case for rebellion was that the British threatened religion and caste. Whether they had a great idea about what would happen once it was all over is uncertain. The inclusion of disaffected officials and even princes tempts a belief that a wider aim was to replace British rule. To do this there needed to be continuous order among mutineers. Caste and religion may have been the excuses the rebels spread, but this historical moment was almost a violent industrial revolution where the lot of the common soldier against the boss class of British rule had to succeed. This may well account for the fact that the rebellious regiments did not abandon pecking orders.

Why did the Sepoy Rebellion fail? Part of the answer is that Punjab did not join in and therefore the European, mainly British, troops were able to contain the uprising. Equally significant, the sepoys could not bring their forces properly together for much time under one command partly because sepoys really did have multiple grievances and therefore a single-minded offensive was harder to achieve. Once the

British, unnecessarily poorly structured themselves, were organised and worked out where the real threats stood and how to respond they appear to have been able to take advantage of the sepoys' command weakness. This was the nineteenth not the twenty-first century. The information pattern of communication and intelligence gathering, plus real time responses, were entirely unknown. The sepoys were not organised into ideological groups. Occupiers and occupied faced each other with little chance of the latter able to gather resources under one grievance banner.

The Mutiny only survived as long as it did because the possibilities the mutineers had expected during the momentum of May 1857 never came together. It was not, though, entirely a failure. The Indians did get rid of the East India Company's rule, although that was in the process of going anyway. The fact that the 1858 Act was displayed so widely suggests wisdom that all should understand that all had changed, albeit in a few lines of parliamentary and constitutional procedure. Indian conditions and relations with the British improved, although many at the level that had inspired rebellion may not have felt the benefits immediately, if at all. It was as a result of the rebellion that Major General Jonathan Peel, the brother of the, by then, late prime minister Robert Peel, became chairman of the inquiry into the organisation of the Indian army.

General Peel, who was also secretary of state for war, worked quickly through written and oral evidence and reported at the end of the first week in March 1859. His report was thorough but very Victorian. Standards could not be standards unless they reflected past reasoning and acknowledgement of precedent. Intentions to change were clearly stated. Promotion of Indian non-commissioned and commissioned officers would – in theory – no longer be based on seniority. A man could now be rewarded for his talents. Commanding officers were to be given more authority based upon their regimental and local knowledge rather than being instructed by central bureaucracy. No longer were sepoys to be dressed up as a facsimile of their British counterparts.

The main thrust of Peel's commission of inquiry was to prevent another rebellion by restructuring the Indian army. Peel decided that the army could no longer have so few British soldiers. Bengal had been the centre for the rebellion. Therefore, he insisted that in future there should be no more than a two-to-one ratio; that is, two sepoys for every one British soldier. The army in the Madras and Bombay presidencies was considered more reliable. Here, his recommendation was that there should be three sepoys to every British soldier. Restructuring meant that the British were admitting how vulnerable they were and, most importantly, how vulnerable was the whole system of rule, especially as the ideology of change was a gathering storm for the British to navigate. In England and Scotland industrial, social and political thinking did not have an obvious work pattern for India, but there were those who would be aware of changes that were making their masters anxious that those changes would never be used to spread similar ideas into Europe. Could the India of the 1857 Mutiny take up the examples that were making industrial and political headway in the British Isles? Almost definitely not. But those changes and ideas would not be contained.

In just a few decades men would learn the new ways and thoughts and read for the bar in the London Inns and there learn more, and would lead the great movements for change in India and succeed, whatever were the tragedies that followed.

There is a footnote to the Mutiny that points to the wider empire. The British wrongly assumed they would always be able to hold their possessions by force if the need arose. Thus it was as well that the British had lost North America because if in 1857 they had still been in that place they could not have raised the armies to rescue the Company. The times got it right for the British. India would still turn profits for nearly a century. America would never have been much for the British unless, of course, the most obvious had come to something: the Georgian monarchs would rule from Washington and the British Isles would have become an electorate of the British Empire with its throne not by the Thames but overlooking the Potomac. It was always too vast for a conqueror to tame. In 1858 Canning and his generals had no need for fantasy history. They had brought the Mutiny to heel and now he was the Queen's ruler of all he surveyed. It was a treacherous task that killed his wife and probably him too.

CHAPTER VIII

CANNING AND THE
FIRST FIRST LADY

Canning was well aware of the perils of the highest office. It was all a grand affair with total privilege and the trappings of exhaustion and the impossibility of ever satisfying ambitions. Canning had his bearers pick up his trappings and he and Charlotte, viceroy and vicereine, moved into the official residence, the first viceroy's 'palace' in the magnificent, almost European, city of Calcutta.

The governor general had lived in modest surroundings slightly beyond the Company capital of Calcutta. This was not much to the liking of Wellesley when he took up office and he put forward the not entirely popular view that the governor general should have a palace. Wellesley understood that although the British did not directly rule, one day they would from the throne; the Indian princes so very conscious of status and position could be in no doubt of the authority and right of the governor general and the British flag that they were to, at least metaphorically, salute each morning at its hoisting and evening at its lowering. Where else to build the British palace?

Calcutta was the capital and the port and city to rival any other anywhere in the world. It boasted thousands of prosperous merchants and minor potentates and hundreds of two-and three-storey residences, occupied by spotless servants. Hundreds upon hundreds of sea-going vessels gave truth to the idea that Calcutta was the commercial capital of the east and that the town swarmed with merchants, traders, clerks noble and clerks ordinary.

If this capital of British India was the noticeboard of imperial ambitions as well as the trading floor of fortunes to be made by the rich and, for the moment, poor, then here was the place for the magnificent, if imperialism can be proud of that. The mansion house of British achievement needed to be sturdy for the coming two centuries and probably another after that.

Wellesley had wanted a mansion and had Charles Wyatt (1758–1819) of the Bengal Engineers model the Raj Bhavan (in English, Government House) on the Curzon family seat, Kedleston Hall in Derbyshire.[1] A century later the Raj Bhavan welcomed the new viceroy, George Nathaniel Curzon, who noted that it was 'without doubt the finest Government House occupied by the representative of any Sovereign or Government in the world' and to leave no doubt put in electricity and a lift. The palace Wyatt created opened for residence in 1803. By even Indian standards it was substantial although not excessive – over 84,000 square feet in twenty-seven acres, with the grandest of six gateways topped by the firmest symbol of all, the lion. Inside, the Raj Bhavan stood well with the palaces of the princes. The centrepiece – the Throne Room – was surrounded on three floors. There were sixty rooms with three drawing rooms, the council chamber, the banqueting hall and the state marble hall. Few would doubt Curzon's boast 100 years on from Wyatt's creation, but many in government objected to what they described as Wellesley's misuse of English East India Company funds.

Canning's lineage was perfectly respectable and uncomplicated other than when his father, the sometime prime minister George Canning (1770–1827), as foreign minister, was wounded in a duel when challenged by Robert Stewart, Lord Castlereagh, the minister for war (1769–1822) during a dispute during the Peninsular War. George Canning had never fired a pistol until the dramatic day in 1809 on Putney Heath and had Castlereagh not committed suicide, he would have gone to India as governor general. Instead he was forced to remain in England and return to the Cabinet. Of such options, history takes its pick. Charles Canning's mother Joan was in a line from the Scottish Dundas and Bentinck families and she was the daughter of a celebrated Scottish general, John Scott. Educated at Eton and Christ Church Oxford (at the same time as W.E. Gladstone, Dalhousie who preceded him as governor general in India and Elgin who followed), he came away with an enviable education in classics and mathematics.

Apart from the social convenience of sending Charles Canning to India, it is possible that Palmerston was sending the son of George Canning because it is always better to give big jobs to members of your own elite. Unknowns, however clever, can surprise you – prime ministers and foreign secretaries do not like being surprised. His background was good family, good marriage, good early career, an urbane manner as a junior minister of foreign affairs in Peel's second administration (1841–1846) and a seat on the British Museum Royal Commission. The image suggested almost a pastoral care for a time in public life rather than the traumatic experience of India. He married Charlotte (Char) Stuart, if not with all good wishes of his future father-in-law Sir Charles Stuart (1779–1845), who became Baron Stuart de Rothesay. He liked Canning well enough but simply could not let his teenage daughter go. Like the traditionally well-intentioned papa, Stuart gave way and his prettiest of three pretty daughters married at eighteen years of age. Canning, with a single-minded work instinct and a mistress for comfort, trod his way through the unremarkable gallery of British politics while Charlotte was at home in the highest of London society.

Charlotte Canning was a gifted and dark-haired, classically beautiful woman. Her mother was Elizabeth Yorke (1789–1867) and her father was the British ambassador to Paris. She was born in that embassy in 1817 – an interesting time two years after Waterloo. Even then, she was said to have made a good marriage. Canning, the son of the former prime minister, had undemanding duties of public office and the two of them led a mostly pleasant if childless way of life in early Victorian London, marred only by Canning having a mistress or two, one of whom was thought to have been George IV's consort, Caroline of Brunswick. This would have explained the King's indifference to, perhaps dislike for, Canning.

Two years after she came to the throne, Queen Victoria set off what became known as the Bed Chamber Crisis. Melbourne, her trusted Whig prime minister, was about to lose the election and Peel was about to become Tory prime minister and hardly one to find favour with the young Queen. The confrontation came when Peel, not unreasonably, asked Victoria to formally dismiss the ladies-in-waiting (ladies of the bedchamber) whose husbands were Melbourne supporters. She refused. Worse, constitutionally, Victoria would not have Peel as prime minister and asked Melbourne to stay on – the last time the monarch has successfully and publicly refused to accept the incoming prime minister. Melbourne fell on-a no-confidence vote. Prince Albert did not care much for the ladies of the bedchamber, whom he found too proud of their position at court and therefore sometimes too forward. But Prince Albert liked Charlotte Canning. He thought her intelligent without being overbearingly clever. He thought her exceptionally lovely, although he did not dwell at all on that. When in May 1842 it was suggested Charlotte Canning would become a lady of the bedchamber to Queen Victoria it was, as was always the value of a court suggestion, readily agreed. Her appointment was to be a very important part of her too-short life. She became a favourite in Queen Victoria's court.

It was not an onerous task. Three times a year, as lady-in-waiting, she attended the Queen for two weeks and would do so for thirteen years. She would go with the Queen to the theatre (but never sit down); she would go for walks with Victoria (but always a step behind). She, with Canning, went to Scotland and the Queen had Charlotte Canning paint and draw every possible view of and from Balmoral.

Charlotte Canning was an activist in many other ways, which was surprising for what was a social station in the royal household. She campaigned for the help and treatment for 'Gentlewomen during Illness', helping Florence Nightingale establish an early women's hospital in Harley Street, London. She helped Nightingale become the first superintendent at the Harley Street clinic and, come the Crimean War, helped helped select the nurses for the Nightingale hospital at Scutari. By the time she was in India Charlotte Canning used another talent more easily admired by the Queen. She became an invaluable scribe during the sometimes wretched moments for the first viceroy and vicereine. She would regularly send her dispatches giving Victoria, who still thought of India as a place of insects and intolerable heat, (this was long before her munshi) a quite different view of her jewel than the more formal reports she was used to, especially after the Mutiny.

The suggestion to 'go out and govern India' was encouraged by those who thought it best that Canning abandon his mistress. The Queen was indignant because Canning's name had not been on the shortlist for India, but constitutionally Victoria could not object – to have done so would have been insulting to Canning, for whom she had high regard. It was a political and personal pickle for the Cannings. For different reasons neither wanted India; for all the romantic writing of the jewel in Britain's imperial crown, India was not always seen as a moment of glory in political and social careers. Certainly, there is no evidence that Charlotte Canning was happy with the prospect of India for the coming five years, the term of office. However, she would be ready to follow her husband 'like a dog' to a society that was duller than she could have conceived possible. The Cannings left in November 1855 with boxes piled high. For Charlotte Canning, the boxes would have been piled even higher to contain enough dresses to change three times a day for informal, formal and washed out in the heat and atop of it all, her two maids, Rain and West. The Suez Canal would not be open until 1869 but the journey that sometimes took half a year depending on the weather rounding the Cape of Good Hope (arguably named) could now be done in two months. One could travel by train from Paris across France to Marseilles and then into the Mediterranean. From Egypt, it would then be across to Suez and, monsoon permitting, onward to Bombay. Even at this stage of ruling, India was undergoing change. Before 1830, East India Company personnel had to go via sea and the Cape.

The Company had, from 1837, an irregular paddle steamer service (the *Beatrice* and the *Atlanta*) but the weather often beat them and there were few bunker ports for the ships. The emerging services meant that expatriates could get back to England on a reasonably regular basis rather than serving out three or four years at once. The Cannings were spared the agonies but the incoming governor general (he became viceroy in 1858) immediately identified this aspec of road, rail and seatravel as a subconscious way of isolating those sent out to govern and directly, those who sent them. The Cannings left London, where anyway they lived well, and were handed on from palace to palace where the towels were so heavily embroidered that morning washing was like drying faces on a field marshal's uniform. The grand parade had begun.

The next stage in the journey was not in the rattling paddleboats with uneasy tween decks. The East India Company packet, the *Feroze*, now a frigate, sent for them. They slept in separate cabins, befitting royalty, even a governor general; even aboard the *Feroze*, Charlotte Canning metaphorically kept two steps astern of her husband. It was also true that the ship had limited accommodation and each was stacked with papers, books, clothes and belongings and the ship's conversion had not much improved the accommodation and what could be heat of 100 degrees in the Indian Ocean. On 29 January 1856 the Cannings disembarked at Bombay. The *memsahib* of India was that night about to become the second most important person in the subcontinent.

> 'It is so amusing and curious and I cannot tell you the strange feeling of such overpowering novelty. But it makes one feel absurdly helpless, not to know a person, or a word of the language, or manners and customs of the simplest description.'[2]

Manners and customs are soon made something of. But precedence and substance in mid-nineteenth-century India was like a concert score. The orchestra of governors general, deputies, commissioners, each knew the music, the notes, when to come in and when to rest. They were as sensitive to position and precedence as the castes they ruled. They were pathetically desperate to preserve position, for only in India did they have position. For Dalhousie this was the closing moment. He had given much to India. He had gone to Calcutta as a man in his late thirties full of hope and the excitement of being sent to rule much of the British world. Here he was, just a few years on, at a time of life when a young man's guise changes little, yet he was worn to almost nothing. Unable to walk without sticks, Dalhousie was yet another young Indian hand aged to nothing before his time and barely able to totter on to the frigate to Suez then, hopefully, spared for home. Dalhousie was dead by 1860. Canning, his friend as well as his successor, could not believe his physical decline.

'D (Dalhousie) is much altered externally – larger and with a thick unhealthy complexion, and the remains of the affliction which he had in the nose; but apparently in good spirits. He is very lame – scarcely able to walk with a stick, and carried in a chair when he has long distances to go *in the house. (author italics)*.[3]

In his final dispatch to the Queen, Dalhousie recorded the arrival of Canning, but not of Charlotte, who had been smuggled anonymously into the residence by Susan, Dalhousie's daughter. Precedence was all. Note the impersonal tense in writing to the monarch.

'The guns are announcing from the ramparts of Fort William that Lord Canning has arrived. In an hour's time he will have assumed the Government of India. Lord Dalhousie will transfer it to him in a state of perfect tranquility. There is peace within and without. Lord Dalhousie is able to declare, without reservation, that he knows of no quarter in which it is probable that trouble will arise.[4]'

This is the virtual eve of the Indian Mutiny and Dalhousie is telling the Queen India is a state of perfect tranquillity. Could this have been what he really thought? Certainly, when the Mutiny started the British and their army commands appear to have been caught off guard. Yet had Dalhousie, known for his insight as the father of modern India, no broad handover warning for Canning? It appears not. Ferdinand Mount, in his family-inspired history, which includes this period, *The Tears of the Rajas*, quotes one officer who lends us some perspective:

'The Mutiny brought home to the British just how little they really knew about the people they were governing. Captain E.M. Martineau, the Depot Commander at Tambala reflected: 'I see them on parade for say two hours daily, but what do I know of them for the other 22? What do they talk about in their lines, what do they plo?. For all I can tell I might as well be in Siberia. Roderick Edwards, the magistrate at Saharanpur wrote: 'Our very servants might be plotting our death and annihilation with every description of atrocity and we be in perfect ignorance of it. Not until now had we ever really felt how utterly we were excluded from the inner life of the people. Not until now had I ever felt what real intense fear was.'[5]

There was the most obvious warning: many, including soldiers, were changing their cash for gold. The signs were there, but the confidence of a witness was not. Moreover, the warnings that were repeated never got high enough up the chain of command. Whatever the weaknesses in the communications system, there was no preparation to start the early warning conversation that was surprisingly absent. Further, Dalhousie in his military reforms had redeployed part of the army around Calcutta and in lower Bengal towards the west. In doing this manoeuvre, Dalhousie could sense threats that would challenge the balance of mixed battalions in the British army. Why did he set up an irregular force and post it to Punjab, which did not obviously need a militia? Pulling out the anomalies and extrapolating shifts in commands can tell us something now because we know something happened – the Mutiny. But at the time Dalhousie saw no threat to British rule and, in idle moments, would have thought more about Afghanistan or even Russia than internal threats More significant in the long run was Dalhousie's work on the Railway Minute of 1853. This document alone did more to spread his enthusiasm for railways among the London directors than anything else he did. It was simple and obvious, thus Dalhousie became known as the father of Indian railways.

There were too many encouraging achievements to think of the dangers of mutiny. Dalhousie's term as viceroy developed more than railways and army reorganisation. He reformed how India was run, giving greater freedom for commissioners to take decisions just as he gave the district magistrates powers to look after police, law and revenue. It was Dalhousie who introduced the first telegraph and electric light. A governor driving himself to the end of his tether misses discontent among people whom he cannot imagine being discontented when so much was being done to give them a better life. Dalhousie's small note to the Queen expressed everything we need to know about the British community from top to bottom. They looked out at India and saw nothing.

Charlotte Canning was during the first couple of days seeing what she had not imagined to be there. Windsor Castle was full of servants at every nook, every turn of a corridor, every door. The Queen had never had to open a door. This image was exaggerated but the contrast with the governor general's house, supposedly the finest official residence in India, was not. It was haphazardly furnished, with not a single lavatory in the building. From governor to commoner the procedure was the same: the potty and a servant standing by to empty – there is no telling where. Charlotte Canning had not believed she was going to India simply to be a wife. She had, as she thought, gone with Canning to help him rule. This image of the finely dressed charity worker was not uncommon.

Instead of the pair of them sweeping brooms of enthusiasm across India, Canning went straight to his room in Government House. There, from dawn to dusk, he sat behind ever-increasing piles of paper trying to understand exactly what it was he ruled, how he ruled and what he was supposed to do with what he ruled. Charlotte Canning was discovering that the British government had selected Canning as a thoughtful (indecisive), clever (theoretical) and unfailingly loyal (slow-thinking) governor general. The government had not imagined the Lord Canning in parentheses but that was what they had sent. As viceroy, he was not very good. Lord Curzon's view was that Canning was one of the worst administrators who ever became viceroy. The longer he sat in his study, the more boxes of papers his staff brought him. The boxes piled higher and higher and Canning – the man who would oversee the defeat of the Mutiny – sank lower and lower with no idea what the papers were trying to say. Canning's reputation was that of a man totally dedicated, a workaholic. Not so. Canning worked long hours because he was inefficient and he worked even longer hours because he was indecisive and unable to delegate responsibilities. He was attempting to run India by himself. There would be changes, and eventually times when he and Charlotte travelled India together and began their masterwork – a record of all he had surveyed with her alongside him. They had travelled, recorded and she had drawn. But the early days were the source of utter loneliness for a vicereine, with a husband home late from the office every night, whose health started to suffer from enormous stress within weeks of the rampart guns sounding the salute. In the last entry Canning had time to write in his diary (for 2 March 1856), he left an idea of his workload.

'Up at 6, but with no thought of going out. Arranged room, papers etc . . . Char (Charlotte) and I breakfasted alone . . . nearly the whole day was taken up with talking over matters with D. His leg is very painful and completely cripples him. We discussed every kind of subject and especially Persons. One great trouble I foresee will come from General Low[6] being about to go home for a time . . . all Military details will fall upon me . . . The pressure of business in these first days has been, and is so great that I have only had time for one look out of doors since we arrived . . .'

Charlotte Canning, because of her position, adopted a formal, even stand-offish pose. She could attend a ball and not dance. A dinner and not eat. Hold a tea and not mix. Some formalities could not be abandoned; here was an indication of the way in which the British saw the Indians as heathens and evil when left to their own ways. Muslims, or Mohammedans as they were called, were seen as liars. Hindus, according to the British, carried out unspeakable acts. Court life in India was as far removed from Windsor as could be imagined. There was no white middle class in the society in Calcutta in which she lived and over which she presided.

For the first lady of India most days were a dull repetition of lunches and dinners and the most testing moment of almost any day would be choosing thirty names for dinner, three times a week. The role of the governor's wife was not exhausting, partly because Canning's predecessor Dalhousie had never allowed a woman to have any authority and Canning did not want any changes at the viceregal household. None of this was peculiar to India. It was the way of colonial life among the white ruling classes in all but the roughest colonies. Charlotte's life was made easier by the company of a series of aides de camp to her husband, particularly Johnny Stanley, who fell in love with her. They rode out when the mornings let them and then rested out of the heat. She kept exceptional sketch books and canvases that created an illusion of a life in India for the British where it was always beautifully settled and wonderfully charming. Yet the letters, the sketches and watercolours, the changing of the drapes and covers in the residence, betray no concern that anything might happen.

'The General at Barrackpore [mid-February 1857, four months before the start of the Mutiny] made a good little speech to the Sepoys of the regiment who are supposed to be rather disaffected on account of the new Minie Cartridges, of which they complain on the ground that the grease used in making them up is beef-suet, and that they cannot touch. There have been mysterious fires at all the places where detachments of this regiment have been quartered.'

It was another sign. What none of the British could understand was that the small incidents that were put down to the ways of India or simple disobedience were unscripted openings of the Mutiny. The cow-fat, the rumour of deploying sepoys overseas, the threatening Christianity with tones of the Inquisition, poor officers unable to realise what could be happening. Charlotte Canning heard what was happening but did not understand, especially the evangelica poison that committed sepoys – Muslims and Hindus – sensed threatening. One incident provoked by the divisional commander, General Hearsey, had all the appearances of a Victorian plundering the souls of the very people they were supposed to be commanding, with the purpose of leading the whole people of India away from some imagined savagery. The British Victorian army never felt safe among non-Christians. They always assumed there was a plot lurking among people whose language they did not understand and religious liturgy they never witnessed. The British nineteenth-century military mind had not moved on since the Crusades. When Lady Canning sent her April duty letter to Queen Victoria, she appeared cheered that a minor mutiny at Barrackpore about greased cartridges had been resolved, the 19th Regiment stood down and that the celebrated Indian army commander, General Hearsy, had the matter in hand. Hearsy, with all the character of a loud minor school housemaster, knew the language, the people and their changing moods. Canning praised him. Lady Canning sent her letter. All the clues were in it.

'Government House. April 9th 1857. The disbanding went off quietly. General Hearsey, who is most fluent in Hindostanee made the men good useful speeches. Lord Canning's general order will be read by this time to all regiments and I trust the matter will be set at rest ... the obnoxious cartridges were withdrawn & Sepoys told to find grease for themselves, but the notion that their caste was to be broken & that they must become Christian spread widely. At least that is the pretended grievance & many most ridiculous stories were invented in support of that rumour. One being that Lord Canning signed a bond to Your Majesty that would make them all Christian in 3 years ... Sepoys are the most tractable good people but any fear that religion or caste shall be tampered with, can always excite them to every possible folly. I do not think the matter is quite at an end but with proper precautions there is no cause for further anxiety.'

A kettle left to boil. Yet even the word mutiny was not as threatening as it might have been. Small, isolated mutinies were not uncommon. The Cannings had not yet seen what might be happening. No one seemed to even ask if the sepoys were rumbling to an outrage. The Cannings saw the sepoys as childlike. Even when news came from Meerut, there was still a reaction of disbelief that this might be an important moment. In England, where distance made clearer the reality, it was difficult for government to be behind Canning's credo that a people must never be governed in anger. Canning dealt justice well, but never with anger. Curzon thought him blessed with 'real greatness'. 'Clemency' Canning, as mostly he is remembered, seems an unfair title, but this came from the British who governed or wrote their newspapers from London. They thought losing India was as unlikely as losing

Manchester and saw a man who refused to overreact with anger.

Three days before news from Meerut came to the Cannings, Charlotte was planning to wear her latest necklace, with its beautiful pearls. Four days later, in a script showing no signs of tensions, Charlotte wrote that

> 'the 3rd cavalry has broken into the prison and released 85 comrades imprisoned for mutiny; others have burnt houses and killed people and were fired into and escaped.'

As for the tragedy of the Delhi massacre on 11 May, Charlotte writes about nothing happening around her, but instead dreams of the

> 'brilliant emerald green of that jungly bit I admire so much . . . like the green of May wheat and emeralds.'

The British were at Evensong on Sunday 10 May when the native regiments of the 3rd Cavalry and the 11th and 20th killed their officers and rode to Delhi. There was no pursuit of the mutineers. The general view was that troops should not leave the camp but remain as its guards to deter other assaults.

In Delhi no defences had been aired. The 38th, 54th and 74th joined the rebellion. Every Christian found was killed and the sepoys murdered their officers. The magazine was blown and thousands killed. The British stiff upper lip could survive even this slaughter. Charlotte wrote to her mother on 19 March,

> 'There is not the least cause for fear here. Many people wish us to put off the ball for the Queen's Birthday – the 25th. I would

not for an instant suggest such a thing. It may not be a cheerful
ball in this time of anxiety, but we ought not to appear in a
state of mourning for this temporary outbreak.'

British understatement? A mother far away to be reassured?
It is the same process.

During the Mutiny, Charlotte Canning told the Queen
what she had seen and not what she had heard. Rumour and
the accounts of eyewitnesses did not exaggerate the terrible
events, but often there was no way that gathered evidence
could put the sometimes grisly affair in context. Charlotte
Canning attempted to do just that and there were those in
high and influential place and status in London who really did
take care to have heard what she was saying through her letters
home and to the Queen. Palmerston, at his patronising best,
noted that, unlike a lady, she kept to the point. The vicereine
was believed not simply because her letters were unfussy as
Palmerston had expected but because they were explicit, literate and she had the eye and thus the mood of the Queen.
Canning, himself under enormous criticism in England from
politicians and the press, might have been thankful for his
wife's talent and intelligence. Her letters, especially those to
Windsor, at least balanced those opinions in England that
dismissed him for making the wrong judgements during the
Mutiny. Following the Mutiny, the constitutional changes
were put in place and Canning, by now further enobled,
became the first viceroy. Together they travelled Canning's
territory and Charlotte Canning painted and wrote everywhere
as they prepared for the final days of their appointment and
posting in January 1862.

As for Canning, he did not see the grand office as a dull
sinecure. He rose while the morning might still be cool and

rarely slept until the night was well on, partly through diligence, as there was so much work to be cleared. In the early months in India, he found his boxes full of unimagined documented responsibility. Dalhousie's view of the governorgeneralship was that he was an official despot. Canning and Dalhousie were like-minded in almost every manner, other than the role of the despot. Canning was a thorough-minded administrator, almost the true example of one who is good at the work because he is bad at it, therefore takes an inordinate amount of time first to understand what he has to do, then think it through and finally get down to work. He understood the weakness in avoiding ideas on the basis that something worked perfectly well as it was. For example, he cultivated the idea that parliament was likely to give reasonable approval to a request from a ministry if members had confidence in the department. The easiest way to achieve this was by introducing the concept of an annual report. A departmental report on a year's work was rare to find. His own report would tell him more than he generally knew about his ministry and, by pressing his people for, they too became better informed and were made aware that much more was expected of them than they had imagined.

Canning took his sound thinking to India and he put this in the context that the changes that were happening in England should not be isolated to Britain. Canning saw himself as an example of how modern ways of running departments and government, together with the emerging movements of sounder democratic thought applied slowly but carefully, should not remain in England but could translate into the Indian system. He was carrying on what Dalhousie had started. India in 1857 prior to the Mutiny was not simply an adventure in improving the ways and means of administering the possession of India. There was also the matter of defending the territory against traditional marauders. His first major task was to make sure that any Russian ambitions in India would be buffered by assuring London that British interests including military deployments into Afghanistan and Persia – this would form a security guarantee for India. Canning deployed troops to the Persian Gulf, the Persians withdrew from Afghanistan and the emir of that place was funded to build an army that could protect its own interests as well as those of the British. Here, alongside the territorial defences of the Burmese territory, were the first signs that the deployments of the Bengal army beyond home territories were unacceptable.

When the Mutiny came, Canning quickly learned that the pitfalls of higher command in times of tension and bloodied uproar could not be avoided. The Mutiny did not come without warning, but because it was not imagined, its warnings were misinterpreted. Well before the outbreak in Meerut that May, unexplained burnings of officers' houses were known to be the work of sepoys. Ill-discipline, orders not really unheard so defied, came in regiments led by officers with no training in leadership. On the question of animal fats in cartridge paper there were too many incidents of disobedience and defiance of orders that followed for it to be ignored. That being said, the cartridge disobedience became symbolic and was exaggerated because the matter was not isolated and occurred daily in some areas and had done for months. The British civilians feared for their lives with good reason – most infamously at Cawnpore. Fear is an imperfect general and the British civilians lashed out to seek vengeance.

The reports of the massacres of women and children in houses at Cawnpore, dusted by further fear and even misinformation, set the British residents on the trail for revenge.

Canning refused to fall into this trap. However, senior officers in the field that Canning could not prevent, took action.

'Not only did the English soldier kill those who happened to come in their way, but they broke into houses and hunted out people hidden in barns, rafters and obscure, dark corners. They explored the inmost recesses of temples and filled them with dead bodies of priests and worshippers. They took the greatest toll in the weavers' room where they killed some women also. At the sight of white soldiers some people tried to hide in haystacks, in the courtyards, but the pitiless demons did not leave them alone there. They set the haystacks on fire and hundreds were burned alive . . . If anybody jumped into a well the European soldiers hauled him out and then killed him, or they would shoot him through the head as soon as he bobbed out of the water for breath.'[7]

A small instance in the thirst of revenge. Canning had no control to convince anyone, especially military commanders, of the long-term consequences of these actions when he understood the coloured memories of war. His determination to more closely identify individual mutineers who were likely to be guilty of specific acts of treason and worse (such as the murder of the officers) prompted the accusation that he was weak. His belief that revenge would do little but exacerbate the Mutiny resulted in his soubriquet, Clemency Canning. In Scotland, the Queen wept. The language was formal, the dialect *pluralis majestatis*.

'Balmoral, September 8th 1857. Dear Lady Canning, I have to thank you for several interesting letters. That our thoughts are almost solely occupied with India with the fearful state in which everything there is – that we feel as we did during Crimean days & indeed far more anxiety you will easily believe. That my heart bleeds for the horrors that have been committed by people once so gentle on my poor Country Women & their innocent little children – you, dearest Lady Canning who have shared my sorrows and anxieties for my beloved suffering Troops will comprehend. It haunts one day and night. You will let all who have escaped & suffered & all who have lost dear ones in so dreadful a manner know of my sympathy; you cannot say too much. A Woman & above all a Wife & Mother can only too well enter into the agonies gone thro' of the massacres. I ask not for details, I could not bear to hear more, but of those who have escaped I should like to hear as much about as you can tell me . . .

The deaths of Sir H Lawrence – Sir Hugh Wheeler & Sir H Barnard . . . are most grievous. The retribution will be a fearful one, but I hope & trust that our Officers & Men will show the difference between Christian & Musselmen & Hindoo by sparing the old men, women & children. Any retribution on these I should deprecate for then indeed how could we expect any respect or esteem for us in future?

. . . we are very very anxious to impress the Government here with the immense necessity of providing a sufficient Reserve of Troops to feed those sent out – and to prepare for the worst & Lord Canning may rely on our urging this unceasingly, for without it I am sure we cannot hold India.'

Here then the Queen, undoubtedly with her principal foreign affairs advisor at her side, Prince Albert, was stating what was not simply imaginable but likely: if it was the intention of the rest of India to follow the mutineers, then without reinforcements – which anyway, would half a year to get in place – British India would fall. Her reference to Christians not behaving as Muslims and Hindus would not get through to commanders in India and certainly not to many British civilians; both groups had a simpler way of dealing with Indians. Not all the British in India from both the military and the civilians agreed with Canning's approach, or the sentiment of the Queen whom they all adored and would die for. They felt ,easier with the natural instinct for revenge. When Dalhousie wrote to the Queen about all being fine in India, earlier that year, this was not the India his successor would inherit. Was Canning's foresight that he may not return to Scotland and London a wand of wisdom in spite of what he was being told in London? What of his vicereine? She never wanted him to be governor general. But there was nothing she would have disliked more than to be told that they would not have two or three more years in India to see the state on its way again to political and not military debate. Yet the Cannings knew India might never achieve that nirvana of a quietly governed country as long as the principles were those of British blessings. The British doctrine, that this is best for you (and us) – was a fragile proposition for two nation states with such opposite instincts.

On 9 October 1857 Charlotte Canning wrote to the Queen.

'It is with heartfelt joy that I congratulate Your Majesty on being once more in possession of Delhi, and on the relief of Lucknow.'

Not such a crisis after all? Matters were still to be settled. The Mutiny would never rest in the minds of the viceroys to come.

In March 1858, Canning declared that in one province, Oudh, there had been almost universal participation in the uprising and therefore with some exceptions, the sepoys, the landowners and whole communities would be punished. Locally and in London, Canning's act was seen as a step too far that would continue the uprising, perhaps at a later date. The outcome was defeat for Canning. The major chiefs of Oudh were too powerful. They got back their land. The peasantry got nothing other than a land title of tenants-at-will. The chieftains of Oudh ruled. The governor general did not. The immediate consequence for Canning was an acceptance that perhaps Dalhousie had been right. Only a despotic regime, perhaps a benign despotism, could rule India with all the advantages of the changes British thinking hoped for. The deeper understanding was that imperial rule could not make do with progressive political and social reform. In Britain, the people themselves were only recently emerging from imperial rule. The major difference between imperial and common rule was universal suffrage. The British in 1857 certainly did not have that.

Canning used the 1861 Indian Council Acts to restructure the executive councils of India and to enlarge them to include the first Indian members. But this was not a preliminary move towards elections or political parties, although Canning saw that as a possibility on a very distant political horizon. There was, however, a need to reverse what Dalrymple describes as the British having lost touch with the people. By putting senior Indians into the governing system, the British would sooner understand what India was thinking and India would think it had a say in government. In fact having a say meant to the Indians they had authority whereas to the British it meant nothing more than hearing what the Indians had to say.

To make this form of consultation work, Canning needed to have the confidence of the council members and a better understanding of the territory. For the former, he certainly had the support of many of the Indians. There was considerable status attached to council membership. For the latter, he had something quite new at hand – the camera. He began to record the imagery of India on film just as his wife Charlotte had tried with her watercolours. Canning's record, *The People of India in eight volumes*, was published in 1868. Here was the example for others to follow and add to: a seemingly never-ending anthropological work on Indian society from villages to palaces.

Richard Beard's portrait of Canning is that of a younger man than the one who went to India. Quite young, he shows thoughtfulness and even solitude. He is certainly not the politician with no memorable achievements apart from the ability to write long annual reports and find the company of a mistress. Canning went to India expressing no doubts but some caution. So too his wife, who did not want to go.

Canning became a better administrator who, in calmer times, might have lived longer and left a brighter mark on English politics. His reputation was that of a truthful man who approached with careful deliberation every decision made, whether by others or himself. He too was asked to stay on in India. Sir Henry Cunningham, in his biography of Canning, wrote that he was

> 'high on the list of those great officers of state, whose services to their country entitle them to the esteem and gratitude of every loyal Englishman.' [8]

Instead he left India in grief.

In the autumn of 1861, Charlotte Canning had embarked upon a long expedition and sketching tour. She went north and then to the Tibetan border. She saw and painted Everest. She and Canning imagined this to be their final trip before returning to England in the New Year, 1862. But she never reached home. In November Charlotte Canning returned to Calcutta with all the symptoms of malaria, to which she would succumb in days. Canning buried his wife in the embassy at Barrackpore. There was nothing for him in India and he returned to London and died at his Grosvenor Square home seven months after his wife's death. They had no children so they left nothing for anyone to carry on, not even his name and title. Did he carry the blame for the Mutiny? Maybe he was not flamboyant enough and so was overlooked. Dalhousie, his friend at Oxford, took most of the criticism. Oxford produced three stewards of India in a row at a time of change, calamity and thankless rebuilding. India took her toll on each of them.

CHAPTER IX

ELGIN, LAWRENCE AND MAYO

Canning, Dalhousie and Elgin were at Oxford together. Elgin's appearance in Calcutta was welcomed. He sat easily with the aristocracy that still ruled the British Isles. The Elgins were used to exercising influence and enjoying the influence of others. In India, that was part of the game. Not who you know, but who knows you. None in the residence was a real stranger, even those not yet introduced. In Elgin's case, he was the son of the man who bought the famous marbles – although in the 1850s, the marbles hardly mattered.

Viceroy Elgin was James Bruce, whose father, the seventh Earl of Elgin, married again after a rowdy London divorce. Elgin's second wife Elizabeth Oswald was Bruce's mother and Elgin's heir by his first wife was George. George died in 1840, the seventh earl died the following year and James Bruce at the age of thirty inherited and became the eighth Earl of Elgin. The family's aristocracy had quarterings enough for any herald to compile an impressive crest. But the Bruce women were commendably fertile and so the family tended to be noticeably hard up, especially as the seventh earl had bought what became known as the Elgin Marbles and had never been fully reimbursed for them by the British government.

The new earl might have spent his whole life trying to make ends meet in the family estates but the well-tested British system of appointing like-minded people to big jobs found Elgin as governor of Jamaica in the year he succeeded his father. Jamaica was not a good place for a caring governor like Elgin. It struggled with the anomalies of the transition of slavery to forced apprenticeships. Elgin had no solution and was largely enfeebled by the sad affair. He suffered in a worse way when his wife of just two years died and in 1846 Elgin, a saddened man who felt that he had failed, resigned and returned to Europe. He made a new and excellent marriage. Lady Mary Lambton was the first Earl of Durham's daughter. Durham was a man of colonial and political influence and comfortably off and had no intention of seeing his daughter (who was to carry five children) living on poor times.

Elgin was offered the governor-in-chief appointment in British North America. In 1837 and 1838 there had been rebellions in Upper Canada and in the Anglo-Scottish communities of Lower Canada with its main city of Montreal. Durham was the man sent to resolve the cause of rebellion; his report famously recommended that Canada should become one and thoughts should be given to a form of independence. Here then was the Anglo-Scottish versus French oppositions. Elgin did get off to a good start. In 1848 he opened the parliament in English and French and announced the two languages would be spoken officially.

Elgin and his family did well and he governed shrewdly, especially through his negotiations with America. But there was little peace in anyone's time. Elgin returned to Britain in

1854, Britain was at war in the Crimea. The other war, the Sepoy Rebellion, was three years away in 1857. In early 1857 Palmerston sent Elgin to China as Britain's high commissioner. It was a very messy business. Elgin did not care for it one bit. The British dispute started with the Chinese boarding a small British vessel in Hong Kong waters called *Arrow*. The Chinese hands were taken off. The British military response, largely with an ill-organised assault on Canton, did not resolve the matter. Palmerston, in one of his less than finest hours, gave Elgin command of a well-fitted-out naval and military unit with instructions to sail with all speed for China. Elgin accepted the commission and sailed for the Far East.

When he arrived in Singapore for stores and further instructions, the Sepoy Mutiny was in full flow. Canning needed soldiers and Elgin was encouraged to send some from his China expedition to help Canning; his ships and men sailed for India. The work done in India, Elgin returned to his original task but with increasing misgivings. His orders were to bombard Canton, which he did with all the distinction of a barbarian but none of the enthusiasm.

In London Elgin was a hero. He had saved India and brought the Chinese to bow before British authority at Guangzhou and Beijing. Elgin had hardly time to catch breath with his family before he was sent back to China. On 18 October 1860 the Emperor's Summer Palace was torched to ashes. Elgin was once more the hero of the London hour. He had hardly time to acknowledge the honours and bows before he sailed for India to become Britain's second viceroy while Canning lay dying in London. Elgin would not be long following his old friend; he could not have known that he would be dead before the next year was out, but before sailing for India, Elgin put his things in order and updated his will.

In the history of the viceroys, there was rarely a quiet time to take up the post. Elgin was better briefed than most. He had spent his short career as a colonial servant. India after the Mutiny was never far from their conversations. It was an impossible place to fully understand other than it was an unsurprising, uncomfortable and unhealthy place for those bred into the temperate climates of Europe's offshore islands. Here was the irony for the family of Elgins. Elgin would seem to have had a premonition that India would do for him. It would be a short tour. Even before leaving Scotland he antici-pated a gloomy tour of duty. At one leaving party he told every-one not to expect to see him again.

'Gentlemen, I cannot conceal from myself, nor from you, the fact that the parting which is now about to take place is a far more serious matter than any of those which have preceded it; and that the vast amount of labour devolving upon the Governor-General of India, the insalubrities of the climate, and the advance of years [Elgin then was fifty-one] all tend to render the prospect of our again meeting more remote and uncertain.'

The view from Scotland and even in the halls of Whitehall was that India was all but pacified, although the Mutiny had been put down not five years. The standard thought in London was that India was in place thanks to Dalhousie and Canning. Here in the 1860s, British India could still be seen as a colony under command. The British had never taken on such an imperial task; there had never been such a direct challenge to British authority. In London, the political view was that thanks to Dalhousie's authority Indian opposition was unlikely to succeed and thanks to Canning the insurrection had been overcome. Thus British colonial authority was in good hands. This perception showed an intriguing set of self-assurances; successive viceroys for the many decades to come would never take it for granted that rebellion was utterly unlikely. Even Elgin with all his experiences, including those with devastating outcomes, had not imagined the reality. He did have one special image – his own health and a reflection on Canning's death. He wrote in July 1862 to his wife, who had yet to arrive in India, about the news he had received of Canning's dying. It was said that Canning had been destroyed by the workrate he imposed upon himself in India. Elgin's was the only insight we have that there was more to Canning's death. It was an Indian death. Circumstances rather than ordinary hard work.

'Is it indeed true? The last rumour of the kind was the report of my death . . . but this time I fear it is only too true! It will add to the alarm to which India inspires. But poor Canning certainly never gave himself a good chance; at least not during the last year or two of his reign here. He took no exercise, and not even such relaxation of the mind as was procurable, though that is not much in the situation of Governor-General. When I told him that I should ask two or three people to dine with me daily, in order to get acquainted with all the persons I ought to know, and to talk matters over with them by candlelight. So as to save daylight for other work, he said: "I was always so tired by dinner-time that I could not speak." Perhaps he was only referring to his later experience; but still it was enough to break down any constitution, to wear oneself out for ever by the same train of thought, and the same routine of business. I think there was more in this than met the eye, for work alone could not have done it. We shall have no confirmation of this rumour in letters for a fortnight or more. Poor Canning! He leaves behind

him sincere friends, but no one who was much dependent on
him.¹'

It was a rare time. Canning, his wife, Dalhousie and his wife
had died in such smart spaces and so briefly after leaving India.
Queen Victoria always made a point of asking if the circumstances of India would suit the health of a new viceroy and especially of his family. Elgin's own health was never strong enough
for him. Elgin's fitness and health were not distressing enough
for him to avoid signs and tensions in India and the opinions
mention him by his closest officers. He was smartly aware of
small incidents that he believed might lead to another uprising.
At the time, political and social sensitivities that were even
slightly out of the norm aroused suspicions. Elgin, newly arrived
in India, was not over-sensitive to conditions in the country, but
like others arriving for the first time, he brought with him an
image of a subcontinent that was not comfortably governed and
therefore one that could never be trusted to provide a new officer
a quiet life. Elgin was in Barrackpore, perhaps from the English
word barracks, as it was an army town and where the first barracks
were built in 1772 about twenty miles from Calcutta. It was a
favourite place of the British, although some viewed it with
mixed feelings. It was, after all, the place in 1857 that a soldier,
Mangal Pandey, attacked one of his British officers and this may
have contributed to the sepoy tensions that led to the Mutiny, as
the sepoys' regiment was disbanded for having no discipline.
There was considerable reported unrest over the standing down
of the regiment. Elgin had gone there to ease his health. It was
then a sad place but Elgin sensed its beauty.

'This place looks wonderfully green. At the end of the broad
walk at which I am gazing from my window, is Lady Canning's

grave; it is not yet properly finished. Who will attend it now? It gives a melancholy character to the place, for the walk it closes is literally the only private walk in the rounds. The flower garden, park, etc., are all open to the public. Although Canning did not die at his post, I thought it right, as his death took place so soon after his departure from India, to recognize it officially, which I did by a public notification and by directing a salute of minute guns to be fired.'

Elgin was not in India to make his mark. He had done that elsewhere, particularly in Jamaica, then Canada and China. And so Elgin had done with medals. When a question was brought to him, it was his style to think about it and understand what others had already tried to do with the conundrum. He would say, 'the first virtue which you and I have to practise here at present is self-denial. We must, for a time at least, walk in paths traced out by others.' It was a good but hard-won philosophy. As viceroy, Elgin had access to everything and to every man he wished to see and could ask every question and demand, if he wished, answers in at least triplicate. The instinct of Indian bureaucracy could not be happier. But the bigger the question, the British way in India was to wave to the furthest borderline, or dip a hand to the religious differences at every corner. The example of both was in the army Elgin found he had at his command.

'To Sir Charles Wood,[2]
Calcutta, April 9th, 1862
When I ask why so considerable a native army is required, I am told that the native must bear a certain proportion to the European force; that Europeans cannot undertaken canton-ment duties, or, speaking generally, any of the duties which the military may from time to time be called to render in support of

the civil power, during peace; that in war, again, they are admirable on the battlefield, but that they cannot turn their victories to account by following up a discomfited foe, unless they have the aid of native troops, not perform many other services which are not less indispensible than great battles to success against an enemy who knows the ground and is inured to the climate.'

Elgin's view was typical of the newly arrived in British India. It was asking the basic question that came through not understanding India. Elgin could not see why there was such a large army. He pointed out to Wood that the rebellion had been crushed and European soldiers could not be expected to put down minor uprisings. Moreover, from what he was told, Elgin could not see signs of India being attacked. The signs that he understood were not good. When he asked why there was a need for such a large army, the answer was well rehearsed.

'You cannot tell what will happen in India. Heretofore you have held the Sikhs in subjection by the aid of the sepoys, and the sepoys by means of the Sikhs. But see what is happening now. The Sikh soldiers are quartered all over India. They are fraternising with the natives of the South – adopting their customs and even their faith. Had the soldiers in a regiment lately stationed at Benares were converted to Hindooism [sic] before they left that holy place. Beware or you will shortly have to cope in India with a hostile combination more formidable than any of those you have countered before.³'

Elgin was paraphrasing what others believed. His interpretation was to prove correct. British India would become that hostile combination not simply in the army but across the country. By the end of the century, signs were being shown of the country splitting into hostile religious parts and portions. He was making all the efforts to ignore easily-come-by conclusions. This was one of his thoughts, that first he trod where others had to find his own way. The army had authority and not a little admiration. The army therefore for viceroy Elgin had to set the pattern for the post-Mutiny Indian communities. Elgin talked about 'judicious' systems of recruiting. Judicious was not a too-easily-come-by label. The army was not for the viceroy either as good as most said it was or could be. It was serviceable and could perhaps be created and officered in such a way that it became 'as little a source of peril as may be.' The army was not the fine disciplined and dependable fighting force that so many military historians tell us. Elgin was no stranger to the military as were other senior colonial men in Victorian times; therefore his judgement could be trusted. India had not recovered from the Mutiny and its consequences were powerful enough to influence the plans for major constitutional changes over the next fifty years. The army could not do all things imaginable after restructuring.

'I do the think they [the army] go far to prove that, notwithstanding our vast physical superiority to anything that can be brought against us, we should find it a difficult task to maintain our authority in India by the sword alone; and that they justify a very jealous scrutiny of all schemes of expenditure for military objects which render necessary the imposition or maintenance of taxes which occasion general discontent, or deprive the Government of funds requisite for carrying on works of improvement that have double the advantage of stimulating the growth of wealth in the country, and increasing the efficiency of the means of self-defence which we possess.'[4]

Elgin's language was still that of the imperial invader. It was still them and us. He wrote of the British having to be willing to maintain authority in India against the Indians. Elgin made it clear that some very basic ideas about the people the British ruled should be examined. Elgin mixed with people who believed all Asians were children; they were amused and gratified by external trappings and ceremonies, impressed by titles and regalia and very willing to give up dignity and their own power if they could be allowed to adopt the image of European power. In other words, some of his own people even in India had a belief that apparently sophisticated people would give up a great deal to mix at an invader level. Elgin's view was quite different. He believed that the eastern imagination was likely to invest outer things with a symbolic character; and that relaxing protocol was valuable because it could mean concessions on substantial matters.

Elgin said that he should travel the country to know the people and they him. All viceroys other than Lytton in 1876 said the same; it was such an obvious task, and for most an impossible one. Yet Elgin's perceptions were realistic enough. Ruling India was not like taking on a few thousand acres of Scottish grouse moor. India, for all its conflicting histories among tribal loyalties, was a place in the 1860s of grand canvases, where the superiority of often hundreds of princes fixed the minds of her people as well as the owners in the boardrooms and government departments of state. Asia too had its principalities, like the more familiar Europe. The mighty wars of Europe fighting for thrones or religion or both would change the complexion of the continent. Since Mughal no one could test the potential for change in India. Elgin understood the wisdom of aristocracies inasmuch as their proprietors knew how far to go in a venture and knew too how

their like in neighbouring places would go. Benign dictatorship, the most flattering of descriptions of the new Crown rule,
was understood by India. While it may have not bound differing societies of the subcontinent or decided which powerful
and warring group to support, it had followed the rules of serf-
dom in signing behind that which was winning until the battle
for proprietorship was settled, albeit momentarily. Again, Elgin
allowed this, as he explained to Sir Charles Wood from the
British summer hideaway, Shimla (then Simla) in May 1863,
a few months before his death.

> 'I have no objection *prima facie* to an aristocracy, and I am quite
> ready to admit that conflicting claims of proprietorship in the
> same lands are an evil; but I also know that, even in our old
> Christian Europe, there are not many aristocracies that have
> had salt enough in them to prevent them from rotting. And
> when I consider what Oriental society is; when I reflect on the
> frightful corruption, both of mind and body, to which the inheri-
> tors of wealth and station are exposed – the general absence of
> motives to call forth good instincts, or of restraints to keep bad in
> check – I own that I do not feel quite sure that, even if we could
> sweep away all rights of sub-proprietors or tenants, and substitute
> for the complications incident to the present system an uniform
> land-tenure of great proprietors and tenants at will, we should be
> much nearer the millennium than we are now.'[5]

Elgin had, in a short time as viceroy, come to question the
phenomenon of bureaucracy anywhere. Elgin also understood
the equivocal situations in which official declarations of the
independence of others, including neighbouring states, were
in contradiction and in which the routine of everyday rule and
the contradictions of debating or negotiating with others were

corrupted by instinctive selfishness and worse, inconsistency. Elgin had arrived not with an open mind but with experience in colonial rule and ambition. He understood the distance between the British at home and the British abroad. He had seen and practised himself the arrogance that he was implying and had felt the reaction of those in whose country he ruled or represented the Crown.

Here was another view of the personality of the viceroy. Elgin had not gone to India for status nor another colonial scalp. By and large the viceroy had a Victorian tendency to improve the lot of the people ruled, to explore ways of getting those subjects involved in making the colonial tract a better place and, of course, a profit. Without the profit, the society forgets itself. However, Elgin also was committed to his primary purpose: the people in England, not the people in India. Elgin, like the other viceroys, was not a missionary who had come to save the Indians. No viceroy was like that. The viceroy was there to rule on the orders of the Crown and that rule would be on British terms and no one else's.

'My modest ambition for England is, that she should in this Eastern world establish the reputation of being all-just and all-powerful; but to achieve this object, we must cease to attempt to play a great in small intrigues, or to dictate in cases where we have not positive interests which we can avow, or convictions sufficiently distinct to enable us to speak plainly. We must interfere only when we can put forward unimpeachable plea of right or duty; and when we announce a resolution, our neighbours must understand that it is the decree of fate.'

Elgin's eloquence was understood in London, especially by Wood. It was not so easily taken in by those who worked and

ruled in India as an expatriate society that, through its experience over the past five or six years, felt constantly vulnerable
and had no guarantees for the future. A successful aristocracy
is acknowledged for its past and assumes therefore its right to a
future. The people who carried on ruling once the viceroy
made way for another had no such guarantees.

Elgin, meanwhile, had formidable sensitivities to overcome
in the everyday management of empire. The India Act promised to temporarily move certain meetings and councils out of
the capital Calcutta to bring government to the people. It
would demonstrate the form of government and show publicly
the importance of rule and law making. There was the plan to
transfer the council from Calcutta to another place, not for a
day's meeting, but for months at a time. But which other place?
It could go to Delhi. It would, but not yet. The first question
for a viceroy in almost everything he did, especially in terms of
administration, was safety. The most obvious place would have
to be Lahore but imagine the contradictions and loss of prestige for other places. However, for the viceroy's council to meet
in Lahore would make most sense because it was under the
government of India and its loyalty could be guaranteed. The
most important reason for moving council to Lahore or
perhaps three or four different cities was that Lahore was not
Calcutta and was not a military city where there was absolute
control of the people and where expression of opinion was
muted. Elgin wanted to hear what Indians wanted to say. That
could not be done in a barracks city like Calcutta.

If Lahore was to be chosen then we should consider that this
was mid-nineteenth-century India. Communications through
the relatively new telegraph were good and the paraphernalia
of council could be carted, albeit crudely, in a half-day trek
from Calcutta. There would be many boxes. The council

would be wherever it found itself for some weeks or months. (A comparison of the European Union parliament shifting all the boxes from Brussels to Strasbourg once a year is not far wrong). Elgin knew that a closed meeting of the viceroy's talking shop as well as his legislative stronghold would need to impress Lahore itself, the whole province and any neighbours with hopes of incursions.

Elgin ordered the lieutenant governor of Lahore to stage a spectacular agriculture exhibition – an enormous version of an English county – which the viceroy would open with an equally grand display of speeches. He then had the army carry out its annual exercise period to remind the nearby Afghan leaders that military reform in India had produced a new model army and potential aggressors would do well to stay at home. They would never do that. Elgin never got to Lahore. He and his wife had first to make the long, sometimes dangerous journey from Shimla towards Peshawar, which meant treacherous passes at more than 10,000 feet, high enough for a stout viceroy with an uncertain constitution. Elgin suffered a heart attack in October, reached the medical centre at Dharamsala fort in early November and died in that place. He was buried there on 24 November 1863.

The British government was in a fix or two. India was without a viceroy. The Queen was unrepresented and the princes without a levee. Sir Robert Napier and then Sir William Denison stood in until the arrival of Sir John Lawrence – not an aristocrat, not a career politician, not an Oxford classicist, not anything that might have been typical of a viceroy. Instead, Lawrence was a tough, muscular Christian Yorkshire soldier who had come to command his division of believers in the British way and had served a good apprenticeship in India to

The Viscount Canning, 1856–62, resolved the Sepoy
Rebellion (the Indian Mutiny) at terrible cost.

(© Metropolitan Museum of Art / © Mary Evans Picture Library)

Charlotte Canning.

*(© British Library, London, UK /
© British Library Board. All Rights
Reserved / Bridgeman Images)*

The Earl of Elgin, 1862–3, was the most experienced colonial administrator to be appointed to India. He was in distant parts when struck by a heart attack and his remains lie in Dharmshala.
(© SSPL / Getty Images)

Sir John Lawrence, 1864–9, kept Afghanistan at a distance, for good reason which twentieth and twenty-first-century Western governments ignored.
(© Mary Evans Picture Library)

The Earl of Mayo, 1869–72, drew up India's frontiers and simplified the idea of resolving local problems by local people.
(© Universal History Archive / UIG via Getty images)

The Lord Northbrook, 1872–6, was a banking Baring who reorganised what he identified as the nonsensical government of India.
(© Universal History Archive / UIG via Getty images)

The Lord Lytton, 1876–80, was something of a poet and started the second Afghan War in 1878.
(© CORBIS / Corbis via Getty)

Edith Villiers, Countess of Lytton.
(© Art Collection / Alamy Stock Photo)

The Marquess of Ripon, 1880–84, is still revered in Chennai as 'Lord Ripon, Our Father'. Europeans in India prevented the enactment of his Bill to allow Indian judges to rule on Europeans.
(© Rischgitz / Getty Images)

The Earl of Dufferin, 1884–88, the eighth viceroy, was liked by Indians but not by the government in London. He was a political reformer, based on a distinguished career in Canada, Russia and the Near East.

(© Lord Dufferin as Viceroy of India, c.1884-88 (b/w photo), English Photographer, (19th century) / Private Collection / Bridgeman Images)

Hariot Rowan-Hamilton, Marchioness of Dufferin.

(© Lady Dufferin as Vicereine of India, c.1884-88 (b/w photo), English Photographer, (19th century) / Private Collection / Bridgeman Images)

Maud Lansdowne.

The Lord Curzon, 1899–1905, was a brilliant viceroy. He saw his role as a divine appointment but overstayed his welcome.
(© Buyenlarge / Getty Images)

Mary Curzon.
(© Illustrated London News Ltd / Mary Evans Picture Library)

The Earl of Minto, 1905–11, whose grandfather had also been governor general over a hundred years earlier. The Minto– Morley Reforms of 1909 meant self-government, if not independence, was inevitable.

(© Mary Evans / Grenville Collins Postcard Collection)

The Countess of Minto.

(© Mary Evans Picture Library)

prove it. The Victorians were content with Thomas Babington Macaulay's version of how the British got to the nineteenth century.

The British way had worked successfully since the Plantagenets and, with the steelier fist of the Industrial Revolution, the political and social reform of the bearers of political democracy would demonstrate that these island people were rightly in charge of the quarter of the world that mattered. The curious mood of island people to assume so much sound authority in their ways of life created a new imperialism based on two premises: the British way was superior and, given that the majority of the indigenous population showed no sustained opposition to the colonial presence, there was a hardly a thought, certainly not at Windsor Castle, that India would not be British for ever.

In John Lawrence, the British had produced a storybook figure rather than an anonymous aristocrat. That did not make him a perfect choice. He was never quite sure how others reacted to his lack of background. First stop was the East India Company's Haileybury College, a place of good learning. Dunces, even aristocratic dunces, need not apply:

'Each candidate shall be examined in the four gospels of the Greek Testament and shall not be deemed duly qualified for admission to Haileybury College unless he be found to possess competent knowledge thereof . . . Nor unless he be able to render into English some portion of the whole works of one of the following Greek authors: Homer, Herodotus, Xenophon, Thucydides, Sophocles and Euripides. Nor unless he can render into English some portion of the words of one of the following Latin authors: Livy, Terence, Cicero, Tacitus, Virgil and Horace and this part of the examination will include

questions in ancient history, geography and philosophy . . . and
the first four books of Euclid. He shall be examined in moral
philosophy, and in the evidence of the Christian religion as set
forth in the works of Paley.'

The would-be clerks would then have to pay their own fares
to India arriving in Madras, Bombay or Calcutta. Then, they
would be given desks and tasks and paid not generously but
better than they would have been at home. For the astute and
opportunistic, there were many chances to do rather well.

The Company's army recruits were sent not to Haileybury
but Addiscombe and then on to join the 5,000 or so British
officers and senior NCOs in the Company army – usually
some 200,000 men. The sepoys lived in wretched conditions
and were uncompromisingly disciplined.

It was into this game of social and commercial chance that
the eighteen-year-old Lawrence, with all the experience of
his family in India, but without the aptitude for languages,
or for the climate and certainly not for the social life,
appeared. He was sent to Calcutta to learn Asiatic languages.
He tried. He managed to get a posting to Delhi and
eventually Punjab. In the Delhi districts he met Charles
Metcalfe (1785–1846). Metcalfe, who was born into India as
well as in India, was rewriting the laws of taxation that he found
had all but ruined the small proprietors, traders needed for
India's future.

Metcalfe's view was that the British in India had done much
harm partly by usurping the Indian institutions. He believed
the British and the Indian ways had opportunities for sensible
co-existence. His view was not always supported elsewhere and
so Metcalfe's influence in the Delhi territory was to set many
British against him. Lawrence took all this, but did not find

himself enough in the Metcalfe camp to be openly criticised as was Metcalfe; perhaps Lawrence was not seen as someone who would go far and so need for higher authority to protect himself for the future. Most of his jobs during the 1840s were in revenue collecting, important for the Company but not exciting lines on Lawrence's CV. What the posts did do for Lawrence was induce an understanding of what Indians saw as the downside of British rule. The turning point in John Lawrence's career was the Mutiny. Conflict often turns up unlikely heroes. The Mutiny turned up a competent administrator and presented him as a hero. Lawrence saw what was happening in Bengal, stood down most of the army and raised almost 40,000 Punjab infantry and cavalry and put them under Indian officers. If he had not been quick enough to change the Company order of battle, the British in the north could have gone down. Lawrence did not get it all right in the Mutiny, which he saw as a a conflict between right and wrong. He made no secret of his Christian ethic. In time of conflict this characteristic is rarely hidden. It was not unnoticed by those sepoys who feared the spreading of Christianity, although Lawrence was no leader of the evangelical persuasions that had reached the subcontinent.

Lawrence made quick decisions that worked in the midst of conflict. His advice on executions, driven by conscience and tactics, turned out correct. Hence the many who saw him as an obvious successor as viceroy when Canning went home in 1881. London wanted another aristocrat. But Elgin became viceroy in March 1862 and was dead by November the following year. Lawrence arrived, still a shaggy-faced hero and still remembering all that he learned from Metcalfe. The Indian peasantry had to be protected partly from the British but most certainly from the historical avarice of the Indian aristocracy.

That he did not conform to the aristocratic seedline of viceroys suited Lawrence, who was exactly how we see him in George Watts's portrait a year before his appointment: a tough, slightly scruffy soldier whose men would follow him anywhere. Watts (1817–1904), a member of the Symbolist movement, would make the point that he painted ideas not things. Lawrence was an idea working its way through a still-rumbling Indian society. The Mutiny was done for but the old order had indeed changed, or should have.

Lawrence was the sixth son of uncomplicated Ulster Protestant soldiering stock. His father Alexander and his two uncles Henry and George served in the 19th. His mother was Catherine *née* Knox, the daughter of a Donegal clergyman. John Lawrence stood in a line of perfect officer breeding, in a big enough frame to take a wound or two and not sensitive enough to feel insecure about a light education at a grammar school and then, thanks to a relative, a not entirely strenuous time at East India College, Haileybury, from which he left in the top ten of his year. He was tough, created for adventure rather than the Church, although innocently devout. A man who could perhaps make mistakes but also many friends and a man who had the imperial sense of authority – to rule rather than to be ruled – as a family pastime. John Lawrence would probably have been equally distinguished as a soldier had he not listened to his sister, who instructed him in his New Testament and prayers rather than daily orders. Nor did he think much of the social life in the capital; at first chance, he escaped to the Delhi province and its villages, where the Indian peasantry lived, as the British saw the people who had been wronged by law and Indian authority. Lawrence was wary of misunderstanding the way in which the British saw India in legal and tax terms. It was relatively simple for the British to apply laws to the people of India as if they were being governed in the British Isles.

It was a dull start to any young man's career in India, which, at this distance, seems surprising because of the experience he gathered far away from decorative norms of the cooler corridors of pre-Mutiny British rule. Lawrence was appointed assistant tax collector of Delhi and even an assistant judge. None of the appointments was as grand as might now seem. He was a junior in the Company, but he was a white British junior in an organisation that lorded it over the Indian districts whose taxation revenues were the main income of the East India Company that had started out 240 years earlier with hopes for spices and silks. India, by the immediate post-Mutiny period, was changing for the British, but not in a manner that in twenty-first-century politics would be notified by treaty, protocol or simply historically assumed custom. Karl de Schweinitz Jr. believed that, however the Great Revolt as he called the Mutiny was interpreted,

'it was a break in the continuity of British governance in India.'[6]

There was, after the Mutiny, little pretence that imperial rule was anything but imperialist. There was an easily imagined combination of imperialism and awareness of the circumstances that had created the Mutiny. Certainly, British rulers measured more carefully the distance between their thrones and the people whom they ruled. One consequence was that by using a government agenda and individual wariness, or ordinary awareness, there was an improvement in the government of the people.

The obvious change was the missing British enthusiasm for a belief that the people of India would be transformed into a more 'modern' society, taking the opportunities and values by then clearly identified in Britain.

'The arrogance of a superior, but exportable civilization now gave way to the arrogance of inherent superiority'.[7]

Britain was hardly relying on the benefits of imperialist authority in India. The Mutiny was not a war against the British in India. It was simply another of the bloody skirmishes in the Great British race through industrial, economic and political definitions of the nineteenth century. So much wasted blood cannot come from a sporting event, yet the British aplomb in victory, however minor, gave Victoria's armies – rarely her Navy – a manner of close-run things and good chases for a class that never hunted south of the Thames. The nineteenth-century battle honours of the British would later become a time line of her imperial history and a reflection of the fact that wars fought at some considerable distance always allowed the centre of colonial power to put out more victory flags but then to draw breath.

Post-Mutiny politics in London and India were no different and the passing of India to the Crown was a constitutional celebration that would intend better management and fewer parliamentary and administrative responsibilities because the template for the relationship was in place. Even the Charter was allowed a good and undemanding time to run its course, not expiring until 1874. Moreover because of the times, the whole matter was one of imperial management and constitutional rearrangement. There was no discussion on taking the opportunity to establish even a talking shop at which the direct interests of the peoples of India would be assured or, at the very least, noted. Britain owned India. The British in India would decide what, if anything, was best for the Indians. This was not a deliberately imperial issue and there was no suggestion that the British rulers were not interested in the state and condition of the different and sometimes differing Indian peoples.

There was no sense of triumph. There was no ambition to rule by the rote of fear. Instead this was the way imperialism worked and the majority of those who ran India saw themselves as a caring bureaucracy frustrated by the contrariness of the people. Why would they not? England itself was run from the grassroots of parishes up through the developing county and provincial city system to national government. Those in command exercised power and even judgement because they were in power to do so. There was no discussion of style or method. This was the late nineteenth century marking time, anticipating the changing way of the world to come. John Lawrence had governed Punjab in the belief that a working rule would be the Christian act of ruling all men equally. Lawrence could say with confidence that this was his way and purpose in Punjab. It may well be that those who decided his future saw little to support this ethic and for that reason he was not chosen to follow Canning. Instead, he was to spend what was, to him, wasted time in an advisory role in London, where he was given the opportunity to repeat his criticisms of colonial ruling methods, and in particular the army in India.

But in 1864, Lawrence arrived at the viceroy's throne because no one was as experienced. The deaths of other candidates and the need for locum viceroys meant that British rule, while not losing its grip, was far from what even the secretary for India's office recognised was needed. Ruling India was not ruling Punjab. In that presidency, Lawrence had the space and the independence he needed.

Lawrence believed that the viceroy should govern with a procedural as well as a bureaucratic principle that was fit for

India, rather than the principle of profit and opportunity that had governed the East India Company and would end up usurping Lawrence's every motive. Lawrence did not have the authority of a viceroy. Nor did he have the social authority of his predecessors. Punjab was, in British social terms in India, a second-class place. It was not a smart command according to the general British view in the then capital, Calcutta. There was too the obvious fact that Lawrence was well decorated but not an aristocrat. India had always been ruled by aristocracy, as had every other state of that period.

For Lawrence, the certainties rather than the social discrepancies were obvious; just five years after the Mutiny the army reeked of little disguised animosities. This was not open rebellion but resentments stretched relations between British and Indian soldiers. Increasing promotions and opportunities for Indians in the three major commands, Bengal, Bombay and Madras, meant that the officers had to be of superb character and understand well the relationship between officer and senior non-commissioned officers. The concept of looking to the personal and personnel arrangements in the Indian army was high on Lawrence's list of reforms.

No matter the capability of the armies, the confidence, sense of security and distinction in the army was of paramount care; if Lawrence got that wrong, then it needed not much scratching at the surface of the system to find another potential mutiny. The British in India had a reasonable enough purpose: make as much money as possible, some just to pay their way, others to make their fortunes. Corruption was a widespread and historic pastime and this irregularity, coupled with the often overwhelming development projection of India including canal, rail and road systems, exposed the lack of capital and much-opposed ways of raising it.

A trader in India was there to make money, not to pay taxes and generally help out with projects that would long outlast the individual British businessmen. Two elements of the reign of Lawrence could easily be examined as examples of modern-day India. What to do about self-sufficiency for the peasant workers and the uncontrollable cause of disaster?

Lawrence was a champion for the rights of farming Indians – as long as they accepted the principle and authority of British rule. For example, he accepted that what he would have seen as the peasantry should have legal tenure of their own land. This was pure Metcalfe philosophy. To give this right, not a concession, would make it less likely that there would be so much animosity towards the rule of Britain. This seemed a simply applied piece of legislation, until the uses of land and right to hold it as an asset were considered. For example, a person could hold land and rent it out. But what happened when a new owner wanted the land himself? The perhaps long-time tenant had no rights and there was nothing the British could do to satisfy the difference. The easily disturbed right to scratch a living from such a holding would never reconcile Indian and British interests. The land tenure legislation was never properly reformed. This was a subject for which Lawrence fought for justice both legally and morally, committed Christian that he was. What Lawrence could not do and most regretted in his time in India was not recognizing and not, with all his powers, coping with drought.

Lawrence felt his part in the handling the 1866 famine was the most obvious failing of his five years in India as viceroy. The famine that stretched north from Madras covered 180,000 square miles and 47 million people and centred on Orissa (now Odisha). A third of the population died from starvation and a cholera epidemic. The 1865 monsoon was not enough to feed the rice crop. The people depended on the rice. The crop failed and worse, the Bengal Board of Revenue, partly because of corruption and the manipulation of figures showing the people who would need the rice, underestimated the consequences for a quickly starving population. When the 1866 monsoon arrived it was hardy and hampered the gathering of the low rice crop. There was little communication across the region and with government about what was going on and what was needed. Imports of rice were mostly wrongly calculated.

A dispassionate view of what happened might be seen in the political awareness among some Indians when news circulated that millions of tons of rice was being exported to England while a million and more Indians starved to death. This period was within a decade of the Mutiny. Political awareness had not been dulled by reorganisations within the army and the legislatures.

Lawrence had been a hero. Now he was no leader. He would not challenge opposition from his own council. He wanted to get supplies through to the needy of Orissa. The decision to do so was put off. The monsoon removed the decision from Lawrence's hands. It could not be done. His indecision was final. It was true that from the very start of his time as viceroy it was clear, even to him, that the job was way above him. This would seem an impossible conclusion given his ambition and determination as a practical man, a burly personality that could seize opportunity in the tightest situations.

Could this have been the same man who commanded so well in Punjab and disarmed the Bengal troops who would have made such a difference to the Mutiny had they joined armed? Was this the civilian who took the guise and responsibility of a battle-hardened commander when he pushed his seniors into action while they loped towards prudence?

Lawrence, the civilian whose soldiering was quoted in honour, took his example in all he achieved from his memory and the record of Clive the previous century.

Whatever it was, it most certainly was the man whose likeness was in Florence Nightingale's bedroom. Miss Nightingale's connection with Lawrence was India just as it was with Charlotte Canning. The dramatic connection was the Crimean War and the ensuing inquiry that merged into the Sepoy Mutiny.

Canning had given way to Elgin but not for long. Elgin was not a healthy man and gave way in November 1863. He is buried in the church of St John in the Wilderness in Dharamsalah. Florence Nightingale forms the connection between Crimea and the Mutiny and the conditions in which even unwounded soldiers lived, trained (when they did) and died. Nightingale was in as poor health as some she dealt with and talked about, but she lived in better conditions and so was a survivor. Born in 1820, she died in 1910. Her contentions about a soldier's lot in India were simple: he was more likely to die of disease than battle. (There are some armies in the twenty-first century where that comparison still exists). Her latest campaign had run with a slogan *Our Soldiers Enlist to Die in Barracks*. Her inquiry for the government was to produce a twenty-eight-page conclusion to which there was a counter-argument. Everything she said about India was true. Many of the details were true and a total surprise at home; consequently, the government pamphlet, *Observations By Miss Nightingale*, complete with diagrams and illustrations (that Nightingale paid for) set out facts that should have been everyday knowledge but in England were not.

In May 1863 when the Nightingale pamphlet was published, the average man could often, if he had a job, work eighteen hours a day. If that same man were fortunate, he would sleep for six hours. India reversed the human day. The soldiers in India commonly spent eighteen hours a day in their beds. An average soldier in an average non-war day would be in bed until daybreak; drill for an hour; breakfast served to him by native servants. Back to bed. Dinner. Bed. Tea. Drink alcohol. Bed. The conditions were the equivalent of locking up a soldier in jail for most of the day. In Bangalore, this routine resulted in alcoholism and disease. The same barracks reported that soldiers who were kept in could not even march on parade. Some barracks, for example the one at Rangoon, had few troubles but this was an exception. One reason the army routine and accommodation were not designed to keep soldiers fit after a fashion, even, was the widespread belief that India was unfit. It was assumed that the miserable condition of the British soldiers was inevitable and was down to India itself. Florence Nightingale pointed out that diversion from drink (often brought about by boredom), physical and intelligence testing training and more time up and less time on their cots would improve physical conditions and make better and in certain provinces fewer mutinous men. The last thought attracted the still nervous British. Her paper *How People may live and not die in India* was published in Scotland in October 1863.

Nightingale's connection with Canning was through his wife, Lady Canning. The Victorian version of 'Ladies Who Lunch' included Charlotte Canning before she went to India. She was chairwoman of the Council for the Institution for the Care of Sick Gentlewomen in Distressed Circumstances and brought Nightingale into the institution as superintendent. It was in this early relationship where Florence Nightingale learned to connive and intrigue behind committee scenes to get what she wanted. Because of this continuing relationship,

Nightingale, even though she was recovering her health in Malvern, wrote to Charlotte Canning during the Mutiny to offer her Crimea-type help. Indirectly, Florence Nightingale had helped by drawing Charlotte Canning's attention to how much could be done so simply to prolong life rather than disease.

When John Lawrence became viceroy in 1864 after the unexpected death of Elgin he already knew Nightingale and; from his earlier times in India, her recommendations for the housing of soldiers; perhaps he was aware that she kept a small picture of him in her bedroom. Within a month of assuming the viceroy's throne, Lawrence had ordered Calcutta, Madras and Bombay – the three presidencies – to form sanitary committees and to follow Florence Nightingale's recommendations in her pamphlet *Suggestions for Improving Indian Stations*. One difficulty was either warfare between the India Office and War Office in London or complete bureaucratic incompetence in one of those places, or even both. Lawrence awaited her recommendations. Seven months later they had not arrived. Miss Nightingale complained to the ministries. Someone, somewhere had blundered. The recommendations were recovered and sent to Lawrence, who had them studied and sent to the presidencies within days; he kept up a correspondence with her telling of progress and conditions. Was this important for the viceroyalty? Yes. Lawrence was not out of the usual drawer for the post. He could get requests and suggestions through the London bureaucracy easily enough, except when there was a tad too much politics surrounding a subject and it needed doing by hand. The delay could have been such a case. It was best to get on with ruling India rather than wait on events to slow you down.[8] All that was admired, until he became viceroy. He was undoubtedly outspoken with a yearning, not unlike

Ripon's, for total reform of the way in which India was governed. But he was not from the school that governed easily when a man is his own and final counsellor. He rode as roughly as a soldier and had no sense of dressage. He misplaced the visual authority as well as the cunning of the viceregal office.

The Nightingale proposal was an example of a viceroy supposedly with almost unlimited power, representing the Crown, being worn down to a point of obvious depression because there was not a good enough system to carry out what were seen not as spectacular projects, but essential if basic changes and the funding for them were to come together. This again was not the 'plumes and elephants' part of the job.

He told Miss Nightingale that all he tried to do was help when and because her plans were feasible. Having reached his tether's end, he wrote in August 1867:

'I am not well and have more on my hands than I can manage. We have so little money and so much to do'.

When Lawrence went, it was Miss Nightingale who said he had 'left his mark on India.' India, once more, had left its mark too.

Lawrence retired to England as Baron Lawrence of Punjab in 1869. It was in Punjab that Lawrence's honour was best left to gather. His tomb is in Westminster Abbey, but even in death all was freckled with annoyance. Disraeli said he should not be so honoured. Disraeli was indifferent in losing that battle. It was some indication that a man such as Lawrence should have deserved more but never gathered it. Lawrence's belief that he failed over Orissa had an echo in the early development of aggressive political activity in India.

Dadabhai Naoroji (1825–1917), the Grand Old Man of India, became the first Asian MP (Liberal, Finsbury Central) in the English parliament and more significantly a founder of the Indian National Congress.

It was Naoroji's *Poverty and Un-British Rule in India* that became the widest-read accusation of the leaking of the wealth of his country into British banks. His study showed that India was vulnerable mainly because it was ruled by a foreign power. His argument was simple: money earned in India did not remain in India. This was a firm challenge to the belief of the British raj that the foremost care was for the people of India. This was never so, according to Naoroji. Few, especially in retrospect, confounded his simple argument that became known as Drain Theory. The money was being drained out of India and so colonial economics had to include the presence of a foreign power that could, for example, introduce a railway that India could not but take the profits the railway created.

The further stage of the theory was when a colonial power made the rules for the occupied state and could, therefore, drain money out of India, reinvest in India using money that it drained away and drain too those profits. Lawrence could identify with these sentiments without losing his principle that he would always do the best he could by the Indian people as long as they recognised British rule. Today that condition seems unacceptably patronising. Then, even in post-Mutiny India, this was not so. The age of the Naorojis, the political and social thinkers who would lay tracks for the likes of Gandhi, was shortly to come. The British had coped with the Mutiny, they had a peace where there were always runs to be had on a good wicket. The raj was not yet confusing to them, nor would it be with the next viceroy, Richard Bourke, the Earl of Mayo, above all, good at sport. Like Lawrence, Mayo too came from a big Irish family at ease with an unquestioning evangelical persuasion. The eldest of ten children, Mayo, like Lawrence, was never troubled by a demanding education other than an ordinary degree at Trinity College Dublin, although his two volumes of notes and diaries on St Petersburg and Moscow were well enough received in 1846. He found work as chief secretary for Ireland in Derby's government; he was a reminder that the second rank usually provides the administrative plank that keeps government in office for longer than might be the case without them. After he succeeded his father as Earl of Mayo in 1868, Disraeli sent him to India. Disraeli then promptly lost office but Gladstone left Mayo in the line for Calcutta. Mayo knew nothing of India, nor did his wife Blanch Wyndham (1826–1918), Lord Leconfield's daughter.

When asked to explain the *Schleswig-Holsteinische Frage* and the complexity of the relationship between the Danish Crown and German Confederation, Palmerston is supposed to have said that

> 'only three people have ever understood the Schleswig-Holstein business – the Prince Consort who is dead, a German professor who has gone mad and I, who have forgotten all about it.'

It was one of the two seemingly irresolute matters of British overseas politics of the mid-nineteenth century producing wars over not much. (1848–1851 and 1864 and the consequence of referendums heard after the First World War). The subcontinent's conundrum, although nothing to do with ethnic history, was Afghanistan. Some knew its origins. Some had known its origins. Some had known but had never known what to do about Afghanistan. It was a conundrum unresolved into the twenty-first century. There had been an Anglo-Afghan war (1839–1842), there was about to be another (1878–1880) and there would be a third (1919). For Mayo, there was too the long period of settling the internal arrangements of the Pashtun-dominated state that would during the nineteenth century's closing two decades mean the unrelenting conquering by the modern founder of Afghanistan, Amir Abdur Rahman Khan of the Hazaras, Kafirs, Ghilais and the Pashtuns themselves. There was no pity in the ambition of 'unification'.

The century was a period of sorting and stretching interests in by then the discoverable world and the authority and demands of the great powers. The British interest in the strategic tournament started in 1830 when Lord William Bentinck was instructed to secure trade routes through to Bukhara and by so doing establish military superiority in the region between British interests and Russia's. It was a disputed region, part of the Great Game, the disputes between Russia and Britain running from the nineteenth century until the end of the twentieth century. On his arrival in India in January 1869, the sporting viceroy Mayo was sent to investigate this Afghanistan innings in the Great Game. He had little experience as secretary for Ireland for such an embassy in an area where mistrust was a convertible currency. Mayo, without always referring back to London, succeeded where others might have and in some cases had failed. He put together simple trade agreements, established border enclaves and had otherwise suspicious princes believing that all Britain wanted was a safe and frictionless *cordon sanitaire* of sympathetic self-governed states. What Mayo understood immediately was distance.

India was long-distance travelling and in uncomfortable conditions. He saw that as long as it was properly maintained and studies were made for its use in difficult circumstances, India had one of the world's greatest military transporters, the railroad.

For India the arrival of the train in 1851 as a temporary run from Roorkee and Piran Kaliyar immediately demonstrated the value of a transport system that could revolutionise the way in which India applied itself to the movement of almost every-thing from pilgrims to beasts, from cotton to soldiery. The Indian Railway Association became the Great Indian Peninsula Railway and the first 'proper' train trip was a three-locomotive and fourteen-carriage rig along the twenty-minute journey between Bombay and Thane on 16 April 1853. The Indian train rides were born.

A British engineer named Robert Brereton linked railways, main and branch lines from Bombay to Calcutta to Madras, an engineering triumph so unexpected that it apparently inspired Jules Verne to include its imagery in his *Around the World in Eighty Days*. By the end of the nineteenth century Indian engineers had been so well taught and trained that they were being sent to built other railroads, first, that of Uganda. The viceroy, Lord Mayo, thought

'the whole country should be covered with a network of lines in a uniform system.'

Of course it would be.

The trains changed the way in which troops were trans-ported. All strategic points had military assembly yards and branches to logistical points and troop martialling areas. The initial building expertise came from the East India Company engineers and was then handed over to the British Indian Army. Yet this too was a burden because, like all major construction projects, the railroad needed to be subsidised. The railroad was introduced then expanded at a phenomenal rate. Labour was plentiful. Design was simple. The demand for steel was endless and the British steel makers profited. The Indian steel buyers did not. Investment, once started, became compulsive – this meant fast financial borrowing and big and unsecured loans. This financial commitment for India would exist well into the twentieth century and, with some reason, the too-fast railroad development was held up as an example of what was wrong with the way in which the British governed. The position as well as the development costs of the train system took away funds that otherwise might have been spent on industrial development and overly influenced where development and therefore employment would be sited. Further, the choice was made to build railroads using funds that could have gone to irrigation canals. Irrigation canals would have, in the second half of the nineteenth century, produced basic foods that would have fed India in normal times and would have saved India in times of famines, as the *Famine Code* of 1883 and the 1901 follow-up on paper illustrated. Mayo's philosophy was Lawrence's in another guise: anything was possible as long as it was thought through and the assets were examined, maintained and exercised. This was not a bad philosophy in the political sense. Anything anywhere was possible for everyone as long as the princes understood that the ultimate ruler was Britain.

This may have worked in the border states; in inland India, however, there were not so easily resolved difficulties that an engineer had a better chance of fixing than a diplomat. Food shortages, transport systems that did not work, lack of funds and an inability to extract common natural resources such iron and salt were reminders that, at a time less than a century before India was handed back, the British still had not built their empire. India was in its infancy as a territory that could be ruled efficiently because in a country so large with social distinctions so elaborate, the subcontinent would only reach some efficiency when government devolved power to local level.

For local government to take any charge, it must have responsibility of the management of local resources. This Mayo tried to introduce. The theory sounded better than it could ever be in practice and one reason was the slowly emerging opposition from a middle class India, an articulate questioning of the policies that may have satisfied the bigger strategic pictures, especially those pasted on the imperial maps in London. Here too was the start of a concept that later politicians would not always grasp or, if they did, would not accept as an unalterable fact. The Crown may by now govern directly and soon, Victoria would be crowned Empress, but Mayo was posing the harshest question to answer: could India ever be governed? Moreover, Mayo's India was, as he would have seen it, being infiltrated by Wahabiism and in ways that would have been suspected by strategic planners more than 100 years later, in the 1990s under the titles of al-Qaeda and Daesh, without the dramatic nature but with recognisable aspirations. Twenty-first-century Islamists declared a caliphate. Wahabis along the northern borders of India declared a crescentade.

Northern India was Wahabi country and subversion was commonplace and it attracted one ever-vulnerable part of society – the taxable. Mayo had far more than anecdotal accounts of the Mutiny. The military had been restructured and the mood among Indians largely accounted for. But if there was a true indication that disaffected taxpayers, the Indian middle class, could throw in their lot with agitating Islamists, then Mayo had few options, starting with the hardest. He reduced taxation by two-thirds in 1871. It worked, for the moment, but Mayo would not live to see the long-term outcome of his politicking. A year later while visiting a prison he was assassinated by an Afghan convict in Port Blair in the Andaman Islands. It was an attack that made no sense. Mayo, who had no eventful experience before arriving in India, became in his short time one of the most informed, the best travelled and the most logically minded viceroys. His appointment and time came at one of the most distinctive periods in British colonial history.

The British are sometimes seen as people always adding to their colonial collection and even after the empire was finally unravelled in the 1960s maintaining that image through the royal stewardship of the Commonwealth (a quarter of the world just as it was in Curzon's time) with its headquarters in the very imperial district opposite St James's Palace and overlooking the Mall along which in gold state coaches presidents ride and wave to Buckingham Palace. Little wonder that throughout the globe, so many still have an image of the British that was drawn by the end of the nineteenth century and coloured in by the end of the First World War in which mounted Indian soldiers of Britain's India clip-clopped to the war their British masters might have prevented.

Mayo had a broader view of that before him than many viceroys who struggled to keep up with India and what London knew it wanted. His thinking was radical and his perspective often too removed from what others thought. If he had not been assassinated, much more would have been done and with it, much more would have had to be explained. Mayo's assassination was not an act of terrorism, not a strike against the British nor against anything else Mayo represented. There had, though, been serious unrest and he had ordered executions by blowing the condemned to pieces by tying them across the mouths of artillery pieces. The murderer was described as a madman. It was a description heard in dictatorships. In developing countries. But then India was exactly that, a dictatorship of a developing country and society.

Mayo's death prompted discussions about what he and the British believed they were doing in India. Mayo believed that the racial superiority of the British meant that there would never be any question of even self-government, never mind independence, for the Indians.

Considering Mayo had a deep knowledge of India it can only be assumed that he did not have an equal understanding. This was a period where the future of India was entwined with India now, or precisely the period of Mayo's appointment. India could not be ruled with dated perceptions, perceptions of India and perceptions of the British – not truly landlords, more freeholders. From the 1870s onwards (roughly) thoughtful considerations of the true state of India from the Indian point of view were conclusively showing that the British were taking and not giving much because they could not. The British were draining India because no matter how hard they tried they governed badly. India with its internal jealousies, and histories contained within a land so big that it could only properly be governed as a federal state, was too complex to be governed to the satisfaction of a government in London concerned with all its other unresolved questions. Patterns in British government were changing. Social, industrial and political ideas were coming from so many sources that governments were rarely in absolute control and anticipations of the future – Irish Rule, the rest of Europe, Russia (all eagerly followed by a monarch with relations in all dangerous political honeypots) – left the British dangerously weak and failing to truly understand the changes occurring in a subcontinent they confidently ruled. One perfect example of overlooking the political and economic obvious in India was the debate on for how long India could be asset-stripped.

Naoroji's *Poverty and Un-British Rule in India* made clear that economic misfortune for Indians began with the fact that outsiders ruled the country and outsiders had a simple logic: was it worth it? Unless it was a strategic judgement that the territory was worth holding on to as a defence of wider interests, the other reason to be in India was to see how much profit could be taken out. Once in power, then the further criticism was not so much about as *how* rule was performed. Hence the Drain Theory, richness on one side. Poverty on the other. Dadabhai Naoroji's thoughts on England's *Debt to India* and British failure to honour its responsibilities to the poor who had made them rich had the single objective of explaining to the British the cause and effect of Indian poverty. There was still a strong Indian view that India would be worse off without the British. But Naoroji argued convincingly that the British were the source of Indian poverty. Curiously, British influence was strong among the nationalist leaders who might have been expected to warm to Naoroji's hypothesis but rarely did so. His six states of governing India were self-explanatory. The opening column was the fact that India was not governed by its people but by a people alien to Indian society. The British were invaders, but the principle was not a direct attack on the British but a reasoning that being governed by invaders meant that dissatisfaction by the people was inevitable. It could be that Indians governed by India could be disastrous. That was not the point. He argued that government by conqueror could not be right because invaders mostly take. India for the people had little to give.

Mayo's encouragement to steam across India was seen as the equivalent of the command 'Put out more flags', in times of hardship and protest. Indians were being taxed at all but impossible amounts – impossible to pay, that is. Income tax was more than 3 per cent. Taxes were increased after the Sepoy Rebellion to pay the cost of restoring damage from the uprising and putting down the rebellion. The *Hindu Patriot* newspaper commented in March 1858 that the people 'are overtaxed and they cannot bear a single pie in addition to it.'[9] Too many could not pay. Mayo understood that for all the advances in daily life, most of them rarely changed the life of the average Indian. Mayo was at some distance from all this. He heard more than the whistle of the trains. He heard too the blast of discontent and the reality that India was too much a land of discontent, including religious strife, for the British to govern safely.

Sir John Strachey (1823–1907), caretaker in the viceroy's residence in February 1872 after Mayo's assassination, did not share Mayo's anxieties. For Strachey the question that India might wonder if the imperial government offered anything to the Indians was hardly one to consider. Confidence was justified.

'It is an inevitable consequence of the subjection of India that a proportion of the cost of her government should be paid in England. The maintenance of our dominion is essential in the interests of India herself, and, provided that she is not compelled to pay more than is really necessary to give her a thoroughly efficient Government, and in return for services actually rendered to her, she has not reason for complaint.'[10]

Strachey was not alone in this view. Expenditure had governing columns decided entirely by the circumstances seen by the British. Mayo had no questions about the need of a large army to send as an expeditionary force to maintain discipline in the subcontinent and to be ready to defend the country from the increasing northern threat from Wahabi infiltration. But many Indians did not accept the considerable cost without question. The army, so obvious in Indian society, was increasingly seen as a drain on Indian resources that was not only judged unnecessary but objectionable too. The second and inevitable stress on justification for imperial demands by the British was the spectacle of the British themselves. As the nineteenth century drew to a close it was an increasingly politically aware and a questioning middle class that watched the drain on resources of the British. All top positions, administratively as well as commercially, were essentially occupied by colonialists, a simple fact of imperial presence in any empire in any continent. India had moved far beyond the acceptance of being ruled as a matter of fact.

There was towards the end of the century increasing understanding of the consequence of so many Europeans with short-term, certainly not lifetime, commitments to India. None of this meant that if the Indians had driven out the British or taken over the decision making in commerce and legislation at this period then Indians would have become richer and would have gathered more of the profits from new industries, for example. Certainly, there is no sustainable argument that the brilliance of Indians as innovators and commercial entrepreneurs would have created a richer and economically expanding society if the British had not been there. For a start, India had not developed a form of political government that could cope with the complex principalities in previous centuries before the British got a grip. The British brought legislation and government to India that had not existed in any national form and would not successfully do so for nearly a century to come. Without that government, there cannot be an economic reforming society. As the raj approached the closing of the nineteenth century, the case was not soundly made that India would be better off without the British. Yet Mayo's question to himself, probably repeated by Northbrook, that asked if Britain could for ever govern India was at the back of the minds of the five viceroys sent out to rule during Victoria's closing years and before the arrival of Curzon.

CHAPTER X

QUEEN EMPRESS AND NORTHBROOK

On 1 January 1876, the Prince of Wales, his feet on a red velvet footstool, invested the Maharajah of Joodphore with the Star of India at the Imperial Hotel, Janpath in Delhi. There was a good lunch to be had and more for the prince with a good appetite. 1876 was a year of much royal celebrations, for Victoria was created Empress of India and the British raj was firmly established in political as well as commercial terms. Victoria's translation to Empress was hardly a surprise, yet it was not until the nineteenth century that the British had the true parliamentary support and nearly enough resources to talk about India as being British. From now until 1947, British India would establish an image that would come to recognition as the time the British were in India far more than the previous 250 years or so. Until this moment India did not salute the British Crown. Until two decades earlier, India had been a commercial arrangement.

Once the Company was set aside and direct rule installed, India became a British possession. There would be education, communications, a world war and then another, Gandhi, Jinnah, political coming of age and, most of all, a tilt in the perception of being owned throughout the world. So, added to the imperial triumphs, 1876 was the year that the British should have recognised that Indian independence was inevitable. Instead the crossing of India by the prince was as if the conquering hero had come in Roman triumph; the future Edward VII, however, was a cautious fellow and understood more than his image allowed. For the moment, the raj celebrated imperial triumph.

There was no image from pageantry, to tiger shoots, to investitures to imperial postures that was not celebrated. The British had been in India since the opening decade of the seventeenth century. Now, the months passed with HRH's honorary private secretary William Howard Russell of *The Times* of London recording every moment. Bertie's Suetonius noted, HRH knew more chiefs

'than all the viceroys and governors together and had seen more of the country than any living man.'

Bombay, Poona, the Bhore Ghat, Baroda, Goa, Sri Lanka (then Ceylon) and onwards to Madras, Calcutta, Bankipur, Benares, Lucknow, Kanpur and Delhi to be, one day, the capital.

Here was a triumph hardly imagined when he left. This was India and Britain glowing in imperial bright confidence. Was there anything so grand as the great prince's progress seen in India and his home? It was not quite parliamentary coincidence when Disraeli presented the Royal Titles Bill on 17 February 1876. It was the Bill that asked parliament to approve a further title for the sovereignty of India for the monarch.

If the Empress matched the people's mood for jingoism it was not heard on the Liberal benches in the House. The phrase 'bastard imperialism' prompted the idea that the title suggested military dictatorship. The Prince of Wales was not entirely comfortable with the phrase 'imperial' – which had associations with past and sometimes tyrannical ruling systems – the Mughal, Roman and Chinese Emperors. In his summing-up in the second reading, Disraeli was cautious.

'Now let me say one word before I move the second reading of this Bill, upon the effect it may have upon India. It is not without consideration, it is not without the utmost care, it is not until after the deepest thought, that we have felt it our duty to introduce this Bill into Parliament. It is desired in India; it is anxiously expected. The princes and nations of India, unless we are deceived — and we have omitted no means by which we could obtain information and form opinions – look to it with the utmost interest. They know exactly what it means, though there may be some Honourable members in this House who do not. They know in India what this Bill means, and they know that what it means is what they wish. I do myself most earnestly impress upon the House to remove prejudice from their minds and to pass the second reading of this Bill without a division. Let not our divisions be misconstrued. Let the people of India feel that there is a sympathetic chord between us and them, and do not let Europe suppose for a moment that there are any in this House who are not deeply conscious of the importance of our Indian Empire. Unfortunate words have been heard in the debate upon this subject: but I will not believe that any member of this House seriously contemplates the loss of our Indian Empire. I trust, therefore, that the House will give to this Bill a second reading without a division.

By permission of the Queen, I have communicated, on the
part of my colleagues, the intention of Her Majesty, which she
will express in her Proclamation. If you sanction the passing of
this Bill, it will be an act, to my mind, that will add splendour
even to her throne, and security even to her empire.'

The tour of the raj should have told both the British and the
Indians that India, like much of the empire, was a commercial
venture to the British that offered risk and, therefore, opportunity. In times recently past, its strategic value was minimal other
than to deny it to others, particularly the Russians and perhaps
Napoleon and, unless judged from a commercial point of view
and in later times, the soldiery it could provide for British wars
elsewhere.

The imperial crown was a symbol that the British felt they
ran most of the world, and that their country was at the centre
of political, social and industrial progress. By the time of direct
rule and the imperial dignity Britain had witnessed a quarter of
a century of changes that were easily remarked as triumph.
Britain felt triumphantly innovative, even down to the street
levels. Fox Talbot's first photographs, the penny post, thermo-
dynamics, the first telegraph line in England, Dickens,
Charlotte Brontë, William Thackeray, Macaulay's history
recording England's greatness at any point during the previous
1,000 years, the conquest of Punjab, sailings to dig for gold in
Australia, the taking of New Zealand and Hong Kong, public
libraries opened, the working men's colleges open, *Barchester
Towers*, the Great Exhibition demonstrating that Britain was at
the very least 'Great', *On Liberty, On The Origin of Species*
and *Adam Bede* all in one year (1859); even a sense of 'we
told you so' with the tragedy that was the American Civil
War. Hardly wonder that the British took and ruled by right.

No wonder that the music halls rang with the anthem against foes in the 1877–1878 Russo-Turkish war.

> We don't want to fight but by Jingo if we do
> We've got the ships, we've got the men, we've got the money too
> We've fought the Bear before and while we're Britons true
> The Russians shall not have Constantinople[1]

Sir John Strachey and then Lord Napier stood in as viceroy until the arrival of Lord Northbrook in May 1872; now, India and her monarch could settle into the reign of the British Mughal. For Britain these were uneasy decades. The ship of British state in India was steadied with the arrival of Northbrook. Thomas George Baring (1826–1904) appeared stern. He was a practical man and a 'doer'. The whole Baring family, full of carefully won City banking money, and his mother's family (she was a niece of the 1832 Great Reform Bill reformer, Earl Grey), were people who did things on the back of considerable school and critical success.

Northbrook had one essential pedigree signature uncommon to many in India and among the viceroys: his family had at one time run the East India Company. One Baring had in the eighteenth century sat as chairman of the Company and had either bought, influenced or both many who sat in domestic politics at the highest level and those who went out to govern wherever the British flag fluttered. Baring's circle was tight and many were related. After Christ Church Oxford (another classicist, another second) the young Baring was sent off to learn his politics in the office of an uncle, the chief secretary for Ireland, Henry Labouchere. Then he went to the Home Office to work for another uncle, George Grey, and for a cousin, Sir Charles Wood, at the India Board. For the last two he eventually became a junior minister. His wife, Elizabeth (née Surt) was the sister of two friends at Christ Church. As for India, he was so keen to go. He was certainly qualified.

Baring was an aristocrat who had done well in the India Office, who understood what government wanted from India and most of the limitations of reform that needed to be better accomplished. Baring particularly understood the need to support Edward Cardwell at the War Office, in which he was a junior minister when the moment came with Gladstone's (his political patron) support for the long-overdue root and branch reform of the army. He realised that it was important to have the army under central control to stop the nonsense of officers purchasing their commissions; discard socially out-of-date practices such as flogging (army officers were against this reform); establish a reserve army to support in a crisis the largely experienced but necessarily reduced manpower during the decades since the Mutiny. This importance of a reserve army was a lesson from the Franco-Prussian War.

Cardwell introduced the army regimental districts, giving structural identity and regimental reform. There was much more to come over the decade because army reform cannot be fixed in one passage of a parliamentary bill and through both Houses. There was not time and understanding to link the detail of the reform to what was necessarily a piece of finance legislation as well as military sense, particularly as many in Whitehall were predicting a future Great War.

For Northbrook (as he had become on his father's death in 1866) reform was more than a late restructuring of an army too far spread across the world, commanded on too many lost principles and trained inefficiently, and therefore limited as a military vehicle to guarantee British foreign policy. India would be important in all these considerations by the Whig political view of the world and Britain's place in it and to send Northbrook to India was a safe choice, especially as Wood, now Lord Halifax, was supporting his cause.

After his wife's death and that of his sailor son, lost at sea, Northbrook took comfort in his lifelong belief in Christian religious contemplation. Northbrook was a devout man and a countryman who could easily have spent his days with his estate. Men of that understanding may be found in moments of ambition or duty in lieu of the more obvious drive in their positions. Northbrook could easily in such a position have decided on a form of semi-retirement in England. He was only too aware of the task in India and was no in awe of the posting. He said no to India but then changed his mind and went.

Northbrook arrived fifteen years after the Mutiny as a reformer in an India that could not, in such a short space of time, have carried out reforms recognised after 1857. Northbrook's thought was simpler than most: reform the idea, not simply the subject. So, he set about reducing taxation. Revenue was a necessity, but how and when and even by whom tax should be paid and gathered was a matter for reform. Often a major project may be considered vital until, equally import-antly, someone asks how it is to be paid for. Unless there is reason for commercial investment (profit) the answer is invari-ably that the people pay, therefore the idea to be studied is not the building but the people and how they react. So he would always be reluctant to raise taxes to pay for something from which few would benefit.

This assessment of the delicate nature of British rule was determined by two long-running factors, both sometimes overlooked during the coming decades: history and under-standing. It was Northbrook who alerted Gladstone and his governors in India to how little the British knew the people they were ruling.

The British gave the impression of caring while ruling with all the sensitivities of a Caesar. They naturally assumed that the people they ruled were effectively conquered. They were brown, they were poor, they had, in spite of councils and legislatures, little hope or consistent demand of and for independence, in even the basic form. The Indians were still the poor being ruled by the wealthy and the British assumed it a natural right so to do.

Northbrook's published view was that the British officer and secretariat showed little sign of understanding the people they ruled and should therefore use their energies to change that. The British at the top should start by getting to know the British at the bottom who had more to do with Indians than any with plumes. This view came from a Whig who had arrived with a notion of reform, if not entirely an idea of what should be reformed and how to bring the British in India themselves all on board.

The second consideration is the historical perspective when Northbrook arrived The British position in India was influenced by the memory of the Sepoy Rebellion, the Mutiny. It was but fifteen years before he arrived or, in another way, it was long ago enough for all to be settled, especially as the princes were on the British side. The first thing Northbrook understood was something that was not understood at home: in a letter home to Lord Bessborough in 1875, Northbrook had to warn that army reform suggested to native troops that they could not be trusted.[2] There was too an obvious conclusion that Northbrook (and some others) voiced about the changes in education for Indians and for the influences of further education in England. Education would open eyes to what was inherently wrong and, probably, unfair about British rule.

Education would provide precedence and possibilities for those inclined to think the time for Indian nationalism had come. It was true also that while education for Indians provided more work and even position, there were limits to what responsibilities Indians might find themselves with. Certainly Northbrook understood there was nothing like a good English or English-based education to give a man confidence to say publicly that change was not simply about the right to own one's land.

Given the popular image of plume and elephant, durbar and poverty, it is simple to see India, even by the last quarter of the nineteenth century, as an over-repeated setting for a novel of the ruler and the ruled, aristocracy and destitute, white leaders carting spoils and reputations back to sweet English gardens, brown servants learning to bow deeper and neither having the true recognition of playing the wizard's cricket on equal terms. From the opening years of the seventeenth century the British had kept as much control as they could of the people in India, ruling on behalf of the East India Company first, and then of the emerging government formed at Westminster.

When Clive thought in the eighteenth century that the princes would want the British to have India, it is not clear whether Britain had the political structure to do anything more than it was doing at the time. Not until the nineteenth century would government in London be structured in the form it needed to be to pay full attention to its ownership of India. With direct rule and the fine tuning of the running system with a restructured army and, most of all, the arrangement of council and more important department of state, the India Office, do we see the punishing peaceful role of the

viceroy and the power play of the London end of governing the
Queen's empire.

Britain too was a country in change and not just industrially.
Innovation, invention and discovery brought triumphs but
puzzles too. India was part of this process. When a change in
the way departments were run and the planning that came
with the resources and innovations within them, India too was
brought into the thinking. Daily life could be influenced by
the personality of the India Office minister in London. When
the Tory Lord Salisbury arrived at the India Office he made it
clear that India was not exempt from his loathing of bureaucracies and therefore his open suspicions of bureaucrats. He did
not like the constant battle between the department in London
and the viceroy's councillors in India.

Under Lawrence, the councillors had acted independently
in some legislation. Northbrook would not have that. Taking
the difference a stage further, Salisbury insisted that when the
council in India proposed either new legislation or an amendment to existing law then they should send that proposal back
to London for the India Office to approve before distribution
to British and Indian members in India. Why would Northbrook
challenge Salisbury? Did he consider his authority questioned?
Northbrook should never have challenged the authority of the
secretary of state, especially Salisbury. But there were often
enough disagreements to make Northbrook vulnerable. The
issues of India were huge, involving commerce (the Lancashire
cotton industry) as well as security (the continued threat
through Afghanistan and domestically) and reflections on the
very society the British had taken. Now, however, the British
could not get quite used to the idea that the aftermath of the
Mutiny did not mean a totally peaceful arrangement between
the indigenous population and the colonist.[3].

But the viceroy sat his seat well and Northbrook believed it important neither to usurp the authority nor to ignore the much more experienced people advising him in India. Yet Salisbury was not a diplomat. His interest was not interference. Northbrook was not an imaginative man. He thought Salisbury's dispatches to him disagreeably stylish. Some on his council supported his mild indignation and so stirred his mood against Salisbury and perhaps hastened his going earlier than expected. When he went, there were family reasons for doing so. Salisbury quite liked him but would not miss him as a thoroughly good administrator with an instinct for duty and what might be best for the people ruled by Britain. But Northbrook was not the dullard some had thought. He served with distinction in his role that Gladstone bestowed upon him – first lord of the admiralty. He was a good voice from India to have in the Cabinet. It was the rarely remembered Northbrook who quietly but consistently warned of the danger of forgetting the lessons of the Mutiny and the sitting threat of not having a good policy in Afghanistan.

When troops were in Afghanistan he supported Gladstone, who thought they should be withdrawn on the grounds that the British had no right to annex Afghanistan. He gave Gladstone good service and himself some very sound advice, when in 1886 Gladstone offered to send him to Ireland as viceroy. Northbrook was in no mood to believe Irish home rule would have a chance at Westminster under Gladstone, whom Northbrook was to think of as the ablest but the most conscientiously unscrupulous leader in the history of British politics.[4] Edward Bulwer-Lytton, who succeeded Northbrook, never thought that deeply about prime ministers, perhaps because he saw himself as a poet rather than a colonial servant, or any other servant for that matter. It was not the most inspired choice but choosing a viceroy was not a game. Lytton was not very good at being a viceroy.

The Lytttons went to India in 1876, the year of the Royal Titles Bill in which Queen Victoria was to be named Empress – a recognition for which Victoria had worked. She was proclaimed so on 1 January 1877 at the Delhi Durbar chaired by Lord Lytton, the newish viceroy. It was one of the British occasions that could be part of the invention of traditions that the British Empire and particularly the period of the raj inspired. The Lyttons – Edward (1831–1891) and his wife, Edith (née Villiers, 1841–1936) – were aristocrats. He of course won the India Prize, an earldom at the end of his time in India, and she was the daughter of Edward Ernest Villiers and niece of George Villiers, the fourth Earl of Clarendon. Their son-in-law was Edwin Lutyens, the architect of the British capital at Delhi. Lytton imagined himself a good poet and a friend of Charles Dickens. He was certainly the latter but not the former. His cultural background was comfortable. In 1849 he had arrived in Washington to become unpaid attaché to his uncle Sir Henry Bulwer. Three years on he went to Florence as attaché, then in 1856 to The Hague and then to St Petersburg, Constantinople (modern Istanbul). Belgrade, Vienna, Lisbon as British plenipotentiary. Yet Lytton was one of Disraeli's poorer judgements when he was sent to succeed Northbridge. Disraeli might have wondered about judgement. Lytton had been offered governorship of Madras but turned it down. A year later, Lytton said 'Yes' to India as viceroy. Irresistible? Why? Disraeli seems not to have asked. In London, many wondered why. This was after all Britain's most imperially spectacular possession at a moment in European history when imperialism was regarded as precious. India was the most prestigious if not important appointment in the world, a quarter of which the British ruled.

Lytton may have been unsuccessful in India, although a yardstick for marks out of ten was difficult to judge. However, his devoted wife, Edith, was memorable. She was stylish, not easy in unattractive temperatures and conditions. The vice-reine had always been judged on style and setting protocols of entertainment even if they did have to walk a pace, even a few places, behind their husbands. With Edith Lytton it was as if the residence had been found in Paris. The daughters and Edith had lived well in court in Europe. They danced, dressed and dined exceedingly well. India was very dull. Edith's upbringing was far from that. Her family was poor even before her mother was widowed with four children. Her uncle was the celebrated foreign secretary Lord Clarendon and he helped, but it still meant that Edith's childhood was learning languages and piano and hoping for a good marriage. She was rapidly left on the shelf and then met the bearded and vain Robert Lytton and discovered, to her delight, that he was the poet Owen Meredith, whose poetry she adored. (She could recite *Lucile*). Lytton's father was not displeased with the engagement but would have hoped for a fiancée with money. These were the times. Robert Lytton however was not in search of money; there was enough. He desperately needed a mother figure (his own, Rosina Wheeler, having wandered off). His father had friends slot him into their embassies so that he could profess diplomacy. It was a good way to fall in love but mostly with wasted affairs. They married and he still fell in love.

When Mayo was murdered, Disraeli had difficulty in find-ing anyone from the usual list to go to India. Certainly, Derby, Carnarvon, Powis and Manners refused the posting – graciously of course. So Disraeli turned to Lytton, who was by then a diplomat in Lisbon but since his father's death was hoping to take up the family estate at Knebworth and write more poetry. He accepted with no great feeling for the instructions to build relations with leading Indians and to recognise the anxieties mentioned by Northbrook. Lytton decided to go to India and spend more time in plumes and uniforms and perhaps one or two light affairs – flirtations, they were said to be – than getting to know the people and hopes for their and India's future. Lytton went to India to enjoy himself. A brief note of the gathering of staff and all that went too is a reminder that not all viceroys and vicereines would advance at a stately pace to obey their monarch's command and go out and rule India.

Edith, not anticipating her social success, did not fancy the future. Apart from shopping in Paris and collecting staff – governess, grooms, nanny, nursery-maid, chef and secretary for starters – Edith, pregnant and with three small children already, had to close the London house. Meanwhile, Lytton called on those demanding that he did so before embarking for India via Italy, a rough Mediterranean, Alexandria, the Suez Canal (opened in 1869) and Bombay at its April hottest. It was the heat season and Edith, distraught at abandoning her husband, who was off to Calcutta to be sworn in as viceroy (and make the first of his protocol blunders by making a speech after the ceremony, which no viceroy ever did) headed for the summer capital of British India, Shimla.

Shimla was Victorian in the Himalayas. Very British, complete with London shopping and Christ Church Cathedral and a roller skating rink. Shimla was the British upper class at play while the rest sweltered below. They played with each other and often seriously so. The viceroy and vicereine lived in the official lodge, Peterhof. The lodge was immediately modernised and it became a refuge for staff as well as the Lyttons with games for everyone. But this was not the viceregal style she had imagined. Shimla was unbelievably provincial with the same people doing the same things, making the same conversations at the same level of social standing, holding the same drinks parties and dancing to the same music while making the same small talk. But then that was colonial life in British India. The greater events that were remarkable and sometimes terrifying gave way to provincial existences; they lived in a style beyond their origins and did it rather poorly and, at worst, sadly.

Into this atmosphere tempered by the greater control London had in many matters Edith Lytton relaxed.

'At Shimla I received every day for an hour which enabled me to get personally known to all the people . . . and to appreciate all their kindness to each other under difficulties.'

Edith Lytton could relax a little from the fear of her husband's affairs that in Europe she had hopelessly called his flirtations, while everyone knew what they were. Lytton had replaced Mayo, who was assassinated. Lytton therefore never stepped outside his room, or even looked out of the window without seeing armed guards.

'I sit in the corner of my private room and if I look through the window there are two sentinels standing guard. If I go up and down stairs, an ADC and three unpronounceable beings in white and red nightgowns with dark faces run after me. If I steal out of the house by the back door, I look round and find myself stealthily followed by a trail of fifteen persons.'

Lytton's memorable event in an otherwise uneventful intro-duction to India was the Great Assemblage. It was the

gathering to proclaim Victoria as Empress on 1 January 1877.
It was also a sign of the determination of Lytton, with London's
approval to remember the Mughal way of displaying power.
Putting on a display was not imperial protocol, it was imperial
pantomime. More than 400 Indian princes arrived for the
Assemblage. Each of the princes brought hundreds of troops
dressed in all the magnificence that could reflect the position,
authority and thus stature of the individual prince. Each
showed off to the others. Each judged the worth and splendour
of the others. Lytton's point was not so much the gathering
itself but the fact that this was the raj who ruled as powerfully
as ever; this was the Queen Empress in whose name they
were commanded to appear. However grand each prince,
he had come to pay respects to the raj. On his arrival in
Delhi, before the durbar, Lytton, courteously as ever, made his
point.

> 'Princes, chiefs and nobles. It is with feelings of unusual pleas-
> ure I find you here assembled from all parts of India to take
> part in a ceremonial which I trust will be the means of drawing
> still closer the bonds of union between the Government of Her
> Majesty and the great allies and feudatories of the Empire. I
> thank you for the cordiality with which you have responded to
> my invitation and trust the close of our proceedings will
> confirm the auspicious character of their commencement.
> Accept my heart welcome to Delhi!'

Everyone was given a commemorative medal sent by the
Queen and draped about each neck by her viceroy: gold for
senior princes, silver for the lesser. The *Illustrated London
News* in its 6 January 1877 edition reported:

'The governors, the lieutenant governors, state officials and sixty three ruling chiefs attended by the suits and standard-bearers, with magnificent memorial banners were grouped in a semicircle in front of the throne. Behind them the vast amphitheatre was filled with foreign embassies and native nobility and gentry and further in the rear was the vast concourse of spectators . . . the whole scene presented a spectacle of unprecedented brilliance. To the south of the dais fifteen thousand troops were drawn up under arms, including contingents from the Madras and Bombay armies and the Punjab frontier force. To the north were ranged the minor chiefs with their troops and retinues . . . His Excellency's arrival was heralded by flourishes of trumpets and a fanfare from the massed bands of the various regiments present.'

There was a very Indian bit of fun to come. The military bands played a march, and Lord Lytton, accompanied by Lady Lytton, their daughters and his staff, proceeded to the pavilion. As Lytton sat on his throne in his robes as Grand Master of the Star of India, the National Anthem was played, the guards of honour presented arms while everyone rose as one man. The chief herald was then commanded to read the proclamation. A flourish of trumpets was again sounded, and Victoria was proclaimed Empress of India, the royal standard was hoisted and a 101-gun salute sounded. The elephants did not like this at all. Off they went.

'The viceroy referred to the promises contained in the Queen's Proclamation of November 1858 and fully confirmed them. The princes and the people had found full security under Her Majesty's rule . . .'

At this stage Lytton answered the question they had asked from the very start of the celebrations. Why was it necessary for Queen Victoria to be called Empress?

'. . . It was intended to be, to the princes and people of India, a symbol of the union of their interests and claim upon their loyal allegiance, with the imperial power giving them a guarantee of impartial protection . . . Referring to the possibility of an invasion, the viceroy said that no enemy could attack the Empire in India without assailing the whole Empire and pointed out that the fidelity of Her Majesty's allies provided ample power to repel and punish assailants . . .'

Durbars were illusions and contradictions. Did Victoria's allies provide ample power to repel and punish assailants? Who were these allies Lytton beautifully invoked? Ample power? Were lessons from 1857 learned? Who had taught them? One example from a durbar was again the divide between those who had much and those who nothing. As the feasts went on, day and night, two guests were particularly honoured: the governors of Bombay, Sir Philip Wodehouse and Madras, the Duke of Buckingham. Rarely had such feats in their honour been seen and eaten. Yet both Madras and Bombay were suffering the worst famines in living memory. For three days Lytton sat on his throne receiving the princes and their salutes. Salutes of another kind were troubling the princes. Gun salutes recognised the standing of a prince. An anxious man would lobby for greater position than just an extra round fired from field artillery could give him. At the durbar, the Imperial Assemblage, some of the princes had their gun salutes raised and four of them were thrilled to be raised to the salute for the viceroy – 21. When it was recognised by the counting of bangs that the viceroy's had been raised to 31, there were fewer smiles.

The durbar over, the Lyttons began to suffer the criticisms inevitably aimed at such an unviceroy type as Robert Lytton. He did not get up early enough to escape the heat and get on with work. He stayed late (therefore so did some of his staff), he was perhaps an incorrigible flirt who went beyond the duty of good manners and charming attention to the sometimes bored wives who felt neglected. Edith Lytton thought her husband's flirting was beyond that excused in a poet. British India talked of him in comparison with the strict decorum of Northbrook and Minto. Lytton was not what they expected in their viceroy. Much of the criticism was idle work and something Lytton had uncovered by his own behaviour and certainly not setting out so to do. The British in India had to some extent lost their way. Dr Marian Fowler in her study *Below the Peacock Fan* concluded:

'The British in India felt so truly affronted by a frivolous, flirting viceroy because of their own guilt. They knew, deep down, that while they still paid lip service to the old raj ideals of solemn and Christian duty, which gave them a rationale for being in India, they had become far too silly and sinful themselves. As they felt their own ideals eroding, they looked towards the man who could best shore them up and set a fine example: the viceroy. When he failed to do so, they became slightly hysterical.'[5]

The reasons for the Mutiny in 1857 had not gone away or were re-emerging in a new generation of British. Arrogance. No true understanding of the people they ruled. No sense of care. A game of British India with excesses as rules. Deep down, none of the people sent from London really wanted to be there.

Writing in 1877, Lytton imagined that the British, although in command and obeyed, were not rightful monarchs over all they surveyed. It was an instinct that suggested time was running out.

'I am convinced that the fundamental mistake of able and experienced Indian officials is a belief that we can hold India securely by what they call good government; that is to say, by improving the condition of the peasant, strictly administering justice, spending immense sums on irrigation works etc. Politically speaking, the Indian peasantry is an inert mass. If it ever moves at all, it will move in obedience to its native chiefs and princes, no matter how tyrannical they may be.'[6]

India ruled by a new British middle class who saw the whole of India as untouchables. It was not true of course, but Lytton's example offered no sterling leadership and decorum that made them safe in the other British game follow my leader. The elephants had got it right. Time to go – but no one knew what that meant. It was empire and there was never a time to go. If the viceroy saw little harm in the manner of his rule, his wife understood what could be happening. Lytton had lost the respect and command of his own British India. Edith Lytton became the stickler for decorum that the British needed from their viceroy. It worked. She effectively became the clichéd power behind the viceroy's throne and assumed the formal role and pose that others could follow and had hoped her husband would have set. Much of this meant nothing at street level where cholera and famine swept British India. Southern India was diseased and starving and the disillusionment among many of the British (during refreshment perhaps) was that they wished India had never been British. If the doubts were anything more than colonial misgivings about the Queen's appointment; what then?

Lytton's declaration at the Assemblage had rung certain enough. By stating that the Queen's allies would protect India, it could be understood that another mutiny would bring the Queen's allies to India to protect India from her enemies within. Were there to be a better organised Sepoy Rebellion would the army stand the test of the responsibility in reorganisation? Salisbury and Northbrook had believed Islam would come to be the internal protagonist and that Islam was more than religion; it was a socio-economic way of life. The evidence of threat was not clear and therefore more likely to induce insecurity in a society that, in spite of ill-thought-through education reform sponsored by the late Mayo that had produced an imbalance of poor basic education and unremarkable higher education, had created a growing half-educated and often out of work distinguished work group; this would be seen as a source of subversive agitation in any society.[7] During the few decades following mutiny, viceroys continuously asked what credibility was given to independently-minded Indian political thinkers not yet finding a place as politicians: what if the British had never come to India? What would Franco-Dutch-Portuguese imperialism have been like for the Indians – would others have colonised or would India have stood its ground as a huge independent state? The standard answer was that India would have been colonised because the thousands of chiefs and princes made independence impossible until the emergence of political parties.

The British had a further interest in India. What made Britain's position in India so special? The answer is somewhere in the late-nineteenth-century insecurities of the British as an offshore European power. The British had extensive military costs in maintaining its imperial rights at a time when it perceived growing threats from Europe, including Russian ambitions in Asia. This extended threat could threaten India – or so the British imagined. Thus the Indian army was not a militia but fitted to be Britain's international police force. Between 1878 and 1896 and then again during the Great War (1914–1918), the British deployed the Indian army to the afghan war, Egypt and Sudan. The British used one of their colonies to maintain imperial power wherever they weakened in the Middle East and Asia.

Durbars with elephants that ran off, princes who craved more gun salutes and a strongly bearded viceroy lolling on a throne for ten hours receiving princes with promises – few of which were truthful – did not cover the weakness of the British rule. Lytton could call out a battalion at will, a British commander-in-chief could take the march past salute, but the British were as vulnerable as they had been in 1857. Those who questioned protocol and the game plan delivered by Lytton and those about him understood the weakness. If proof were needed, the tragedy of Kabul was at hand.

In 1878, Lytton had stood his ground with the Afghans when his delegation had been refused entry into Afghanistan. The result was the second Afghan war. Lytton had lost his way from the guiding instruction given him by Disraeli. Disraeli saw the ever-present dangers in Afghanistan and wanted Lytton to be firm but bring about a peace accord of some form. The entry refusal at the border was an affront to British authority. A declaration of war on their own territory seemed inevitable to Lytton and he had been warned as much when the delegation travelled. The British army dealt swiftly with the Afghans, whose escaping leader Sher Ali the Amir died at the beginning of 1879. Lytton was advised that the new Amir, Sher Ali's son Yakub Khan, would talk peace and he put an experienced campaigner and deputy commissioner of Punjab, Sir Louis Cavagnari, in command of the negotiations. Cavagnari, a Frenchman by birth from a distinguished Parma family, was grand and trusted. He had been naturalised as a British subject and joined the East India Company and fought in the Mutiny. He was in the negotiation team turned back at the border. Now in May 1879 in Kabul, Cavagnari negotiated successfully a peace treaty with the Amir that allowed the British to have a permanent envoy and residence in Kabul. He was knighted and praised continuously. If the truce held, then with the new blood in Kabul the long animosity between Afghanistan and the British could be over. Lytton appointed Cavagnari as emissary. He left Shimla for Kabul on 6 July 1879. On 3 September 1879 he and all those at the embassy residence were massacred.

Lytton, his wife Edith and so many in the Shimla summer sanctuary were astounded. They could not believe what had happened. Even those who had seen so much in India had learned little of its recent history. It was as if they danced in ignorance of what the next hour might bring.

Lytton sent his army under General Frederick Roberts (later Field-Marshal Earl Roberts of Kandahar) to Afghanistan to seek reprisals, but not too dramatically. Bobs, as General Roberts became known, saw no campaign winnable without drama; this would not be a reprisal, but revenge. Roberts's army burned wherever they could and hanged whenever they thought fit. Yakub Khan escaped as princes often do. Lytton too. The 1880 general election gave the newly elected Liberal prime minister Gladstone the opportunity to get rid of Lytton,

whom he disliked, whom he thought treacherous and even a
fraudster. Gladstone was wrong on the last point. The mismanagement of war funds for Afghanistan had been Strachey's
mismanagement rather than fraud. But Gladstone refused to
back down after he blamed Lytton for what had happened in
Afghanistan. Lytton knew he had to go, so resigned. Gladstone
told him to get out of India there and then and his successor,
Lord Ripon, to go with all speed, which because of the heat
he did not want to. Gladstone ordered him on to the next
boat. Queen Victoria,who did not care at all for Gladstone,
told the Lyttons not to rush their departure. Ripon arrived, the
Lyttons had nowhere to stay and the departing viceroy had to
borrow a house from his general. Then, the carriage arrived
and the month-long journey to Knebworth was on to the
English countryside where, as Edith Lytton said,there were
'no flies, no glare, no biting things.'

Their friend the poet Wilfrid Blunt met the Lyttons. Blunt's
diaries show the two men reflecting on the future of India.

'We are both agreed that the day of England's empire is fast
ending, for my part I do not care how soon. Lytton has more
patriotism.'[8]

But then Lytton had never read Drain Theory and its consequences. Blunt had.

Lord Ripon, the man who followed Lytton, was only one of
two viceroys who truly tried to change the way India was ruled
for the benefit of India. Lord Curzon was the other. By their
times, both were among the most powerful rulers in the world.
Denis Judd, in his *The Lion and the Tiger*, sees the British viceroy of India in his own way by the end of the nineteenth century
as powerful a figure as the Emperor of China.[9]

Ripon was George Frederick Samuel Robinson (1827–1909), a large, straight-nosed, shaggy-bearded Liberal. He was a son of the rarely remembered Viscount Goderich, who introduced the Corn Laws in 1815 and was prime minister for barely any time at all – between August 1827 and January 1828. His son, the future viceroy, was an only child who stayed at home in the Lincolnshire countryside instead of going away to school and university and was suffocatingly adored by his mother Sarah, a pious woman and the daughter of the fourth Earl of Buckinghamshire. He was an uncompromising Christian socialist who converted to Rome after his mother's death and, in spite of a whole shelf of titles, believed that aristocracy was bad for the nation and therefore good for class warfare.

Ripon's enthusiasms for workers' cooperatives, of free education at the highest levels for all who demonstrated an application to be taught and to exploit their learning for others, knew few bounds. He believed that self-government should be the highest and noblest principle of politics. Robinson who became Goderich who became Ripon remained a radical devoted to like-minded parliamentary souls (Henry Bruce, Austen Henry Layard, Edward Horsman) scheming the downfall of Palmerston. Everything Robinson stood for was found in political radicalism even when in later life, age, titles and social position brought together his two flying characteristics – radicalism and respectability. Could a radical be respectable in British society? Fashionable, yes. Radical? To be taken seriously as a radical it was necessary to have an intellectual base and position, otherwise the title would be altered to 'working class agitator'; and therefore one was unlikely to achieve a thing. Ripon achieved much. He lost much as well. He did so through doubt.

There was a period of some fifteen years between 1865 and 1880 when so much confronted him with demands to explain himself to himself about why something had happened and why he had taken deep decisions in the way in which he had. His single trusting figure, his mother, died in 1867, leaving him in a deep mourning that lasted far longer even than people who thought they knew him well understood . His role, three years later, as Grandmaster of English Freemasons had him wondering about his own beliefs and contradictions within those beliefs. For example,his conversion to Catholicism came at what he wondered was a didactic time for himself and the Church into which he was about to go. Exactly at this period and hour of commitment the First Vatican Council (1869 to 1870) contained the dogmatic declaration of Papal Infallibility. It might be remembered that even 100 years later, the then prime minister, Tony Blair, delayed his reception into the Church of Rome because the political consequences of the prime minister effectively renouncing the persuasion and doctrine of the State Church was too controversial not to get in the way of the day-to-day instruction of government. A century earlier, the conversion of a minister of the Crown was controversial and sensitive.

Prime Minister Gladstone thought this could be the end of Ripon's political career and Ripon thought the same. The debate was about the test of his loyalties. In the end they agreed that Ripon was the last person to doubt his duty to Queen and country. Cardinal Manning suggested that it was now time for relative anonymity and Ripon slipped away from politics. This was the complex figure who was, on Gladstone's return to power, sent in June 1880 to India as viceroy. The matter of class distinction and equality would be tested for four years.

As a senior man in government with such radical views and instincts of Christian justice, he knew about India. Most British minds, associations, commercial, politicians and media were

very aware of India. India was more than a historical possession. Newspapers and journals covered India and its military,
political and social issues and had done so when, for example.
Hick's Bengal Gazette appeared in 1780. *The Times of India*,
India's oldest English-language newspaper, appeared in 1838.
Papers in India carried news from Britain as well as India and
responses and major issues were carried. Prior to the Mutiny
in 1857, the British press and its political and social readership
imagined India was a relatively trouble-free part of the imperial portfolio. In early- to mid-nineteenth century Britain,
strong party politics revolved around individual political leaders. In India, there was no major political Indian figure. If
names sold papers, there were few British names newsworthy
enough to command more than a social mention. Moreover,
the time it took news to reach London made it harder for an
editor to find a space for almost anywhere beyond Europe.
Even the shock of the Mutiny had its own pace.

The Sepoy Rebellion started on 9 May 1857. First reports
arrived in London on 20 June. Even with reports arriving, the
attitude of the British press was defensive. *The Times* spent
considerable effort attacking the French press for saying there
was a revolt against the British when, according to *The Times*,
it was clear that because the whole of India had not joined in
then it was a low-key affair. As the Mutiny proceeded, so did
the British press. It was as if they had found India. Men such as
Robinson made judgements about the treatment of Indian
society to include the changes in Britain, as if India was not to
be treated separately. Ripon was more sensitive than most in or
on the fringe of government. He had seen the India Councils
Bill through the Lords as a junior minister in 1861. The Bill
came about as part of the promises to India that there would be
changes and that those changes to the administration of India

would be to the advantage of Indians and not simply as re-modelling of the council. It was during this time that Palmerston died and Russell changed his cabinet, giving the Secretary of State for India to Ripon who, under pressure from Florence Nightingale, tried to introduce legislation that would have been expected to update sanitary and health services in India. But Russell's government fell before the legislation could be heard.

It remains a contradiction of late-nineteenth-century imagery of the raj that Ripon was there at all. He remained a total radical and a viceroy in whom Indians came to trust. Some in London and on the council did not trust him. They felt comfortable with the viceroy when kept at a distance, someone who acted like royalty and therefore was not vulnerable to factional loyalties to the system and imperial protocols. Ripon was before his time. Ripon had not forgotten the causes of the Mutiny, nor had he missed or ignored the grievances widely imagined. He saw India's future in the same way that he had understood the necessary changes in British society. The obvious difference in his judgement was the consequence.

In Britain, the day of revolution was gone and would not return until the organisation of workers in the trade union system. In India, the consequences could not be judged by British standards. Any protest could involve millions of people and could, by manipulation by the few, get out of control inasmuch as the British Indian Army would not be able to cope with the disturbance. In a note to Forster he effectively predicted the future.

'Unless we provide these men with outlets for their political aspirations they will become most naturally our bitter and very dangerous opponents. It is our duty to raise the people of this country politically and socially – making the educated natives the friends instead of the enemies of our rule.'[10]

Ripon cared for India and Indian people. Every Liberal instinct suggested to him that those people had a need to be given every advantage of being part of the British Empire. He had every influence that might have been imagined in someone who had served in Liberal government for almost all his parliamentary career. His time as first lord of the admiralty under Gladstone and then secretary of state for the colonies gave him not a unique insight but a deeper understanding than most of what might be needed to maintain and protect imperial power and responsibility. Imperial responsibility in Ripon's colonial lexicon was the acceptance that whatever the existing system and however both those governed and those governing imagined their role, there was an inevitable conclusion: one day the governed would be independent of those now ruling them.

Therefore imperial responsibility was a purpose to govern, reform and create a good lot for the people and so prepare for the day that independence would come. It was hardly a policy that fitted the arguments of the majority, who saw India as a huge commercial and professional recreation in which even the most indifferent players could make their fortunes and live in a manner to which they were hardly born.

Any interruption to this parade of expatriate position and opportunity, where the the white settler feared little from the Indian, was rarely accepted and invariably viewed with suspicion. So it was with the attempt to introduce the Ilbert Bill. Here was exactly what could have been expected from a man who effectively was saying all should be equal under the law and no one should be able to hide from justice from their social, including racial, position in society.

The Ilbert Bill, named after one of the viceroy's council, Sir C.P. Ilbert, caused a legal, political and social stir at all levels of influence in India and Britain. In present times it might have been called explosive. The Ilbert legislation had one main aim: Indian judges would be able to preside over cases and hearings involving the British. A brown judge could hear evidence for or against white colonialists. For the time, this was unthinkable.

Resistance came from all sides, including the considerable oppositions of Anglo-Indians. In a land of castes, there were those, often wealthy or at least comfortable, who would always be seen or think they were seen as inferior. At times, the Anglo-Indians had few rights that might have been expected for others in India. During the early nineteenth century thousands of Anglo-Indians were excluded from social and castes and had no legal position in courts. In some cases, they were subjects of Islamic law rather than British law. Later, they were assumed to be Christian supporters of Britain, especially when the independence debate came about. Anglo-Indians had their own society in language (English), customs and persuasions (mostly Christian) and even a professional identity as senior clerks in customs and railways.

It is difficult to identify Anglo-Indians as people without the support of the ruling classes or the majority of countrymen, but they stemmed from a pre-Mutiny time when there were few British women for East India Company officers to take up with and therefore had to tolerate sometimes prejudicial readings of their origins and standing after the Mutiny. The Anglo-Indian in society and professional position was an anomaly inasmuch as the British had not thought where such a person fitted in with what might easily have been seen as British rulers on one hand and Indian subjects on the other. In the early nineteenth century Anglo-Indians were not subjects of the British legal system. Moreover, it was not until an 1833 parliamentary act that Anglo-Indians, whatever their education and qualifications, could be considered for government employment. Certainly one consequence of the Rebellion was the drop in Anglo-Indian marriages and the very real fear of being segregated as a minority, having little sympathetic recognition from either Indians or British. While Courtney Ilbert's thoughts on an Indian judge being able to hear evidence for a white accused were clear, little explanation was given to the position of the Anglo-Indian. The Ilbert legislation, had it gone through as intended, would have been revolutionary as it was; the debate that interrupted the legislative ambition was enough to help if not determine the level of political awareness among Indians throughout the subcontinent and in 1885 indirectly help towards the establishment of the Congress Movement.

In 1885, the Indian National Congress was established and would become one of the foremost political movements, then parties, in India. This was not a rebellious movement. There were those in the British imperial government, tasked with the administration of colonial possessions, who recognised that India had to develop its own movements if the task of independence was to mature; this is a somewhat immature observation, but the school of liberal administration of India should not be overlooked. One member of that 'school' was Allan Hume (1829–1912), a political reformer and a man wedded to truthfulness and his boyhood chum John Stuart Mill.

Hume was a character from the old school of Indian service – East India Company College (Haileybury), Indian civil service and district officer, ornithology. He was a reformer who saw British ignorance and arrogance as contributors to the Sepoy Rebellion and afterwards mounted his own ideas for free education and reforms in policing. Good men, perhaps too well-meaning men, antagonise the back office seemingly without trying. After major initiatives to regulate salt sales (not nearly as mundane as the phrase suggests), Hume was taken up by the then viceroy Mayo and together they structured a new department of agriculture to guide India through the necessary imaginative work of reform. Hume wanted model farms throughout India. London was not much impressed and simply insisted on more effort to raise taxes; in many cases, the senior men in the Indian provinces agreed and turned aside Hume's ideas on conservation (for good commercial reasons) and poverty reforms. In 1879, London said no more of this. The India Office decided to run down his department and demote him to an administrative job that allowed him no authority to promote dangerous ideas.

Hume swallowed his pride and stayed on, probably for one reason. The job would fund his three volumes entitled *The Game Birds of India, Burmah and Ceylon*. When he did go, he gave his collection of 80,000 bird skins and nests to what was to become the Natural History Museum in London. There was more to Hume than birds' eggs, agricultural reform and theosophy (a common enough interest among those thoughtful or even curious when serving in India). Hume was not alone in seeing in the 1870s and 1880s that one day India must be alone with its prospects. The resources, including the vast manpower and intellect, would move India into a time when it must break from colonialism into even, perhaps, its own form of imperialism without the condition of invasion.

Hume reasoned that India and those who cared about and for it must introduce the new Indian generation of intellectuals, and those who questioned the status quo, to the foothills of the politics that would need climbing before the future could be realistically imagined. Hume changed sides. Instead of his obligation to London he found a duty to India.

The educated needed to be carried on the way to political organisation and Hume more than most became responsible for the formation of the National Congress in 1885. Hume the political activist organised reformist thinking in wide parts of India's social and commercial life. Would that this had been the quiet revolution he thought likely. The British Establishment, while caring for some of his ideas, could not condone the concept of Indian emancipation. Nor would some of the Indian leadership. There were no cries of freedom. In 1894, Hume went back to England where he died eighteen years later. The importance of this period was the storytelling that came later of the raj being sensitive enough to understand that the day would come when India would be set free. The servants of the empire, which had been so easily milked for its profits, had a unquestionable duty to ready the people, their leaders and the British in particular for independence.

Individuals had gone and still went to India to make their fortunes and better their reputations. They had no feelings for the future that just might come after their own times were up. They would take their profits and leave India to the next generation. Ripon may not have gone to India to make changes, but he would when chance and reason closed forces. With Afghanistan partly resolved (in spite of opposition from some of his people still wary of believing anything that came from Kabul and never believing anything said by a leader in

Afghanistan), Ripon saw the inevitability of independence in some form but found no clear sign when or how this could come about. He began at the beginning; by 1884, with the exception of Bengal, British India would have the provisions for self-government at a local level in each presidency. To get anywhere with a policy and procedure that would eventually have to have freedoms for voting, Ripon removed the press laws that Lytton had inspired. How could there be freedom without first having press freedom? These were day-to-day measures that were less controversial than his proposals that Indian judges should sit in cases where the accused was European. But his own judgement in allowing the freedom of speech to consider both arguments calmed as well as excited debate; this was a very European view that worked in India as well as it did in Britain. Ripon went home in 1884 to his own Liberal Party devouring itself over Irish Reform and he quickly saw what he dreaded most: India becoming a similar political and militant mess, which was Lord Dufferin's view when he arrived to be viceroy shortly before Christmas 1884. Dufferin would also see through the formation of India's first lasting political party, Indian National Congress. It would take more than a half a century passing through two world wars, but the caravan of independence was rolling.

Frederick Temple Hamilton-Temple-Blackwood, who was Lord Dufferin (1826–1902), could be seen as the typical Victorian public servant. He was spoken of as a fine, successful British diplomat – the two going together. His first posting was to Syria as commissioner (1860). He was in government as under-secretary for war and in 1872 he was sent to Canada as governor general and then to India as the eighth viceroy and was enormously thankful that he had been chosen. He had no passion for the land and the people. He did have enormous

longing for the winnings, as his Irish cousins would have it.
Dufferin needed the wealth ruling India would bring and his
motives were purely eighteenth-century. He would have kept
good company with the financial privileges of Hastings.
Dufferin had rid himself of a reasonable fortune and was now
quite broke. The viceroy was going just as ne'er-do-wells and
those in dire straits had before gone. India in the late 1880s was
still a place to draw one's financial breath. But the one-eyed
man – and so he was after a childhood accident – was no wast-
rel. He gave as well as helped himself.

Dufferin was the son of Royal Navy Captain Price
Blackwood, later Lord Dufferin and Clandeboye; and the
Countess of Gifford Helen Selina. His mother gave birth when
she was eighteen and they grew up together. He was a slightly
built figure with a usually quiet lisping voice and preferred to
deal with the person rather than the paperwork all others
seemed to collect or worse, create. In everything else Dufferin
was standard aristocracy: Eton and Christ Church Oxford and
president of the Oxford Union Society. He was very Irish,
whatever that might have meant in the middle of the nineteenth century. As a lord-in-waiting to the Queen, Dufferin
was in Lord John Russell's debt as indeed he was so much
during his early life, including for getting him an English peerage, Lord Clandeboye, that gave him his seat in the Lords.
Victoria thought him agreeable but too handsome and sometimes (often?) forgetful of his courtly manners. For a one-eyed
Irish peer rubbing by on a few thousand and falling in love
often, he did well in political circles and was admired as something of a polymath.

The log he kept in the yacht *Foam* during a long and round-
about voyage to Iceland was acclaimed and supposedly admired
by D.H. Lawrence. The apparently ever-broke Dufferin was

always nearly financially finished. His friends, though, could be relied upon to come up with something. Prime Minister Russell had him appointed lord-in-waiting to Victoria. Apart from any recognition, the appointment suited his pretentions. When he married his distant cousin Hariot Rowan-Hamilton he found his perfect companion. They had lots of children, he travelled as ambassador to conferences and was ever at state occasions. He had hoped for India but Gladstone saw no backbone in Dufferin. His friend the Duke of Argyll, the then secretary of state for India, gave Dufferin the consolation of going to Canada as governor general. He was debt-ridden and so Argyll's influence was a financial blessing. In 1884 the Dufferins got the prize they'd long hoped for, India.

Dufferin could speak any language that mattered. He understood (and enjoyed) Egyptian hieroglyphics and was a great believer in frivolity (or so he told Lady Agatha Russell). He was unlikely to meet casually anyone who had read as deeply or knew more of painting and music, and danced lightly. That he was vain and lazy gave his critics something to work on. He was, in short, very good company with the charm of someone who had put to rights most of the world he had touched from Russia, to North America, to the Sahara, to Paris and Turkey. He distant cousin, his wife, lacked his laziness and vanity. She went with him to India and established the National Association for Supplying Medical Aid to the Women of India – the Countess of Dufferin Fund. Across India there are nursing schools, colleges, streets and funds still in her name. When the Dufferins went to India they needed the funds but they gave in return.

The pomp without any circumstance would have appeared to suit Dufferin down to the imperial ground. However, he set about the appointment with considerable caution. He also noted the reality of the late-nineteenth-century position as viceroy. Mostly it was boring and the politics were potentially treacherous and from his point of view, largely irresolvable.

'. . . dullness is certainly the characteristic of a viceroy's existence. All the people who surround him are younger than himself; he has no companions or playfellows; even the pretty women who might condescend to cheer him, it is better for him to keep at a distance; and, except occasionally, the business he has to deal with is of a very uninteresting and terre a terre description, for, though he would make a great mistake if he drowned himself in too much detail, it is well that he should know everything that goes on . . .'[11]

Here was a reasonable reminder that the viceroy was not sent to create new issues in the governance of the subcontinent but to progress the work already in hand. Thus when Dufferin arrived he was faced with a country in many parts divided over Ripon's ambitions for their self-governance. The bureaucracy that had split largely between Anglo-Indians and Indians over Ripon's plans for change would split on any issue; nations divided by race will rarely come together. In India, the ethnic national groups would stand together whatever the advantages; the religious groups were united by their persuasions but split by the differing expressions of liturgy if not belief; all would be against the occupiers of their land but would not necessarily oppose the same irritant.

The more liberal of the Europeans knew what skin differences meant while others did not lose sleep over the simple fact of white people having, by creation and European descent, unquestionable authority over the indigenous population. It was not a sophisticated argument, but it was taken seriously for

another century generally and longer in some less liberal
minds. In the 1880s, Dufferin had to protect the ideas encased
in the Tenancy Acts and similar legislation.[12] His Irish history
lessons and his own history as an Irishman gave him the option
to protect the landowner or protect the tenant – the argument
was not much more sophisticated than that, given the status of
landowner and tenant in India, not so different as they had
been in his native land:

'We are irritating the natives out here in exactly the same
manner as for hundreds of years we have been irritating the
Irish'[13]

Dufferin's sensitive Irish view was that the English instinct
was to flex muscles as well as diplomacy when dealing with
what they saw as inferior people. In November 1888, when
Dufferin was about to go, he produced a minute on the British
policy to move, to some further rule of the country in council
by, inevitably, middle-class Indians with an infusion of
European education, European political ideas and European
literature. He simply could not see how it would ever work.

'They neither represent the aristocratic sections of Indian society nor are they in special contact or sympathy with the great
masses of the population; they do not understand their wants
or necessities, if indeed they are not indifferent or even opposed
to them – as was evidenced by the strenuous resistance of the
important Native Associations to our recent Land Legislation
– and they are very imperfectly fitted to grasp any of the larger
questions which affect the stability or safety of the Empire as a
whole. To hand over therefore the Government of India either
partially or otherwise to such a body as this would simply be to

place millions of men, dozens of nationalities and hundreds of the most stupendous interests under the domination of a microscopic minority, possessing neither experience, administrative ability, nor any adequate conception of the nature of the task before them. Already it looks as if the Mohammedans were rising in revolt against the ascendancy which they imagine a rival and less virile race is desirous of obtaining over them, while there are signs that the Native Princes, Magnates and Land-holders are becoming seriously alarmed at the thought of a small class of Barristers, Native Newspaper Editors and University students intervening between them and the just, impartial and powerful administration of the British Government'.

It was a minute full of frustrations. True, India was finding its way through the jealousies of political lobbying to produce parties that would come to govern the subcontinent. In the 1880s India did not have clever and experienced people running the groups that would one day take India back and for the first time have to prove that they knew what they wanted to do with it. Dufferin was showing in this short minute that, while many people may have talked about the future, it was true also that there was no emerging leader with the corroborative corporate, political and constitutional experience that could take India and run it as the first opportunity of government. More and more Indians were going to London as students – exactly what Gandhi and Jinnah had successfully done. They heard and studied the brilliant ideas floating in journals and classrooms. They had come at a time of changing European, especially British, views among younger lawyers, academics and economists. People were being encouraged to plead for universal suffrage. The viceroys were each reporting back, from Lancaster onwards, that if the British rule were to be sustained then Indians had to take responsibility for running it without any suggestion that one day it would be theirs. Yet no viceroy even contemplated the future without thinking that at least self-government was at hand – if they could do it. Dufferin's view was that the very class of bureaucracies in India was not at close to forming a reliable government because the middle classes were simply not up to it – or, at least not yet. And at the end of 1888 Dufferin was replaced and by the next year was sailing his beautiful yacht, The *Lady Hermione*, in the Mediterranean – a civilised pastime for one who had just been appointed British Ambassador at Rome, where his task was to keep a watchful eye on Italian ambitions in East Africa. Dufferin as viceroy was a first-class example of what the British and French have done better that any other nations – he was a superb diplomat. Kind, considerate, learned, charming, culturally at ease: Dufferin was all these and more. He was, also, quite lazy and probably equally vain. He spoke English, Latin and French and was also a Persian scholar.

There were tragic moments, for example the death of his first son in the Boer War, but even this forlorn time would deepen the image of a deeply cultural figure with tired ideas that betrayed tragedy as well as triumph in irregular parts. The perfect subject for a portrait.

The British never had to look far in the nineteenth century for a Dufferin or two to send to India.[14] The fifth Marquess of Lansdowne was not a true copy of Dufferin (there could not be) but was in waiting.

Henry Charles Keith Petty-Fitzmaurice (1845–1927) was an upright fellow whose father took him away from Eton when his son got in with the boating set. He had the background and family that said that one day the boy would be a great statesman of some sort. As it turned out, he was not a great man but very much in the top drawer where greatness is found.

Lansdowne was born Viscount Clanmaurice and as the Earl of Kerry in Lansdowne House (in 2017 a celebrated London club – if not exclusively for gentlemen) the elder boy of the fourth marquess and his second wife, Emily Jane Mercer Elphinstone de Flahault, in her own right Lady Nairne. His great-grandfather was William Petter, Earl of Shelburne, who was for some months (1782–1783) a maligned prime minister to George III. Having been rescued from the Eton boat, he was privately educated and then off to Balliol, during which time his father died and, as an undergraduate, he became the Marquess of Lansdowne and inherited the family estates and incomes across the United Kingdom.

When Lansdowne went down with a good enough second it was time to take his seat in the Lords as a Whig during what seemed a moment of great political change; it was an even more radical and far-seeing period than the years before and after the Great Reform Bill of 1832. His Liberal political masters Gladstone and Granville – the Leader of the Liberal Party in the Upper House – had awaited his coming and in 1869 (Gladstone's first administration) Lansdowne was given a job as a junior whip – the standard post on which to carve a young politician's arrival initials. In 1872 he was a war minister. The times of Europe were uncertain. The Franco-Prussian War had finished the previous year and France, with little honour and so helpless resentment, would smoulder until reparations were satisfied after Versailles in the 1920s. William of Prussia was the first German Emperor that year and Bismarck his chancellor. The way to safeguard British interests in Africa beyond brutal reaction was unknown and in his second year as war minister the Ashanti Wars began. In 1880 he moved his desk into the India Office and became under-secretary. Within weeks Lansdowne was out.

As one of the biggest landowners in the British Isles and, in particular, a large Irish landlord, Lansdowne was on course for a collision with Gladstone over the Irish Land Act. The government was determined to change property acts and therefore faced opposition from the landlord; so, as a politician, he would always be vulnerable to attacks by other landlords. He resigned. Gladstone sent him to Canada as governor general, a common enough testing ground for a future viceroy of India. Five years on, with Salisbury's government in power, Lansdowne was the simple choice for India. It was also for a politician a good time to get away from mainstream politics. Lansdowne was a Whig. He liked better the policies growing from a more confident Tory administration. He cared for Salisbury and imagined that, by picking up experience in India after Canada, he would keep out of the Westminster in-fighting and might even be considered for higher office as one with no record in the internal conflicts of the Liberals.

There had always been an opportunity to go too far in ruling India. Canada was usually a simple posting where the only serious issue had been the consequences of the borders – both land and sea – with the United States. Lansdowne had good diplomatic skills naturally gathered through his good and often thoughtful instincts in his family and an advantage of classical French. Lansdowne could easily have done Canada for the rest of his life without putting a foot wrong. India had never been such an easy vessel to steer. There were as ever two ongoing concerns for the viceroy: a possible Russian incursion across the Indian border and the mood of the Indians.

His first sense of mood was all about him when he arrived at
Bombay on 3 December 1888. His destination was Calcutta,
but Bombay had put out the flags and was not going to let him
go so quickly. George W. Forrest, the Director of Records to
the Government of India, noted:

'The leading inhabitants of the city – European as well as
Native – had assembled at the pier to give him a welcome
suited to his dignity, and the Municipal Corporation presented
him with an address. After staying three days in the capital of
Western India, spending his time in making himself acquainted
with the people and the city, and in visiting its many noble
institutions for the promotion of literature, science and art,
Lord Lansdowne proceeded to Calcutta. On the ninth of
December His Lordship took over charge of India.'

It was a gentle welcome. That is how it always was at the
handover. The important business of sorting out what the
incoming viceroy was to buy from the outgoing viceroy had
been done. It was often the hardest task (or shock) of the
handover to realise that the new man had to buy the viceroy's
carriage and horses and even the tablecloths. The logic was
very simple: an outgoing viceroy was not going to take home a
carriage and pair. The bartering started from that point. What
could not be bargained was the need of a viceroy to know what
he wanted to achieve and whether or not he had, or could rely
on his staff to provide, the knowledge of India to know what
was and what was not possible to achieve. But where to start?
As Lansdowne found immediately, even a basic idea of what
he was about to rule was hard to come by when a census took
place only once every ten years.

The official programme for Lansdowne was

'the promotion of a systematic enquiry into the facts and
circumstances of the Empire . . . a knowledge of the country
and its people is the foundation of all sound administration.'[15]

To understand religions, social customs, satisfactions and
anxieties were important matters never to be fully known by a
viceroy. He was there for five years and in that time, with the
changing society over which he ruled, there was simply not
enough time. However, to get a clearer picture of Lansdowne's
kingdom, we might rid ourselves of any preconceptions about
India being a backward imperial outpost. In one area, medical
education, started by Lady Dufferin, Lansdowne produced an
improvement that was greater than that in Britain at the time.
It was what a viceroy could do as would an entrepreneur –
taking a subject, deciding the need, supplying the fulfilment.

In a manner that would be called an initiative in the twenty-
first century, Lansdowne authorised a simple essential for the
treatment of common malaria. Quinine vaccinations were put
into post offices. Such a simple medical supply that needed
the nod from the viceroy. Lord Dufferin's vicereine had started
women's medical education. When she left it would carry on.
The Lady Dufferin Fund supported twenty-seven hospitals
and dispensaries when Lansdowne arrived. By the time he left
there were sixty looking after 550,000 patients and the native
princes were paying for a quarter of them. When Lansdowne
arrived in India he was told about 100 female students were in
medical schools. When he left there were more than double
that number. The story was similar in other institutions, with
higher education for women breaking into the thousands.
General education had improved by more than a quarter.
These brief statistics may in modern times seem little more
than party political references, but for India it meant

advancement; the whole country was still hopelessly poor and many lived in wretched circumstances. Nor were the advances contradicting Dadabhai Naoroji's Drain Theory, yet the running of India did in many ways represent something that is distinctly more sophisticated than often described. It was, even in 1890 with the emphasis on caste-based clerical and administration occupations already there, something that in twenty-first-century visits to India are so much admired and longer thought a curiosity. Perhaps this clerical education and status for so many produced the solemn passion for the report. For example, monthly reports were being published of the Departments of Forests, Surveys, Inland Trade, Geology, Meteorology, Veterinary Sciences and Agricultural Chemistry. The Vets department was set up in Lansdowne's time and if it fails to offer the attractive story-telling often imagined (hoped for?) during this period, it does represent a different view of India under the British in the 1880s. Figures, records and stock lists were being produced for vaccine procedures for destructive epidemics, especially rinderpest, which alone every year destroyed many millions of cattle. The report on the Marquess of Lansdowne's term as viceroy contains a last-minute update on one of the most important records and the instructions it reflects still.

'During the past four years [Lansdowne's time as viceroy] the formation of the Imperial Library has been the first step towards supplying an urgent administrative and intellectual want. At the capital of the Empire there has hitherto been no institution in which the administrator or student could find important standard works in any single branch of knowledge. The Government possessed departmental libraries, but, owing to the want of proper catalogues, it was not known what books

they contained. About sixty thousand volumes, gathered from
these different Departmental Libraries, have been brought
under one roof, arranged and made available to the public. A
catalogue of the Imperial Library is in course of preparation. It
is no unreasonable expectation that, in the course of time, by
the generosity of benefactors and a judicious expenditure of
state money, the Imperial Library, founded during the
Viceroyalty of Lord Lansdowne, will not be unworthy to rank
with those of those great storehouses of learning which it is the
privilege of Europe to possess.'

Lansdowne was of course pleased and supposedly not flat-
tered but, as the recorder noted, this considerable moment in
supplying an intellectual want was not as satisfying as taking
on the biggest weakness in India when he arrived – not the
school reform necessary, not expanding what the previous
vicereine had started, but how to enforce law and maintain
order. Lansdowne's view was that the first problem of law
reform was to define what was meant by the administration of
justice. It was a simple proposition for a peer of the realm in
Great Britain, with all the simple definitions including the
exclusion of religious and social differences. In England, for
example, the district and collaboration of thieves was an easy
project for the reformers. Having taken on the centre of the
British Empire, it was not enough to rely on the experience of
staff, district and provincial management of India. The viceroy
had to make up his mind and therefore understand the people
who saluted. As the official report of his administration
acknowledged:

'The difficulty of administering criminal justice in India arises
from the character and habits of the people. Their passive and

timid natures make them unwilling to take an active part in bringing criminals to justice, and the great power which must be entrusted to the police is fraught with considerable danger. Measures have been taken, during the administration of Lord Lansdowne, to reform what has hitherto remained the most faulty part of our system in India.'

Lansdowne's view was based on what he saw before him. Libraries, nursing, agriculture and even the formal separation of interests of the people of India were everyday issues but not the stuff of national debate for a viceroy. In 1888, with the memory of 1857 still very much alive, the new viceroy understood that his daily interest was law and order. The previous year in London, the first Colonial Conference had convened. It was the forerunner of the British Commonwealth and coincided with Victoria's Golden Jubilee. It had no powers to institute anything agreed among the 100 or so delegates, apart from creating a new title for Victoria: Queen of the United Kingdom of Great Britain, Ireland and the Colonies, and all Dependencies thereof, and Empress of India. India was not represented. Considering imperial cooperation and naval defence were major issues for discussion; this was a reflection that India was not ready, as it would be in twenty years' time, for a formal coming-out into the personality that would be the first to go its own way as the the biggest part of the British Empire.

Lansdowne's signature on the restructuring of Indian law and order was not going to be effectual. Lansdowne's hopes really did rest uneasily with the new Indian Councils Act and the creep towards more Indians onto more legislative groups.

Lansdowne's policy was that everyone should understand that the Act meant that even small advances were advances, not simply token democracy. The Councils Act gave members of the legislative councils the right to be involved in all financial discussions – this had not happened before. The Indian Legislative Budget would be given to every member and they could pick it apart if they wished. First interpretation suggested that members would have no restrictions. This was not so. Anyone wanting to raise questions could not do so from the floor. There had to be six weeks' notice. The questions could not be used to start a debate. They were meant as points of order and information. The immediate objections facing Lansdowne was that the Act did not give members, especially Indian members, much authority. What is worth pointing out today is that the restrictions were simply the same as those under which questions could be put to the government in the British House of Commons. This is a reminder that, while criticising the level of democracy in India, the levels in Britain in the 1880s were very far from those in the twenty-first century. Lansdowne's interpretation of the Act was theoretically encouraging:

'The Government of India have freely availed themselves of the power thus conferred upon them, and have framed regulations by which the number of non-official members has been materially increased, and thus the first steps have been taken towards introducing the electoral system into the institutions of India.'

When Lansdowne left India, he knew that most of the country was not searching for the full freedom to vote and appoint those voted in nor to expect legislation to appear into law on the say-so of universal suffrage. But then why should Lansdowne have expected idealistic democracy? After all, it most certainly did not exist in Britain. It would take thirty years to the 1918 Representation of the People Act before men over twenty-one and women over thirty got the right to vote. The 1928 Act gave women the vote at twenty-one. That franchise did not appear in India until the 1951–52 election.

Lansdowne's constant wariness of the undercurrents in Indian society made him more concerned with what had to be done about the army than any spread of so-called democratic institutions and the Indian membership of governing bodies and councils. To Lansdowne, the army was the single important institution in a society that, just three decades before, had boiled over and threatened the heart of empire. The army was inefficient and financially all but insolvent. In 1879, in Lytton's time, the Army Organisation Commission told the viceroy that the system was obsolete. Considering India was at war in Afghanistan, that was not encouraging news; yet nothing was done. Dufferin recommended the army be restructured into four: Punjab, Hindustan, Bombay (Sind and Baluchistan to be included) and Madras (to include, as always, Burma). Nothing was done until Lansdowne arrived. In addition, two testing questions remained: what was to be done about the caste system in the army and what would be recruiting policy for the 'warlike classes'.

Lansdowne had a complete picture drawn of the different and differing classes in the army. The general view of his regimental officers was that the class system made for fighting efficiency. But which class and where to put one class? What to do with the next class? What to do with mixed class? Once the deployment of which-class-where was agreed, it was going to be impossible to improve efficiency with anything but individual regiments and companies using the system. Moreover,

Lansdowne agreed that it would be undesirable to apply any one system to the whole of the native army of India, composed as it was of men drawn from so many different races and professing different creeds. It could work perfectly well to constitute class regiments of Tamils, Telegus, Pariahs in the Madras army, but it could well be inexpedient to introduce a similar mix in other parts of India. Something along this methodology was agreed. The purely military advantages were undoubtedly on the side of the class regiments; the comfort and welfare of the men were more assured. There would be a greater *esprit de corps*. There was one caution that normally did not raise its head in army structures that existed outside a society with so many conflicting social and religious differences. A class regiment might be more radically and rapidly 'infected' by movements among people of their own class or creed. Consequently there might be, more difficulties in officers obtaining information as to what was going on in a class regiment where there were so many different interests and jealousies.[16] Indians had some very warlike classes. Lansdowne could either say leave them where they are but keep a weather eye, or ask how best to use them in the army. The question was simple, the answer almost as simple. In times past, the army had gradually set aside from its ranks the warlike races and recruited those of peaceful, instead of warlike tendency:

'It is obvious, however, that this policy cannot be carried beyond a certain point, as although from a military point of view it may be desirable to have the finest soldiers that India can produce, political considerations forbid confidence being reposed entirely on one particular class or race, and the difficulty is to form a force in which no particular race shall be of preponderant strength.[17]'

Lansdowne had a simple outlook: make the army feared, but not by us, its masters. It can be seen again that the viceroy was very much a working, politicking figure. Some would leave the work to their staffs but some like Lansdowne, who does not always get good historical press, was far from the ceremonial image. His dawn-to-dusk workload was on big complicated issues such as law and order and army reform, which was not completed until he had gone. The continuing task from viceroy to viceroy was to know whom he was governing and for the governed to know British motives. There were plenty of people of all persuasions in India who knew perfectly the motives of the empire makers. Paradoxically, as the century drew on and there was a mood of questioning how long it would be before self-government was possible, more small states were being drawn into British India. The not quite continuous war with Afghanistan had meant districts such as Pishin, Sibh and Thal Chotiali and the Khetran Valleys, that had hardly been shown on the viceroy's map, were now in the empire. Both sides had reservations mostly based on trust. This uncertainty had Lansdowne answering the question no one ever asked but most of the new princes wanted explained. It was a question also for himself.

'During these years you have had ample opportunity of judging what British rule means. You will I hope, have learnt that this is founded on justice, that the British Government neither exacts heavy taxes nor interferes with your private affairs, that it has no wish to meddle in your religion, and that it desires to respect your ancient customs, so far as it is possible to respect them without injustice to individuals. The British Government desires to see its subjects prosperous, contented and happy.'[18]

Dufferin's point was not original; British arrogance or insensitivity – a generous description of attitudes towards the India populations – was antagonising relations between the British and the various societies. Ever since the Mutiny, there was not a viceroy who failed to remind his staff that the rebellion had happened because the British had not been close enough to the people to see what was coming. The consequence of the British still being at a distance from an emerging political class needed a special understanding of, and responsibility for, what the future most certainly would hold. Lansdowne understood as others did that India was moving towards a new desire – more say in the running of their own country even if all Indians were not agreed an what that should entail. Some were not aware that change was perhaps only a generation distant. It was longer than that of course but perhaps a First World War made a difference.

Lansdowne was a Tory in Whig's clothing. His interest in the conditions of Indians did not dissuade him from condemning a small uprising's leader to death. He would consider the divisions and difficulties of Indians and their sometimes wretched differences. He would not tolerate insubordination from leaders who thought their actions beyond treason. Lansdowne would return to London to swap his Whig coat for a Tory position. Salisbury made him secretary of state for war in 1895 and unsuspectingly Lansdowne had to face demands for his resignation because the British army was in a hapless state of preparation during the second Boer War. The lamentable condition was not Lansdowne's fault, but he did not excuse himself. He could, after all, always retreat to his estates.

Lansdowne had no need to retreat. He went across the road and became a distinguished foreign secretary and is mostly remembered as the minister who negotiated the first of the twentieth century's lasting diplomatic achievements, the *entente cordiale* in 1904 with France.

It is hard to make the connection with modern Europe, but the bilateral understanding with France was the first modern demonstration of the British place in Europe. Its origins were in the settlement of who owned what in the world; it was the audit of colonialism that would within the half century begin to give back that which had been taken. Not all has yet been returned and some people yet prefer to stay as colonial possessions because the difference offers little. But the *entente cordiale* may have stretched the point towards the European Union because the reasons for its coming about were quite different; nevertheless one came shortly before the first modern world war and started in Europe and the other before the Second World War also started in Europe.

Lansdowne's career was one of right to rule and as the century closed he was a reminder of the power of the viceroy, not simply by the authority invested in him but the distinction in the politics left briefly behind. The viceroys were not sent to sit on elephants, despite what the images might suggest.

India was changing as fast as it could ever be imagined. Before the end of the nineteenth century the Congress Party had found its feet and, although not always sure footed, it would be in the forefront of the change that Canning had imagined would lead to independence in some form. Education, formal conditions of Indian employment for the better off and the appearance of the Anglo-Indian minority would change even how India sounded. Curzon would see British India as a miracle. In 1895, the British, keen to show the miracle was British, decided to show to themselves an extravagant tableau of its colonial achievement.

The Empire of India Exhibition opened in London in 1895, symbolising all those things which Victorian England believed they had brought to this subcontinent. The British saw themselves as beneficent masters who had delivered to the Indians prosperity, happiness, the virtues of mercy and even wisdom – none of these, of course, had existed before the British in India. Hundreds of thousands of people passed through the turnstiles at Earl's Court to witness not a parade of the glories of India and her peoples, but an extravagant tribute to the British themselves. The subcontinent was their proudest possession. Everything that was good in India was good because the British had made it so.

The sense of eighteenth-century Protestant self-importance that urged Britannia to rule the waves had not dimmed a hundred years on. Very few would carry that view forward two generations in appointments that expressed the sentiment so easily. Elgin, who followed Lansdowne, did that. Elgin's father had been viceroy in 1861 and died of a heart condition not two years in post. His son, a quietly but financial successful man, had no remarkable political distinction although he did follow Gladstone on home rule for Ireland, but even that needed little thought. Why he was courted as viceroy has never been clear – it was Lord Rosebery who persuaded him and he went to India in 1894 and drew no great attention that he had done so. Yet this was what India needed at the time. A safe pair of hands. He moved the development of the railway another 3,000 miles and he saw no reason for the plan to pull out the army in the sensitive outpost of Chital. By cancelling the withdrawal, he a considerably added to the security plan of British India. His biggest task was to cope with one of the most serious famines India had witnessed in living memory. Much to people's surprise, Elgin coped, then succeeded in reducing the consequences to a minimum. Very few have recorded the success and it was Curzon, on Elgin's death in 1917, who so fairly put him in right perspective. Elgin was

'one of those well-endowed but unassuming men whose abilities and services are not less useful because they are to some extent concealed by instinctive modesty from the public gaze.'

CHAPTER XI

CURZON

India easing into the twentieth century was not just about India; it was about the British. India represented a 300-year-old investment that the British could no longer afford, in spite of what turned out to be India's contribution during two world-wide wars together with the cultural contributions to British society. India, we should remember, was considered one of the top ten industrial countries in the world. Britain was overwhelmed by domestic considerations and had been the previous century too, but in those years politics, although as eventful, had a different pace and had fewer consequences for fewer people. Whatever the form of government, every administration was occupied in its own parliament with seemingly weekly challenges – Ireland, the economy prior to and after the First World War, the Gold Standard debate, emergence of new political rivalries, the failure of the League of Nations, the emergence of Communism after that war. It took a lot of optimism to believe that India would always be there and that the road to it not being there would be free of confusion and continuing tragedy. Few had imagined the social legacy of post-empire.

Some images were suspect. There were questions about the long-term consequences of the Mutiny even to the extent that it had been more than a single event. The fact that nearly forty years on, both Indian and British still wondered if there was unfinished business and that there only had to be a single incident to set fire to India. Equally, there was no real everyday tension about Britain's position as ruler of India; there was, however, an active debate about what it would take to challenge British rule. People were asking when India would begin to demand self-government and who would lead the Indian side in that debate. The part answer was that Congress existed and the Muslim League was about to be formed. The bigger questions therefore were when and who. Within a decade the names Jinnah and Gandhi would be known to all India. Throughout all this, the country would run reasonably well because the best apparatus devised by the British, the Indian civil servant with testing entry standards, was on the whole remarkably efficient and a fair way of book-keeping India.

As for the white Mughal, he was one of the most powerful leaders in the world. He ruled without real question 300 million people who knew the rules of his reign; the most efficient of all Asian armies kept the less agreeable in step. Meanwhile the civil service explained or made mystery of every regulation and collected not all, but enough taxes to run the country. When Britain claimed to be a great power it needed to be reminded that the strength rested in a developing industrial power in which Britain had invested since the early seventeenth century and from which it had taken generous dividends ever since.

These conditions and industrial, constitutional and political facts had not each and every one come to pass when Curzon ascended the viceregal throne (none other did it with such majesty in spite of his bad back) but they were discussed by those who saw the new century with some fear that Britain may not after all be quietly goverrned.

When Curzon arrived in 1898 the Boer War was about to begin and would be fought until 1902. But war or not, the Queen Empress was omnipresent although she would go before those guns fell silent. Lord Curzon believed that his monarch ruled by God's command. He expressed the same sentiment of authority, in grand viceregal terms, as Thompson would have done a century and a half earlier.[1] Curzon came to represent an image of the British raj. Durbars would come and be celebrated in India as the British turned by the gift of some magician from Victorians into Edwardians. With this scene change came the magician's assistant, the man who would be the most famous viceroy until 1947 – Curzon.

Everything about Curzon was a symbol of the British in India: purposeful, inbred with arrogance and an exquisite belief in his right to rule everything. He looked the part and acted it out. No one was superior to him and he married a beautiful and bewilderingly rich American.[2] He was thirty-nine, the youngest viceroy ever. Leonard Mosley, his friend, painted the Algerian picture.

'In his train followed long strings of elephants and retinues of gaily coloured servants . . . For the rest of his life Curzon was influenced by his sudden journey to have at the age of thirty-nine and then by his return to earth seven years later, for the remainder of his mortal existence.'

Curzon was never overwhelmed. Mosley, close as anyone to the pageant, had it that when Lord Salisbury sent Curzon to

India he had done so because he believed that he was an amenable subordinate and would make no major moves without securing the consent of the government at home. But a change came over Curzon the moment he 'felt the warmth of the viceregal throne on his breeches.' Curzon, the junior minister who had so often stifled his principles in the interests of office, now felt himself strong enough, and far enough away, to act alone, and, if need be, in defiance of Westminster. He viewed his position in much the same way as a Roman proconsul had done, in Britain or in Gaul, during the time of the Caesars. He had time and distance on his side. And as the government became increasingly involved with the difficulties and disasters of the Boer War, Curzon became less heedful of any advice they might offer him.

Leonard Mosley thought of the transformation in Curzon on the day of his welcoming banquet in Calcutta. The regalia, the bowing and scraping – to him. He had always assumed wives were inferior one-step-behind creatures; now there was a protocol to prove it.

If Curzon needed a reminder of his great inheritance – which, really, he did not – he got it on the afternoon of 3 January 1899 when the state carriage containing himself and his wife drew up at Government House in Calcutta. All around him, in the streets and squares, the brown bodies of his subjects were jammed together like a colony of ants, squeaking and shrieking a welcome to the newly arrived overlord. From the reviewing stand at the top of the Government House steps he watched his armies marching before him, soldiers from every regiment in India, men from the Gurkhas and leathery Pathans, Dogras, Sikhs and Mahrattis – most of whom his predecessors had fought to a standstill of submission and servitude. Soldiers before him on foot, soldiers on horseback, soldiers on lumbering painted elephants. Curzon, a man rarely at a loss for tears of self-pride, was nearly, just nearly, overcome.

> 'I suddenly saw what had come into my hands, and what prod-igies of energy and inspiration would be needed on my part to guide them.'

That night he was dressed in the court dress of a viceroy: silk tights, gallant gold and crimson jacket, heavily jewelled sky-blue cloak and sashes of office. His vicereine, Mary, wrote to her sister that 'never before has George looked so beautiful.' One by one vassals presented themselves: first the governors of Bengal, Bombay and Madras, the lieutenants governor and the senior maharajas and nawabs, Hindus, Muslims, Sikhs and Buddhists. The formality was sure footed and represented what the viceroy saw as novelty, brave hopes and high aspirations.

George Nathaniel Curzon was born on 11 January 1859 at Kedleston Hall, the family Derbyshire mansion built by Robert Adam. The Curzons 'came over with the Normans' and had lived thereabouts since the twelfth century. The name comes from Notre Dame de Courson in Normandy. His father Alfred Curzon (1831–1916) was Church of England rector of Kedleston and known as the fourth Baron Scarsdale. Curzon's mother Blanche (1837–1875) was a lovely woman who bore eleven children and died at the age of thirty-seven having run out of energy. Curzon's nanny, Ellen Mary Paraman, was not described as a lovely woman and by the time Curzon was ten she had insisted that he remember his heritage and thus his obligation to honour it and imagine the great heights that an ancient name should achieve. He was packed off to Wixenford Preparatory School and then Eton, where he was liked (by tutor Oscar Browning, who regarded Curzon as outstandingly gifted) or utterly disliked (by his housemaster C. Wolley Dod who thought him objectionable).

Curzon excelled in almost everything he touched other than sport – his spine was unreasonably curved and from this he suffered much pain for the whole of his time. Oxford schooled him well in oratory and the confusions of political government. The conclusion of contemporaries was that Balliol under Benjamin Jowett was maturing yet another political titan, although Jowett himself thought him cocky. Curzon would have it as self-assured and determined to make his name as recognisable as the stately home in which his family had lived for longer than parliament itself.

After Eton and romantic fumblings and political leanings, Curzon won a seat at Southport (not his local constituency) in the 1886 general election and then displayed an instinct to travel the world as none other of his friends had even thought to do. He would be known as the most well-travelled man of his generation, who searched thoughtfully for origins and understanding, particularly of Asia and British occupation of India and where that venture might lead. It was not that surprising that, in late 1891, albeit with not much political experience, Curzon was given the job of junior minister in the India Office. Six months later the Conservatives were out of office but Curzon's mark was made and when in 1895 the Conservatives were back, Salisbury appointed him as junior foreign minister.

Salisbury was foreign secretary as well as prime minister and sat in the Lords, so Curzon led for the government in the Commons. Where might he go from here? Salisbury was not letting go of the Foreign Office but he sat and he listened when Curzon spoke on India. His observations and constructive advice to the Cabinet were carefully prepared. An example might be his advice to maintain a considerable military force on the North West Frontier at a time when there was a general feeling that the Russians would move into the region should the British show signs of losing interest. His advice was taken and the considerable cost of maintaining an army in the Chitral area was approved. By his mid-thirties, Curzon was an established political feature at Westminster bur realistically chances of promotion were slim. There were two posts to his liking, Foreign Secretary and then Prime Minister. Hence, this was the time to achieve his ambition for now, viceroy of India. Curzon lobbied without shame. He told everyone who mattered, most obviously Salisbury, that he, being the most qualified and brilliant man to go to India, should be appointed with haste. A little maturity needed? Certainly not. A young, vigorous figure with unparalleled authority should sail for India as soon as could be arranged. In 1898 Salisbury proposed that Curzon should succeed Elgin. There was never such a contrast in viceroys.

Self-esteem does not easily sit alongside humility. Being viceroy was the nearest one could get to be monarch without the advantage of inheritance. Many who had been appointed wrote, lobbied and hinted and even put together learned papers on India. Some took India as a grand design. Mayo saw it as a place where he could change matters, even the lot of the Indians and generally do good. Others with long connections to India saw an appointment as an expected honour, although Northbrook never really wanted to go. As for Curzon, no candidate wanted India more. He knew the subject, he was born at Kedleston and the viceroy's residence in India was based on Kedleston.

Curzon saw India as one destiny answered. He never made the second. Not even Prime Minister would come with such an immediate elevation of status. From countryside station-master to Constable of the Tower, all caps would be doffed at his very passing-by. The very seniority of ruling the empire on behalf of the monarch in such imperial guise was a reason to bow at the sound of viceroy, but there was some added distinction, some unknown and mostly unimagined status reserved whilst still in England. In Britain, the monarch was mostly safe. The sound of gunfire would be ceremonial. Since the Sepoy Rebellion there had been retold stories of the dangers of murder, rape, pillage and terrible violation as well as grand and uncompromising respect due to the viceroy and his vice-reine. The Queen was someone ever grand and probably elderly, safely locked down with burning night light at Windsor. The viceroy appeared as a warrior, even a great warrior defending the very empire every day and night, living among those who could whisper rebellion in dark and strange places. This and more were all true.

The viceroy would have daily reports of uprisings, disease, famine, floods, threats and misunderstandings spawning crises. The people understood this. They understood also that only the most trusted and distinguished in the land would have been chosen to dress the part and therefore a metaphoric finger would be ready to touch a forelock. The viceroy travelled in a mythical chariot and then to a far-off place where Kipling knew one might risk their life to defend Great Britain's empire. No one believed the Sepoy Rebellion could not come again and, as Curzon had debated at Westminster, there continued to be a real threat from the Russians in the north. No imagination was left alone. No possible treachery dismissed.

And once appointed, the viceroy and his vicereine, his beautiful American, his adoring Mary, began the round of formal recognition with balls great and small, dinners rarely fewer

than 100 sat down, a City of London banquet, Oxford feasts, a
court ball, royal invitations to dine and stay (i.e. sleep over-
night at Windsor). So openly in awe were the British of their
viceroys that there was ever a question of associated identity.
The British have always seen their monarch as a reflection of
national identity. The only other figure to mirror with that
distinction has been the viceroy. The monarch and the viceroy
were untouchables with whom all had an imagined first-name-
term relationship. The viceroy was treated as royalty long
before arriving in India.

Curzon was created Baron Curzon, an Irish peerage. If it
had been an English title, then he would not have been able
to return to the House of Commons at the end of his term in
India. It was in this title and with his vicereine in waiting that
he started the round of official and private occasions to mark
his appointment. Lady Curzon, as now she was, was the daughter of a Chicago multi-millionaire storeowner, Levi Zeigler
Leiter, and Mary (née Carver). The Leiters, of Swiss Mennonite
backgrounds, were frequent visitors to Europe and during a
visit to England in 1890 she fell in love with Curzon. They
became engaged in 1893 but Curzon, ever preoccupied upon
his voyage to greatness, made her keep their tryst a secret.
Nothing could interfere with his ambition. Not until six weeks
before their wedding two years later were their intentions
widely discussed. They were married in America and Mary
never returned. She never lost her sense of being an American,
but her duty was now with her husband. It was not an easy
time, even with family. The long-faced rector had seen no
great reason why George should take a foreigner as a wife and
could not hide his disappointment. Curzon's friends did not
dislike Mary but their social group was mostly men and
marriage did not bring even visiting membership.

This then was the society into which Curzon led his wife, a woman described on both sides of the Atlantic as an almost divine creature blessed with breathtaking looks and, frustratingly, a mind of her own. It was very new and her letters home presented an insight into moving from high society to becoming the subject of the highest in society as they arrived by ship in Bombay.

'On Friday we land in Bombay, we go to the Governor's House & stay Friday night for a great banquet & reception and on Saturday we proceed in our train to Calcutta [the then capital]. George and I drive in a state carriage with four horses, postilions outriders & escort and behind two Syces [servants] running holding parasols above our heads – our drive is through wild masses of people for five miles, behind our carriage come all the staff & officials sent by Gov. of Bombay and Viceroy to meet us, the procession is about five carriages – babies in one with a hood to keep off the sun, all this time salutes of 31 guns firing & all the warships in the harbour cannonading – so it will be thrilling'.

The incoming viceroy was still expected to take over more than the appointment from the outgoing man. The Curzons had to buy from Elgin his horses, carriages, silverware and anything else that was considered too much to expect to return to England and would be too much effort to replace. The new man had to pay for himself and his entourage to get to India and foot the costs for uniforms and livery. It was a costly business taking up residence and Mary's father came in very handy, or his wealth did when dressing the new vicereine in the best Paris haute couture could (and did) offer and the finest jewellery, including a newly designed tiara. When the Curzons arrived they faced a bill of some £835,000 at 2017 prices. The government gave Curzon a grant of about £300,000 towards the costs. Within three months of arriving it was decided that a pair of carriages were looking shabby and a new rig had to be ordered. Cost? £85,934 including harnesses. The vicereine was soon sending begging letters to her enormously rich papa. Very simply, a viceroy could not skimp. His wife could never be seen in last year's style. The pressure on health, social standing and protocols was demanding, although mostly taken in viceregal stride.

The difference between the Elgins and Curzons illustrates that there was a sad price to pay for the privilege of being the Queen's appointee. This is in spite of a recent view that the viceroy was a reflection of a sometimes reprehensible imperial British occupation of a land that was never theirs and represented a now unthinkable attitude to the people whose land it most certainly was.

The first viceroy Canning and his wife were broken by the experience, which, considering the Mutiny, can easily be imagined and perhaps explained. The Elgins and Curzons had no such traumatic events with which to cope; even the notorious famine from which more than four million Indians were said to have died did not directly threaten the way of the Elgins, although Victor her husband, the ninth earl of Elgin and thirteenth earl of Kincardine, was criticised for never mounting an effective 'rescue'. Such a task would have perplexed any leader, although later critics allowed that he had succeeded where others would not. Elgin was not an inspired choice and there is no evidence that he took to the role or found even the ceremonial part of the appointment appealing. They had every family and historic advantage except the stamina and health to cope. He appeared to be a good appointment. His wife

Constance (1851–1909) was bred well as the daughter of the ninth earl of Southesk and married well. She was totally devoted to the care of their eleven children and suffered from the experience. The Elgins never quite managed India. They never wanted to go and had neither the wealth nor the imperial style to make a mark. Constance Elgin was constantly in poor health and never recovered. She died in 1909.

Poor health was common enough and there are many gravestones in Calcutta, Bombay and Madras to remind us of this. Mary Curzon, in spite of wealth and a healthy background, suffered as others but her seemingly bottomless private means and beauty matched anything that had been seen before in India. In Mary Curzon's first eight weeks as vicereine she held a Drawing Room (a full dress presentation of the leading ladies and families as well as the not-so-leading ladies and families); one grand garden party; an even grander state ball for more than 1,500 people; a state evening party for the same number; a dozen dances – and no dinner sat down without 100 guests. Curzon thought little of these occasions and rated them by the attendance of those he remembered from many days gone by – from Eton or Oxford.

The official viceroy-making ceremony was never as grand as supposed and often not as gorgeous as those that followed with the state meetings with princes and maharajas. We can thank Mary Curzon for a letter home.

'At 9.30 on Friday all the Staff fetched George and marched two and two, he following alone, through the Marble Hall into the Throne Room at the end. There all Members of the Executive Council shook hands with him and the procession re-formed, they joining it, and proceeded back through the Hall to the Council Chamber in the north wing. There the procession divided, taking their places to right and left and George walked up between them, turned round and faced the room. It was crowded with officials and Maharajas on either side of a passage roped off. I had come with Lord Suffolk and taken my place at the end of the room. George stood under Quentin Hastings' picture while the Home Secretary read the Warrant, which took about five minutes. The Warrant proclaimed him Viceroy; that was all, there was no oath taking and the whole proceeding was very simple. As soon as the Home Secretary had finished Lord Suffolk signaled to the Guard out of the window, and the band played God Save the Queen and thirty one guns went off; then the procession re-formed in the same order, Lord Suffolk and I bringing up at the rear several paces behind, and we marched back to the Throne Room.'[3]

And that was about that. However, from that moment the protocol of the status of the viceroy and all standing by was clear. For example, the viceroy always sat in the right-hand side of the carriage. The vicereine would never get into the carriage before her husband and would always follow him through the door. Curzon was a grand figure. His predecessor Lord Elgin was small. Towards the end of the nineteenth century a grand Curzon was a perfect image when taking the salute, when going about or, most importantly, being gazed at.

'Last Thursday we held a drawing room – where all the high officials were grouped either side of the throne – the throne was covered with a perfectly magnificent solid gold carpet which was laid over it, the ends coming far out of the carpet of the room – on the dais were two immense chairs, one of which was silver with gold tigers behind G. A smaller one for me. We

stood in front of them and all the entrée ladies filed past making
two curtseys – they then took their places to the left of the
throne beside their husbands who were already there – as each
lady came up her name on a card was given to the ADC who
handed it to the Military Secretary & he called out her name
– she then proceeded to courtesy to G. who bowed solemnly &
then another curtsey to me & I bowed & smiled. We did not
shake hands with anyone – just bowed.'[4]

Curzon was not a ceremonial viceroy. His imperial gait was
natural enough but with it came a determination that, between
him and the secretary of state at the India Office in London,
India could be a better place for the British and for the Indians.
Here was an understanding that India was too complex a society and place to rule without the Indians on board. Some of
Curzon's achievements seem of no outstanding importance,
but they were of the time and tended to be new. He had a
direction to implement twelve administrative reforms. He fell
short of his bureaucratic dozen, but those he accomplished
were of the time and a warning that nothing in the government of India – a local affair, a time for persuasion, an
understanding with London thousands of miles distant – was
easy. A durbar was simple by comparison.

Furthermore, pressure and dilemma in India were equally
matched by British security uncertainties on the borders.
Curzon was faced with a border conundrum that could not, it
was thought, end in anything but calamity.

During Curzon's time in India, there had been an almost
continuous rupture in relations with Tibet. The story of Tibet
and British interests was linked to the seemingly continuing
belief that the Russians threatened India or, more specifically,
British interests in the subcontinent. By 1902, there were

reports that the Russians were sending guns into Tibet. Little enough was known about that state and the idea that the Russians were building up influence, which, if necessary, could threaten the British on that north-eastern border with Tibet, was taken seriously.

Historically, China had authority over Tibet. In 1902, China was unable to govern itself, never mind the fiercely independent Tibetans. Moreover, just three years earlier, there had been a complete rupture of relations between the British and the Chinese in what became known as the Boxer Rising. The Boxers were members of a secret organisation called The Society of Harmonious Fists. They did not like the Europeans taking over important elements of Chinese institutions. Western churches and embassies were attacked. With the help of the Americans and the Japanese, who also saw their interests threatened, the British and some other European states put down the Boxer rebellion. In 1902, if Curzon thought the Chinese were going to help him keep control of the Tibetans, he was wrong. As for the Tibet authorities, they said that if Britain had complaints they should address them to the Chinese. The further possibility for Curzon was to negotiate directly with the then Dalai Lama.

Curzon wanted Colonel Francis Younghusband to lead an expedition into Tibet, and negotiate with the Dalai Lama and establish a British legation in the Tibetan capital, Lhasa. It was a good scheme on paper. Curzon did not have support from Broderick, the India secretary, nor Prime Minister Arthur Balfour. Relations with Russia were difficult. Balfour, who faced opposition on so many policies, did not want to do a single thing that would further weaken relations with the tsar. The difference between Curzon's view of what should be done and Balfour's was simple to understand: Curzon wanted to get into Lhasa and establish a British presence. Balfour wished to do nothing more than resolve any local border incidents. If Curzon thought he might be on a collision course with the Dalai Lama (who anyway, by this time had fled into Mongolia) he must have known that the real confrontation would be with Balfour.

In 1903, Younghusband was given permission by London to go no further than just inside the Tibetan border to talk about trade and local disputes. The Dalai Lama, having run off to Mongolia, limited the scope of Younghusband's negotiations. Moreover, Balfour's government had expressly refused permission for any questions about Russians. In July 1903, Younghusband, with a military force of about 200 Sikhs, crossed the border, much to the annoyance of the local Tibetan commander who had no physical power to stop them. They then waited in Khamba Jong for what they expected to be a large Tibetan and Chinese representation. Although Younghusband met the Panchen Lama, others failed to show. This was all very frustrating for Curzon, who seized on a border incursion by the Tibetans in the autumn of 1903. This was something even Balfour understood.

Curzon sent a signal to London that Younghusband should move further in and, if necessary, show the Tibetans that they could not go into British territory without retaliation. More troops were sent to Younghusband and by the time he moved on from Khamba Jong, he had more than 1,000 British and Sikh soldiers, artillery and machine guns and, apparently, as many as 7,000 labourers. This was all new country to Younghusband and his force. It was also the end of November and therefore, sub-zero temperatures. They spent that winter fighting the cold rather than Tibetans. Younghusband's target was to get to the lesser city of Gyantse. It was not until the end of March 1904 that Younghusband halted his troops before the small township of Guru. Two thousand Tibetans, led by a general, confronted Younghusband's force at point blank range. A shot was fired, it was later said, by the Tibetan commander. The British machine guns opened up. Rather than flee, the Tibetans, utterly powerless, walked forward as a mass into the machine gun fire. It was a massacre. More than 800, some reported 900, Tibetans were killed or seriously wounded. There were just six slightly wounded British. Younghusband stepped across the dead and dying and contin-ued on his way to Gyantse. The Tibetans attacked. Younghusband's troops swept aside the defenders. Given the action against the British forces, Younghusband believed he had the authority to go on until he reached the holy city of Lhasa.

On 2 August 1904, Younghusband entered Lhasa. The Tibetans were overwhelmed. On 7 September, he eventually signed an agreement that gave the British trading advantages and excluded, in theory, others from Tibet. Younghusband was upbraided by Balfour and so, therefore, was Curzon. The British would honour nothing in the Younghusband agree-ment that might upset the Russians, who at the time were at war with Japan.

If this period was the apogee of the British Empire, it was certainly one of the last times that the British felt they had the authority, both politically and morally, to teach savages that they should not mess with imperial masters.

Curzon is only imagined at grand occasions; but there was the humdrum too. One of his first tasks was to push through an Indian Coinage Act and put India on a gold standard. A single and simple Act that set a new pace for India as a trading nation in its own right, British or not. But when the British went off the gold standard India was wounded. Her economic standing suffered, as did London's. And if all failed, there was always the railways. Curzon's view was not original but it was nonetheless sound: the railways carried India's people and goods distances that no other form of transport could begin to achieve and so kept India on the move. They had to be extended. They were. He considered the extension a triumph. There was too in Curzon a deepening sense that India's heritage must not be abandoned and become little more than a by-product of ruined antiquity. India 'was there' before the British. Curzon perfectly understood the meaning of India's history and that it should be restored and then preserved as part of Indian identity and, most importantly, that the identity was not British. In 1904 he saw through the Ancient Monuments Protection Act; Agra would become a beneficiary.

The final long-lasting Curzon action reflected the continuing unrest and vulnerability of India and the British control. The frontier tribes had been at war in 1897 and 1898. The answer was not a continuing turn-around of soldiery. Instead, Curzon created the North Western Frontier Province. For decades the area had been claimed, fought over and even acted as a buffer zone with Afghanistan after the Second Anglo-Sikh war (1848–49). To govern the territory (Peshawar, Dera Ismail Khan and Malakand) it had to be a province with all the authority and resources of its own administration and capital, Peshawar. Curzon's province survived Partition and existed until 1955. Governing with understanding towards tribal and religious pressures gave Curzon reason for his final and most difficult legislation. Muslim eastern Bengal was portioned from mainly Hindu western Bengal in October 1905. It was a sign of the sadness to come. He was rightly proud. In 1903, when it was time to go, he begged to be reappointed and reminded Prime Minister Arthur Balfour, Salisbury's nephew, that he had done well as viceroy but needed to finish the job.

Curzon should have gone in 1903. He may have done better politically at home. Moreover, he could have gone on a spectacular moment. In 1903 came the greatest event ever organised by Curzon – the durbar to celebrate the coming and succession of Edward VII and his Queen, Alexandra, as Emperor and Empress of India. Here was Curzon setting the stage and parade of his, as well as the people's, India. Here was the event planning and staging of what would be seen in the early twenty-first century as the opening of some Olympic Games. On the Delhi plain a mystical tented city was built.[5] Medals were minted and struck, electric lights were rigged, railways were laid, telegraph poles planted, hospitals and courts, stores and watering holes opened. Galas and balls, dinners and revues to bands and dances and games and banquets were everywhere. The glittering and white block infantry at their most colourful paraded and countermarched to the fit-to-burst bands of the regiments of the moment.

Elephants trumpeted their coming and maharajas dressed in all that money could buy swayed from the royal chorus line of power, affluence and bejewelled ostentation. The coronation ball was the grandest remembered among those who remembered well. It was Curzon's finest moment. But the King never came. Instead he sent his brother, the Duke of Connaught.

Curzon went back to England. His extra two years would not be a triumph and he would lose Mary. India did it for Mary Curzon. Socially she was at once brilliant, dazzling and an irritant to the many who saw her lapses in protocol as typical of an American. Curzon was a stickler for rules and protocols and was often minded to lay them down for all to see. From the first months in Calcutta, Mary Curzon was writing to her parents about the heat and not being able to cope with it. In 1904, the year before the Curzons left, Mary was ill and complained of a constant cough and during the spring before Curzon returned to India for, as it turned out, a short second term as viceroy, she moved into the dank and drain-troubled Walmer Castle overlooking the Channel at Kent.

That same year, saddened by the death of her father and perhaps a miscarriage, Mary Curzon fell badly to phlebitis and peritonitis and notices of her health described her condition as grave. In November, Curzon returned to India and Mary followed, hoping that she would be better at her husband's side. Curzon, on reflection, was wrong to return for a second turn believing that he could tidy up unfinished work.

He believed he still had work to do in India and hoped that he would be supported from London by the new secretary of state for India, St. John Broderick.[6] At first he was, but the period between the spring of 1904 and 1905 would be a miserable time for Curzon and for British rule in India.

It began with both London and Curzon being faced with the need to reform the governing of Bengal. Curzon's view was that Bengal was too big and too heavily populated to be governed as one state or province. He wanted to divide it. At first, this might seem simple administrative logic, particularly in the hands of one who had made sure and steady decisions during his time as viceroy. It left one part of the division with a Muslim majority. The Hindus in Bengal disliked Curzon's decision. It would, in theory, weaken their political strength. This was not a local difficulty. Curzon's reputation as a man who was sensitive to religious balances was damaged for all time.[7] There was more to come. This time, there were two areas of contention between the viceroy, London and the commander-in-chief of the army in India, the recently appointed Kitchener.[8] That difference centred on who had absolute command of the army, especially when the c-in-c was away campaigning, the viceroy with his military advisor or the commander-in-chief. To even raise the matter was something of a brave judgement by the viceroy. For that reason alone, Curzon's time in India was not to be long.

Curzon had taken over India from his own government. He made decisions and acted upon them without consulting his governors and without seeking the views of London. On one occasion he made what was in effect a state visit to Oman. There word was out that Oman was about to sign a cooperation treaty with Russia. Salisbury's government was indifferent. Curzon was not. He forestalled the Omani–Russia treaty. Salisbury, who by now understood that he had lost much control of the viceroy, decided to tell Curzon that he should have been consulted on such a commitment. Curzon told him that he knew Salisbury was very busy (wars and things) and so had simply anticipated what his revered prime minister would have done. Salisbury could be heard 5,000 miles away offering a weak sigh of 'I suppose so'. (The relationship Curzon established exists into the twenty-first century, Salisbury would be pleased to know). Curzon saw himself as royalty and regarded the inability to delegate as a sign of strength. Immediately that meant that as viceroy and as Curzon anyway, he would make it clear that Congress was interfering and of no value to India; Congress had a different view of what India should become to Curzon and it was therefore not much short of nonsensical. Curzon had no doubts about the future of British India. Just as God had commanded Nelson and his like (certainly the admiral's predecessors) to rule the waves, so he had commanded Britain (i.e. Curzon) to rule India. No one should misunderstand that view because it was here to stay; not even the high-end Indians should think that they would one day have India back for themselves.

'If I thought that it were all for nothing and that you and I, Englishmen and Scotchmen and Irishmen, in this country were merely writing inscriptions in the sand to be wiped out by the next tide; if I felt we were not working here for the good of India in obedience to a higher law and a nobler aim, then I would see the link that hold England and India together severed without a sigh. But it is because I believe in the future of this country and the capacity of our own race to guide it to its goals that it has never hitherto attained, that I keep courage and press forward.'

Curzon was now obsessed with his role as viceroy. Dalhousie would have recognised him without his robes. Napoleon would have greeted Curzon as a kindred spirit, but one content with his empire. Salisbury may have doubted Curzon by now. Salisbury would have been wrong. Curzon was the ideal, if picturebook, viceroy for the time. The century was changing and so was the way of political Britain tumbling from one battle report from Africa to another in search of victory, with Salisbury giving way to A.J. Balfour. Balfour, said the rumour machine, was about to recall Curzon and have him as foreign secretary. It could not have been because Balfour was one of the few who saw through Curzon. The rumour did Curzon's self-esteem no end of good, as if he needed it. The Indian media believed the rumours and wrote lengthy articles and leaders begging him not to leave India but to stay and finish his task. Mosley, intrigued by the image of an Emperor who

believed in his own greatness and surrounded by acolytes at
the gates and with palms wafting the energies their master
needed, understood why Curzon was

> 'convinced more than ever now that he was India's only hope,
> the fulcrum of her present, the keystone of her future. He had
> no doubt at all in his mind now that he would reach the heights
> and be remembered through history as the greatest viceroy of
> them all; and he settled down to his desk, writing away steadily
> through the hours, almost welcoming the blood and tears
> which lay ahead, convinced that they would result in greater
> glory for himself and India. He had no inkling that what lay
> ahead was disaster, humiliation and tragedy.'[9]

The British army in India had a commander plus a senior
administrator, a sort of adjutant general. The commander-in-
chief in 1904 was Kitchener. When he picked a fight with
Curzon, whom he thought on first meeting in India nothing
more than a toy viceroy dressed in blue silk, he was like
Curzon: he could not imagine losing. Curzon thought
Kitchener something out of a Gilbert and Sullivan operetta.

> 'He seems to think that the military government of India is to
> be conducted by concordat between him and me. Accordingly,
> he comes and pours out to me all sorts of schemes to which he
> asks my consent. It is all so frank and honest and good-tempered
> that one cannot meet these advances with a rebuff. Here and
> there I head him off to steer him into more orthodox channels.
> But as yet of course he does not know the ropes.'

Arrogance is rarely but a step from patronage, which is but a
step from bitter surprise. To believe Kitchener was bringing

naive plans to the viceroy's table was to miss the fact that Kitchener was Curzon with more self-belief, but one who was tortured that self-belief was not enough. Kitchener had made a public note that he thought the viceroy's MA, the Military Assistant, was unnecessary and a meddling appointment in the command structure. The viceroy's view was that the MA stopped the commander-in-chief getting absolute control of the army and therefore he, the general, and not the viceroy would be Emperor. Kitchener wrote home to friends in high places that Curzon was 'all that one could wish and as kind as possible.' Kitchener was not naive. He thought Curzon a well-shod viceroy but with feet of clay. He was confident that Curzon was the naive one. How could he imagine that a general as famous as Kitchener could not like the idea of having a mere major general as a joint administrator of the Indian army? Kitchener wanted to be commander-in-chief of everything military.

The general's further objection was that the other administrator was also a member of the viceroy's council. This had always worked and the double authority had been strengthened by Curzon, who believed that the commander-in-chief should be responsible for war-fighting capabilities and that the major general on his council (the one Kitchener objected to) should be the much-needed logistician. Moreover, if the commander-in-chief was campaigning, then the viceroy would have at his side an immediate military advisor. Kitchener was not the sort of man to delegate the authority of his command, especially as, the way he saw it, a junior general would be in a position to influence the viceroy while the commander-in-chief was not there. Curzon said that the system had worked perfectly well before Kitchener's arrival in 1902 and so he rejected the famous general's demand.

Generals rarely become famous without having a grasp of
tactics, both military and political. Kitchener thus lobbied the
political hierarchy in London. St. John Broderick was won
over. At the time that Curzon discovered what was happening,
he was in England, where Mary was seriously ill. She would
die in July 1906 and suffered the bad treatment of her husband
at the hands of Kitchener in a relationship that could have
been so triumphant in Curzon's final spell. Instead they knew
they had been outwitted, lied to and abandoned by the very
friend they had once had, Broderick.

But Kitchener had not finished. He had got his way, but then
said he was going to resign. Kitchener was out to ruin Curzon.
He knew that a threat of his resignation would be close to
devastating for Balfour's unpopular administration. Curzon
returned just before Christmas to India. In the following
spring, 1905, he led his viceroy's council in rejecting any plans
to scrap the military department and thus, Curzon's major
general. Kitchener had anticipated this and, determined to see
the end of Curzon, had already primed his London supporters, who forced the government, in spite of civilian and military advice, to support Kitchener. Broderick wrote to Curzon,
by now no longer his close friend, explaining that the viceroy's
council could no longer have anything but a very weakened
military department. There now came a curious ploy from
London. It was clear that the government wanted to get Curzon
out of India, but to do so without being seen to dismiss him.
That would have caused ructions in India and in the British
press, which the government did not believe it was popular
enough to disregard.

Kitchener, still in India, appeared to be backing down from
his original demands. Then, within a few weeks, he went the
other way. The test came when Curzon nominated a new

major general as his military member of the committee. Broderick vetoed the nomination.

This was happening when Mary Curzon was ill and in London and Curzon was not giving the matter all the attention that he might. More than this, Kitchener openly detested Curzon and was determined to get rid of him. The simplest way was to threaten to resign. Kitchener was a national hero. Curzon was hardly that. Surely he was too great a man for them to accept his going. On the morning of 16 August 1905 Curzon was at his breakfast when he received a Royal Command from King Edward VII.

'With deep regret I have no other alternative but to accept your resignation at your urgent request. Most warmly do I thank you for your invaluable service to your Sovereign and your Country and especially to the Indian Empire.'

That was it. Go now prince. Curzon had been outwitted. There had been no need for the matter to get as far as it did. But it did and, although Curzon returned a hero, although his higher peerage was held over, his career did not perish. He outlived Kitchener and glittered as foreign secretary but never higher.

CHAPTER XII

MINTO–MORLEY REFORMS

Lord Minto, who followed Curzon, led the life of a steady, hardly ambitious Borders Scot aristocrat with 16,000 acres, who was quite capable of looking after British interests when asked to by successive prime ministers.[1] Minto was a Murray and like his ilk tutored before Eton in Minto Castle near Hawick, a town of good, sometimes rough, cloth people devoted to the field. At Trinity, Cambridge, he properly spent much time in a boat or on a horse. He had an almost distinguished racing record. He won the French Grand National in 1874 but two years later an accident stopped all that. With a commission in the Scots Guards he spent two good winters hunting and at other times performing mostly ceremonial duties. Minto, as he became, and Lord Melgund as he was until then, was not exceptional. He was one of the blessed characters of the late Victorian and Edwardian times who seemed to do things with little effort as if by some hand that foresaw a distinguished future. In the 1870s he tried out as a war correspondent, found himself as aide de camp to Major

General Frederick Roberts and during a skirmish hurt his hand, a brief inconvenience that won him his majority.

While still Melgund, he married Mary, the daughter of General Sir Charles Grey, Queen Victoria's private secretary; consequently, Minto would never be forgotten at court, the exchange of all interesting jobs that allowed time for other interests.

Lord Lansdowne was going to Canada as governor general and as Melgund was at a loose end following lunch he accepted the offer of military secretary to the new governor. In Canada he found the opportunity to recruit almost 400 Canadians to join Sir Garnet Wolseley's force making for Khartoum to rescue General Charles Gordon. He joined a committee to examine defences against the United States and found himself as chief of staff to the general fighting against the north-west rebellion. He left Canada hoping to return as governor general, which he saw as his right to a pleasant appointment. He settled in the Borders to look after the family estate. His not quite earnest ambition to be governor general in Canada needed a little campaigning when word spread of the pending retirement of the sitting tenant Lord Aberdeen. Mary was good at court. Minto became governor general.

For Minto, Canada was something of a love affair and he considered retirement in the Rockies but whispers at court meant India was his. Curzon had resigned and in the summer of 1905 Minto was, as Mary put it, appointed out of the blue. At almost the same time, Burke's biographer, John Morley, was appointed secretary of state for India. It proved to be a good if competitive partnership between the radical Morley and the conservative-minded Minto, with both working together but eager to take credit. Minto was a good example of the viceroy who was out on his own and travelled with his preconceptions.

He understood that nationalism was key to the future of India inasmuch as nationalists had to be taken on board when discussing new planning, thus establishing nationalist authority. He was a new generation that could see the obvious hazard of government in India: it was too backwards to govern without board representatives of the seemingly endless line of interests in every province. Something of his Scottish Borders instincts surfaced in his respect for Indian princes and landowners. There was a difference of scale but not of principle. India could not be run without the people with local power. For decades, previous viceroys had believed that India was the ideal society in which to develop the purest democracy, the mother of all parliaments, Westminster. Minto did not believe this.

India was too big for British parliamentary democracy as practised in Westminster, with each member in theory knowing his constituency and even personalities in its 94,000 square miles. India was then 1.58 million square miles and Minto saw that different groups in India should have representative status. He also believed that those who would govern in any parliament should know more about their often scattered constituency. Minto believed that, by combining Indian and British political systems, a nurturing and early form of democracy could be created. Earlier viceroys had helped form groups such as Congress, which would become major political parties. This meant the emergence of the new generation of Indian council and group members who were the founders of what was not always to be a political system but would be the generation that took the reins of government from the British. Furthermore, here was the example that showed that India was governed directly and not from the viceroy's residence.

Just as Hamilton, as secretary of state, and Curzon had worked well together and Broderick and Curzon should have done, so Minto was supported by his secretary for India, Viscount Morley.[2]

Minto had been governor general of Canada for six years until 1904 and so he was used to colonial administration. He is remembered in India as reforming, with the support of Morley, the way Indians were brought into the various ruling bodies of their own country. So, for example, elected members, both Hindu and Muslim, joined the viceroy's council, all the provincial councils and the Legco, the legislative council.

This reform was in place by 1909 and once more reflected the political awareness of a middle class in India that had, especially following the development of the Indian National Council of the late 1880s, become an obvious part of the future governing of India. Discussions with those who thought through the possibility of independence one day were no longer seen as subversive or surprisingly progressive.

Morley saw reforms as best coming from the Indian government and put it that way when he talked with men like G. K. Gokhale. Gokhale (1866–1915) was a pioneer in Indian politics. At twenty-two, he was secretary of Sarajanik Sabha, the main political group in Bombay, and seven years later, in 1895, Gokhale became secretary of the Indian National Congress. It was in this role that he went to England to make clear to the British that the future of India was as an independent state. In London he met Morley and was back again to go through the Minto–Morley reforms. Gokhale was a moderate, though sometimes feared as a reactionary that he was not.

Minto could understand what would come, but many others in influential places in London and within the expatriate population in India condemned the ambitions of the Indians who saw independence as the next stage of India's development, not because there was an established political history

The Lord Hardinge, 1911–16.
Through Hardinge, India fell in
alongside British troops in the
First World War.

Winifred Selina Sturt, Baroness Hardinge.

ATTENTAT CONTRE LORD HARDINGE, VICE-ROI DES INDES

Hardinge was sitting on his elephant when a bomb was thrown, presumably at him. His shoulder was badly wounded, but he carried on as best he could. The elephant was fine.

(© Mary Evans Picture Library / © Illustration London News Ltd / Mary Evans Picture Library)

The Attempted Assassination of the Indian Viceroy

During the State Entry into Delhi, December 23, 1912

LORD HARDINGE--WOUNDED IN SHOULDER

LADY HARDINGE--UNHURT

The Lord Chelmsford, 1916–21, was the viceroy who had to explain the 1919 Amritsar massacre.
(© Topfoto.co.uk)

The Earl of Reading, 1921–26, was the first Jew to be viceroy of India, attorney general, ambassador to America and Lord Chief Justice.
(© Hulton Archie / Getty Images)

The Earl of Reading with his wife and the Maharajah of Patiala.
((© Keystone / Getty Images)

The Lord Irwin, 1926–31, the one British
politician who might have become Prime
Minister during the Second World War instead
of Churchill.
(Lord Irwin Lord Halifax (b/w photo), English Photographer,
(20th century) / Private Collection / © Look and Learn /
Elgar Collection / Bridgeman Images)

The Earl of Willingdon, 1931–36, was good at cricket.
(© Illustrated London News Ltd / Mary Evans Picture Library)

Lord and Lady Willingdon.
© Fox Photos / Hulton Archive / Getty Images)

The Viscount Wavell, 1943–47, was the Field Marshall who should not have been replaced.

The Viscount Mountbatten, 1947.

(above) Inspecting the troops. Mountbatten never did a quick march-past; he had an eye for a rumpled collar, an improper order of medal ribbons and a failure of officers to instil a sense of pride and modesty in valour.

(Keystone / Stringer / Getty Images)

(left) Gandhi recognised that Mountbatten was not impressed by a reputation that had done little for India other than to force it into something no one who cared beyond their own political ambitions could possibly desire.

(Topical Press Agency / Stringer / Getty Images)

The conference table: they all sit behind their name plates, but Mountbatten knows them all and their worth. He has the inkstand, the symbol of agreement.
(Keystone / Stringer / Getty Images)

By the authority of a viceregal handshake comes the promise of success and tragedy.
(Universal History Archive / Getty Images)

but because a gradual movement towards independence had more to do with the way Indians existed under British rule.

The British in the immediate pre-First World War period could not be seen as cruel frustrators of what would later be called human rights, but it was clear that the reforms rehearsed in the United Kingdom that were creating universal suffrage as well as shifts in the class system were not going on in the same manner in India. One reason was that leading Indians themselves, through the caste system and an inbred trust in superior and inferior groupings in public and private lives, had no intention of bringing India into a movement that supposedly hoped that all born equal would become equal.

Liberals who championed the cause of Indians to enjoy better conditions had only to look at the viceroys before them and those to come to be reminded that equality was a mark of good nature perhaps, but most certainly did not begin with equality of birth and all that followed. When Gokhale went to South Africa to talk to Mohandas Gandhi it was about rights for Indians, not hopes for independence. No matter how many looked forward to independence at this stage (1912), the emerging Indian political leaders accepted that nothing in India was in place that would allow any chance of a peaceful transition to even self-rule, never mind the full hope of democracy. All political thinking is radical although easy labelling of left, right and centre politics obscures that impression. Gokhale was none of this; he was, in modern labelling, a moderate.

Where Gandhi let the British all but consume themselves by their reaction to him as a 'dangerous' figure (which he was), men like Gokhale introduced modern politics into the Indian system while at the same time understanding the dangers of practising extremism; not an easy task in a society that could rouse half a subcontinent at rumours of British arrogance.

Gokhale is not enough recognised as one of the fathers of modern political thinking in India.

Minto's reforms meant the expansion of all the legislative councils in India and for them the right to debate major issues including the budget. The legislative councils brought Indians into the administration of India with everyone seeing where this could eventually lead to constitutional reform and, one day, independence. If British policy was to change Indians into people who followed the British code of society, then among a certain class it was successful. Necessarily this was no over-night transition.

Firstly, the British control of India had been brought about over more than two and a half centuries. Secondly, many of the families and individuals who became westernised were probably from parents whose family had gradually adopted western styles over two or maybe three generations. This change of style among certain Indians meant also that a group in society did not see itself as other Indians saw themselves. There was a period in the nineteenth century when an aspiring elite was rethinking what it meant to be Indian and indeed, what India had become. Although the college system was, by the mid-nineteenth century, well established in India, with some in Calcutta having university status, necessarily the best students were also going to London.

The sons of the best families, properly educated, would become classical scholars, medics and lawyers, practising in London teaching hospitals and called to the capital's legal temples. An inevitable consequence of this was a continuing comparison of style and opportunity. A son could not return from London to India without an image of the British middle and upper middle classes. The emergence of a middle class in any society produces a mainstay that can cope with social turmoil and act as a centrepoint from which society recovers when damaged. In India, above all colonies, the influence of middle-class thinking, its combination with professional and commercial levels of Indian society helped to create a unique colony; one that came nearest to creating the original ideal of a colonial little England.

An obvious danger as seen by the British was the authority of this Indian middle class. Certainly in nineteenth-century India there were those British who could not imagine themselves being subjected to jurisprudence exercised by, say, Indian magistrates. Thus Lord Ripon in the 1880s was effectively bowing to the insecurities of the British in their own raj.[3]

Half a century earlier, Macaulay had floated the idea that educating Indians would inevitably suggest to them the possibilities of being independent from the British.[4] By the end of the nineteenth century the whole politics of Europe, and certainly Britain, were changing. An emerging socialism in Britain would early in the twentieth century lead to the Labour Party. Political thought was being exercised in areas previously safe from radicals. The question of home rule in Ireland was not one of the safe havens. The move to Irish independence was more than a gymnasium to exercise pamphleteers and idealists. Home rule was a big political issue, as any supporter of Gladstone and those who followed in all parties would testify. The educated Indian civil servant and professional could not but miss a temptation to compare the Irish home rule movement with real possibilities for India.

Britain and India were advancing towards the great debate on independence without the crude proposition that imperialism had had its day. Few had even defined imperialism as a transition from separate identities that come together when one conquers the other. Dadabhai Naoroji, in 1901, was writing about British India being under a 'dishonourable' unBritish system of government. He appealed to the British instinct of fair play for a change that would not mean the two nations going their own and different ways; instead, he encouraged an avoidance of an explosion of the British Empire and envisaged a form of self-government that would lead to 'a great and glorious future for Britain and India'. By 1904, Naoroji, who had served in the House of Commons and was still at odds with the Curzon view of how to develop India within the British influence, declared that India would remain a land of hopeless poverty. He saw self-government as being the answer. Self-government did not mean independence just as self-government does not mean an independent Northern Ireland. Naoroji was accepted by Curzon, who disagreed with the argument but saw its inevitability.

If the British were to remain in India would they have to change the way in which the subcontinent was governed: would there be an extended form of self-government or increased provincial responsibility that would serve both interests? European economic philosophy at this time (1900–1914) did not influence Indian nationalist leaders in the way it might have, probably because in practical terms to transform the British way of justice and the Indian way of life into a equal partnership that the the British would accept could not be accomplished. Moreover, many of the Indian leaders were part of the British system and understood that India could not be left to her own devices without a remarkable transition of power, justice and commercial authority. There was not the system to achieve that. The economics of India as a developing nation were quite separate from the political progress to a point where it was difficult to even guess how such progress would develop. Simply, nationalist leaders in India had no practical applications of power for India in this pre-First World War period.

No colony had at that time alternatives to the imperial systems. Even with the enormous advances in political and economic thought and the British willingness to employ them, even the two decades of independence after the Second World War, people forgot that independence was about freedom. Many new leaders took to the seats, desks and habits of the departing British and the people they had freed remained with nothing. There was in pre-First World War India a reluctance to press for self-government, never mind independence, because the nationalists who wanted both were not confident that they had the ability to do it and were not sure of what they could do and what support they had. The leaders were in a minority. This was understandable: other than the events in eighteenth-century America, no one had attempted to gain freedom from British imperialism. (Neither Australia nor Canada were victims of imperialism, nor did Naoroji travel with the opinion that self-government in the British white colonies was industrially, economically and politically more advanced than the British-governed Indians).

Self-government and even Dominion status seemed such an obvious way for India. But opposition and determination for political change comes from a small radical group, not from a population. Countries seek independence because a small, educated and politically motivated group says the time is right and that they have the means and wit to take up the government of their people. In India in the early years of the twentieth century, this confidence and capability was emerging but had not yet established itself, so there were idealists and political activists, but none had the confidence or support of the people. People have to be governed and only feel safe when they are strongly governed.

During the Curzon, Minto and Hardinge period, Indians felt safely governed and none had looked elsewhere, or could look further than their own people, to find the alternative. This was the apogee of the British Empire. When the Great War was done, India through educated, single-minded voices would make its demands. Thirty years on, India would be free. A new generation of viceroys kept the plumes and elephants but the political science of India and British imperialism was being written virtually day by day. There was no established text to draw upon.

The natural progression of Minto from Scottish castle to India via the governor's seat in Canada and kindly friends at court is a reminder of the steady tread of privilege. This was so accepted because it was with few exceptions the likeliest source of educated, experienced people and commanding figures who were needed to send off with the minimum briefing to run the British way across the world.

The aristocracy or something close to it provided a ready supply of available people used to command and superiority and with enough money to spend five years in post with some style. Stylish entertainment and comfort among the most important in far flung empire posts was essential management of that empire. There was not enough supply of any other class to do the jobs in Calcutta or New South Wales. It was unthinkable to appoint someone viceroy or governor unless he had this background; unless he had reached the most senior rank in the army he would not know how to do it. An appointment such as Minto's did not rouse bureaucratic objections or suspicions that all might go wrong. The latter was par for the imperial course anyway. The two camps, pro-Curzon and anti-Curzon, were examples of the never-ending debate on that subject. But Minto was different inasmuch as he had immediately stepped aside from the diplomatic line in Canada, where he had told everyone in Government House to smarten up and adopt more formal styles than his predecessor Aberdeen. It made no difference to the issues that needed to be solved or their outcomes, but it meant that the people in London who had supported his appointment had not known him well enough. His appointment to India had supposedly been covered by the promotion of Morley, who would keep an eye. He did – on his own legacy. Reform in India would always have a date on it and a name. Morley made sure that his would not be smudged by Minto.

Morley saw India from the banks of the Thames; he believed India did not quite grasp the possibilities for the future. Minto saw India from where he stood every morning and believed, correctly, that London did not understand.

Gone were the days when a governor's position was put on paper and took weeks to reach the East India Company directors. Communications were now faster and clearer but did not always mean differences and confusions were resolved. The language of the diplomatic pouch has always been a mysterious text that was tacitly encouraged by the India and Colonial desks, who adopted the code that it is often best to do nothing. The argument being that by the time something is ready to be done, rather like Schleswig-Holstein, the question is forgotten. This was not the way of working for Minto and in a single act he was responsible for something that would later be tracked back as the cause of the tragic circumstances of 1947 and Partition.

Minto's diplomatic history suggested that he became involved with causes and did so when he displayed a certain naivety over the rights and wrongs. He did so in Canada when exhibiting an almost childlike belief in the two parties involved in trying to settle differences over the Alaskan boundary. When what he thought was an honourable settlement fell through, he believed England's lord chief justice Lord Alverstone had produced a convenient ruling rather than a judicial settlement. He had it out with Alverstone in private but never believed it had been settled honourably. In India, Minto's preference for the Muslim view was thought, again, to be naive. His reaction to potential dangerous sedition following a breakdown in talks between the moderate and radical wings of the Indian National Congress was deemed simplistic. Minto's life was threatened, or so his people perceived. He pushed forward the 1910 Press Act to restrict what could be printed and political leaders were imprisoned. Morley in London, an ineffectual redoubt, thought Minto overreacted and was quite wrong, but he never put up any alternative plans to forestall uprisings. Radicals attacked minor officials who were easy to come by, but nothing terrible had to be recorded. Minto's position on relations with the Muslims had already alerted Morley and the India Office that Minto might not have been the wisest choice for India.

The Indian Muslims were worried by the influence of Gokhale and the Hindu majority in Congress and how much more they would get from the constitutional reforms. Minto had the answer. He invited the Muslims to the summer residence in Shimla in October 1906 and heard them out. The Muslim argument was concise: in all reforms the Muslims should have two preferences. The viceroy should consider that Muslims must be given separate considerations in any reforms because their religious persuasion meant they had positions that could suffer if they were thrown into a general reorganisation. For example, being a part of joint decision making procedures could mean their own followers might be at the least suspicious that the Muslim interest was not being followed. Furthermore, Muslims felt they had beliefs, traditions and ways that would either be overlooked in a reorganisation or even banned.

Secondly, the Muslims wanted a separate vote to guarantee a Muslim would be elected who would look after their interests. Minto saw no reason to reject these views. He was either very smart politically or overwhelmingly sympathetic to the Muslim view. Having agreed to their demands, the viceroy now had the loyalty of Muslims who immediately set up as the All-India Muslim League, in direct opposition to Congress. This was 1906 and to demonstrate the wide reach of the organization, it was called the All India Muslim League, although it was later knows and referred to as the Muslim League. The confrontation that culminated in 1947 between the two religious-based political movements was indirectly Minto's doing. He would know nothing of 1947. Minto, the epitome of muscular aristocratic Christianity who went out to rule the Empire with the same instinct and hopefully decency with which he ran his estate, died in Minto Castle in 1914.

In 1910, when Minto went, Charles Hardinge arrived. This was much to the delight of Curzon, who believed that Hardinge would carry on where he had left off. It did not quite happen that way. In five years the role of viceroy had shifted. Certainly, Hardinge was not from the same tray as Curzon or most of the earlier viceroys. There were plenty of titles, both military and aristocratic. His father was the second Viscount Hardinge and his mother Lavinia was the daughter of the third earl of Lucan, who, even as a field marshal, had done badly in the Valley of Death during the Crimean War. His paternal grandfather was also a field marshal and in the 1840s had been governor general of India. Charles Hardinge thought that being viceroy of India would do very well for him, but he accepted the disadvantage of not having much family money and no serious aristocracy in the blood. Indeed on that latter matter, there was certainly a disadvantage. He married his first cousin Winifred Selina, which was not thought to be a good idea. The wedding went ahead, partly thanks to lobbying by the Princess of Wales, the wife of the future Edward VII to whom Winifred became lady-in-waiting. This royal connection, once more through the wife of a viceroy, became a fortunate friendship for a man who was enormously able as a diplomat in European embassies (Berlin, Paris, Constantinople, Bucharest and Sofia). In each post he excelled his calling, in spite of his apparent formal manner.

Orpen's portrait captures a man of lean, unimaginative formality and one who allowed nothing to compromise his sense of duty. In 1896, Hardinge went to the embassy in Tehran and learned for himself the practical and not always trusted rules of British relations with Tsarist Russia in Asia. Grasping how that strained understanding between Russia and the British worked at the most delicate level, Hardinge was sent to St Petersburg in 1898 as secretary to the embassy. Here he exchanged the views of one monarch for another, albeit cousins. The Hardinges were well received at the Russian court and there was immediate agreement about a threat by Germany to European peace, such as it had been.

Although his chance in India was still a few years off, Hardinge then moved back to London. Here, with broad experience at seemingly every important level of diplomacy (it had also included a spell in Washington), Hardinge in 1903 was appointed, in spite of much internal Foreign Office opposition, as one of four under-secretaries at the FO. It was said that the King wanted him and so got him and made it clear that Hardinge was a confidential advisor. So high was Hardinge's stock that he was sent to St Petersburg as ambassador. It could not have been at a tougher time. Russia was at war with Japan, Russian warships were attacking British merchant ships and the fishing fleet was also attacked by Russia's Baltic Fleet off the Dogger Bank. Hardinge's diplomatic and political skills were tested. He enjoyed the examination, but then he was exceptionally successful by securing peace with Russia and France and strengthening an alliance with Japan. He had effectively laid the ground for the 2007 Anglo-Russia Alliance. Next stop was the Foreign Office itself as permanent secretary, in other words head of the FO. This may have seemed an odd appointment, when everything abut Hardinge suggested that he did not care much for foreigners. His entire professional philosophy was based on the notion that the British did things better and why should they not when in fact they were better?

This then was the man sent to take up his right to govern India, as a Hardinge had once gone as governor general. He was now Baron Hardinge of Penshurst in Kent and arrived in India with an air of self-confidence. India was the most complex problem he had ever imagined. Plotting and charting solutions over dinner with salt spoons, forks and napkin rings was not going to work in India. In addition to minor successes in further technical education, opportunities in the civil service and two new universities – one Hindu, one Muslim – Hardinge needed to draw a deep political breath for the real conundrum: what to do about the seemingly irresolvable trouble caused by Curzon's partition of Bengal. Hardinge was confronted by a consequence of one of Curzon's 'triumphs'. Curzon had divided Bengal to stop internecine warfare. Muslims on one side. Hindus on the other. The separation of the two was a short-term measure and when Hardinge arrived in India Bengali Hindus were running bombings and even assassinations. There was, however, a solution in the offing. Hardinge grabbed it. George V planned to visit India and celebrate his succession in a grand durbar.

In much secrecy Hardinge, on the advice of one of his officials in India and in particular Sir John Jenkins, decided that the British had to remove central government out of Calcutta to Delhi. Calcutta had always been the capital of British India and the senior British governor of the East India Company had lived there[5]. A century before Curzon, during the second Maratha War, the British East India Company army defeated the Maratha in what became known as the Battle of Delhi and retook the town in the Siege of Delhi during the Sepoy Rebellion in 1858. It became a district province of Punjab[6]. But the capital of the British India Empire remained Calcutta. Now, in 1911, Calcutta was the most dangerous place in India for that empire.

In modern times, it would have been as controversial as moving government from London to, say, Birmingham or Manchester. But why get out of Calcutta? The growing opposition to British rule was in Calcutta. Curzon had split Bengal in the belief that that divisions between Hindu and Muslim would be tempered and that would reduce the direct threat to Britain's authority. That threat was increasing. Jenkins suggested that Britain's capital in India should be moved to Delhi and that Curzon's divided Bengal should be reunited. The decision to recommend this to the India Office in London had to come from the viceroy. Hardinge's first instruction was to demand secrecy in his own office. If the proposal leaked, there would surely be a violent reaction in Calcutta. The spectre of 1857 was never far from a viceroy's thinking even though a full-scale rebellion was unlikely.

Hardinge was a practical soldiering viceroy. He plotted and planned for unwanted contingencies. He was being pushed for a response because the obvious time to break the secret was the pending arrival of the King for his durbar. Therefore, again in secret, George V had to be approached for his permission to do such a thing. Hardinge, as so many of his predecessors, was able to test unofficial opinion as well as the formal channels. The viceroys had the best-connected wives at court in the British Isles.

Hardinge's next question was about Delhi itself. Could it cope with the exodus from Calcutta? Delhi was certainly a fine place but where were the grand imperial palaces, buildings, department stores, guest houses and the very residence for the viceroy? Was Delhi ready to be the centre of the British Empire? His staff went back to their desks. They returned. Yes, they agreed, it would take time. How much time? Not weeks. No. Months? No. Years? Yes. Did the perceived crisis allow them years? No. But the move had to begin. As for Delhi, the great event would be the building of a new Delhi. Using the imaginations of Edwin Lutyens and Herbert Baker could take how long? Years. How many? No one knew at the time. The answer turned out to be 'twenty years'. In the meantime, Hardinge had to think through how this was to be explained.

The British had created Calcutta. It had heroic and recent memories including the Black Hole and the punishments that followed. Curzon had ordered the Victoria Memorial to be built, not in Delhi but Calcutta. Its Britishness was indisputable. But the decision was clear in Hardinge's mind. As he wrote to Lord Crewe, his political master in London:

'It has long been recognized to be a serious anomaly that we govern located as it is on the eastern extremity of our possessions'.

There was little other than public formality in that sentiment. But then it came clean. The anti-British sentiment was mostly in Calcutta. It was expected to grow. Calcutta would still be the centre of trading and commercial fixing. Ironically, it was the return of India to the people that damaged Calcutta the most.

The centre of the empire was on the move. The matter was kept a secret until George V's durbar in Delhi. The fury and the excitement came from both sides in equal parts. The Hindus, with all that Delhi meant to them, were pleased. The commercial interests in Calcutta were displeased. *The Times* of London reported on 28 December 1911 that 'The commercial classes view with apprehension the removal of the Government from all contact with mercantile and manufacturing interests.' Ironically, it was the return of India to the people thirty-six years later that would damage Calcutta. When the nation was partitioned raw materials on which Calcutta industry had thrived, such as jute, were in the new state, Pakistan. Calcutta had few choices and a new poverty appeared almost overnight. Now, on 12 December 1911 in the grounds of Delhi's Red Fort, George V announced the move. India's premier city of commerce had lost the undoubted cachet of being the nation's capital; it was as if the Bourse had lost Paris or the Stock Exchange had lost London.

Hardinge and Curzon, who had not been warned over the move, had been close friends. Curzon even believed that his unachieved plans for India would be successful through Hardinge's understanding of the wisdom of where Curzon had seen India travelling. But in just six years, India was a more threatening place for the British. Curzon could not forgive what he saw as Hardinge's treachery. Of Hardinge and his advisors he told the House of Lords, 'They desire to escape the somewhat heated atmosphere of Bengal.' He was exactly right. Hardinge would agree. However, Curzon's sentiment was unhelpful. Curzon was right to point out that the move of government into the centre of India was abandoning the insights, influences and long experiences of Calcutta as a commercial, business and therefore well informed community. In Delhi, the viceroy would, according to Curzon, be 'shut off' from the rest of India. Hardinge might have believed that rebels and even assassins would be contained or scattered in abandoned Calcutta. A year later he was to find this not so.

Delhi was Hardinge's project. He had not much wanted Lutyens and Baker and pestered them both. The clash of authority and strong personality was testing. Hardinge enjoyed detail but could not have imagined the amount that had to be made public soon after the King's announcement. Government and people were watching. What was happening? Who to ask? Who to say? Who to do things? Who to pay? It was an achievement that could only have been brought about by military-style leadership and more than a century of faceless bureaucracy working at full pelt with thousands of hands at every command. They had just twelve months to get the government ready to move to Delhi. In 1947 a similar energy appeared but with tragic consequences rather than the triumph of two days before Christmas 1912. On this day, Hardinge and his vice-reine arrived at Delhi station for the opening of the new city capital. What followed could well have been a tragedy.

The couple mounted their state elephant and headed towards the Red Fort with rolling gait. An easy target. A Bengali atop a roof along the procession threw a needle bomb. One of Hardinge's servants was killed, Hardinge nearly so. The bomb hit him full in the back and neck, ripping him open from shoulder to backbone. Hardinge, almost as every film director would have had it, drew attention to his bloodstained speech and ordered an aide to have the speech read. He was then rushed to the new viceregal residence for surgery. Hardinge survived. He made a recovery of sorts. Further sadness was to come soon. Winifred Hardinge died in 1914 during an operation for a cancerous tumour. Their daughter Diamond took her mother's place as vicereine, but it was the best that Hardinge could do to stay until recalled to London; agony was greater because he was asked to stay on a year and, out of duty, did so.

It was at this period that Hardinge's second dilemma as viceroy had been tested. He of all people might have been expected to show military judgement. Some since have thought he did not and in a matter that extended beyond India. As in the years immediately before the Mutiny, there was a matter of what could be done with the Indian army, what might it be used for and, particularly, in what state was it to answer both questions.

In 1910 General Douglas Haig arrived in India as Chief of the Indian General Staff. Kitchener had been followed as commander-in-chief by General Garrett O'Moore Creagh VC (his Cross was won during the second Afghan war 1878–80). Here then was some new thinking about the Indian army that was in an unhealthy and not particularly well-trained condition. Haig's view for some time had been that India was under threat not from Russia, as British policy for decades had supposed, but from Germany. Haig believed Germany would take over India to become the new world empire. Creagh supported Haig's analysis, which included the belief that France could be overcome and thus leave Europe uncertain. Turkey, then, could be brought in on Germany's side with the promise of finishing the German–Ottoman project of a railway from Berlin to Baghdad.

This was not an uncommon view in the British army. Where did India come into this? Haig's belief was that the Dominions (Australia, New Zealand and Canada) would be called up immediately into Europe and so would the Indian army because the British army was too light and too thin on the ground. According to Haig, it was very likely to be decimated and no amount of territorial reserves could replace the regular troops. At this stage America was not considered as a viable army.

When Hardinge arrived in India, Haig and Creagh told him at their first meeting that the Indian army should be re-funded to see where the money was needed, retrained because it was untrained and given increased manpower and up-to-date equipment. Hardinge, who understood the army, dismissed Haig as harebrained. Hardinge believed there would be a war in Europe and he thought it could start as early as 1913. But he did not believe that the Indian army should get involved because his policy as viceroy was based on the defence of India, not Europe. The 1907 Anglo-Russia Treaty and the 1902 Anglo-Japanese Treaty (renewed in 1911) were, he believed, sufficient to protect British interests. If there were to be threats, Hardinge saw them coming from Afghanistan, the Pathans and maybe China. Hardinge, like most newly installed viceroys, was thinking about spending budgets on social reforms in India. Social policies made Indians happier people and so reduced chances of insurrection – except in Bengal. The reform would improve the standing of his own regime as well as the general view of the British. The quickest way to do that would be to do just the opposite to what Haig demanded.

When Hardinge arrived in Calcutta, about half of government spending went on the army. He was going to cut rather than add troop numbers. After all, Hardinge saw no peril other than insurrection. London agreed.

There was a further difference in opinion that had nothing to do with the chances of war. It had more to do with who would, or could, fight whom. British troops who were not white (so the Indian army) were not allowed to fight white troops in case a black soldier killed a white soldier. That, so the belief ran, would suggest whites were inferior. Indian soldiers, who had been deployed overseas, for example in the Boer War, had been kept away from confrontations with whites. Herbert Asquith, prime minister when Hardinge went to India and Crewe, secretary of state for India, both supported the colour bar rule. Therefore, Hardinge did not have to seriously consider Haig's case. Haig was appalled and resigned from the legislative council wondering how such a great man as Hardinge could be so blind to Germany's intentions. How was it that others felt the same, for example, the Army in India Committee? Hardinge's position was clear. Two infantry divisions, about 20,000 men and a cavalry brigade, could come under command for a war in Europe but only if they were deployed to Africa to fill in for troops redeployed to Europe.

Hardinge had accepted that there could be war by 1913. Curiously, he seems to have changed his position on deployment once war was declared. He offered troops to fight in the Middle East and saw a value in a European campaign that may have done well for the Indian army's reputation. None of this enthusiasm, if that is what it was, was tempered by the clear inefficiency of the Indian army. Hardinge and the commander of the Indian 6th Division, General Sir John Nixon, persuaded London to let them send the army to fight in the Mesopotamia Campaign that was appearing to be going far better than it turned out to be. The objective was simple enough: advance on Baghdad.

Like many simple military objectives, this project was edged with treachery. The 6th Division engaged in the battle of Ctesiphon in November 1915. Of the 14,000 Indian troops deployed, 4,600 were killed. Of those who were left and survived their wounds or disease, most surrendered to the Turks in April 1916. A commission of inquiry in London into the conduct of the army was critical of Hardinge and, as was the way of these things, he was appointed ambassador to Paris, the place and post he had longed for. As a postscript, Hardinge became a special constable during the 1926 General Strike. He died in loneliness in 1944. Such was the end of plumes, wounds and living another age in another age. Hardinge was never imaginative, never likely to be anything else that matched up to it. Thesiger, who followed, was just the opposite.

Frederic John Napier Thesiger was born at a good London address (Eaton Square), did well at Winchester, did better at Oxford and, better still, captained Oxford at cricket. A blue was always better than a first, but he took that too (law). He succeeded his father as Lord Chelmsford in 1905. His eldest son was killed in Mesopotamia. He was part of the governing aristocracy, the people you know and they know from birth will get big jobs and who mostly were good at them. He was a governor of the London School Board, governor of Queensland, governed New South Wales, governed Australia and was viceroy of India. He followed the sad figure of Hardinge and so was told to go to India and calm things down. After all, there was a war on. This was 1916. Gerald Kelly's 1922 portrait showed him as most remembered him: tall, elegant, suited to frock-coated uniforms and medals and gold and the sort of man they expected in India. However, the elegance of a new viceroy, the style of his vicereine Frances who was through her mother a Marlborough, did not settle India in days gone by.

Chelmsford's time as viceroy could be counted as the very beginning of the end of the British Empire. Indians would have a public statement from the British government that self-government of India was possible. And as Chelmsford finished his time in Delhi, so Mahatma[7] Gandhi moved to the national stage and began his nationwide campaign and tours demanding reform and Swaraj, self-rule, independence.

Chelmsford was to keep on track the dinners, balls, meetings and privy tea dances as if no war would touch India and any misunderstandings were just that. He set up committees to look at army efficiency records, raise the standing of the Indian officer corps by having them opened for full king's commissions. The radical change that once stated could not be retracted came not from the viceroy but London. Chelmsford wanted his executive council in Delhi to think about the single important point in future Anglo-Indian relations: what was it that the British intended for India?

Had anyone thought that imperial rule would continue? If so, for how long? If so, to what aim? Was the idea that the British would always be in India and the Indians would be expected to live with that? Or, should they be thinking not so far off and should they, the council, be thinking there was an ultimate plan for Britain and India and what had to happen to reach that goal? Everyone at that meeting read the code. Some more acutely than Chelmsford himself, who knew that people in London were talking about the long-term ambition of Britain for India and so he should be thinking about it as well and sending council thoughts back to London.

The council had thoughts, not everyone agreed, but a summary was prepared and sent to the India Office. The proposal sent to London included legislative authorities with more powers and bigger constituencies; more places for Indians on legislative councils; more Indians everywhere in the public services. The paper was not badly received.

The India Office particularly agreed for bigger representation for Indians but on the understanding that there should be considerable responsibilities and they had to be assured. Power and responsibility was the watch-phrase. The India Office's reaction to the proposals from Delhi was delayed. As ever, there was a war on, Austen Chamberlain was leaving the Office and the new man, Edwin Montagu, was not quite in the chair. Montagu's views on India were well known. In the summer of 1917 he had told the Commons that India was poorly administered and that he would back with a declaration on how Britain saw India and on the future of the Anglo-Indian relationship. In August 1917, Montagu was back in the House. He took with him what has since been called the Montagu Declaration. The open title clearly stated Britain's intentions, or was supposed to:

'Increasing association of Indians in every branch of administration, and the gradual development of self-governing Institutions with a view to the progressive realization of responsible governments in India as an Integral part of the British Empire.'

Here was a declaration that was the start of the road to 1947 but was not intended to lead the way it did. The British were not washing their hands of India; they had no intention of leaving.

The British had no plan to break up the empire or abandon ideas about the global role they saw for themselves. Montagu and his India Office and Chelmsford and the British ruling caste in India were not striking the camp of imperialism that they mostly saw as working well and expected to do so for the foreseeable future. What they wanted most of all was better government made possible by bringing an educated English-speaking Indian middle class into key points of government. They were repeating the understanding of so many of the diaries and papers of late-nineteenth-century viceroys: India is too big, too complex to rule without the right Indians taking part, balancing the anomalies and inconsistencies as well as the sheer complexity of India, not least the need to maintain some peaceful existence between Muslims and Hindus.

In the British autumn of 1917, with the war in Europe not yet done, Montagu took his declaration and notes to India to talk them through with the people who would have to bring India together with what the British were thinking for the future. For the first time, in November we could see the reality that agreement would rest very much in the hands of two people Montagu met that month, Gandhi and Jinnah. These two men could begin to answer the question: could Hindu India and Muslim India govern together? From these visits came Montagu's Indian Constitutional Reforms, to be published in July 1918 and from that document came the truly historic Government of India Act the following year. This Act brought together the three documents that would be the first Magna Carta of India. Was there total acceptance? Congress split. The nationalists called it unworthy of England to offer and India to accept and wanted the reforms to go much further towards nationalism. The moderates said it was just fine. Many, especially among British Conservatives, knew for sure that the reforms gave too much away. Praise heaped and criticism thrown had been predicted.

The British were not being generous. There was a single purpose for the move towards self-government: they could no longer govern India. Equally, they could see the advantages of staying with India in some form to take advantage of the economic and commercial potential as well as having some Dominion status that would, as in Australia, throw the running of the country onto the Indians but allow the closest of ties. For example, there could still be a governor general, thus tying India to the British monarchy. The guideline was in the Montagu–Chelmsford Proposal; no matter what was agreed on devolution of powers, the viceroy would always report to London and not to an Indian legislative council. The Crown still ruled but recognised in its Constitutional Reforms Summary that the Montagu and Chelmsford workable proposal was not 'lost' in the sometimes dense evidence and discussion that would follow.

'Far-reaching changes in the principles and framework of the Government of India are recommended to His Majesty's Government.'

There was, as Chelmsford had all along made clear to the government in London, to be no doubt that the time had come for change that would mean India having a constitutional independence of some practical sort and which all Indians would understand. Edwin Montagu and Chelmsford met at

Shimla (then still Simla) on 22 April 1919 and signed the '300 octavo' pages that would be the basis of India's constitutional step-change. Signed and sealed, the Montagu–Chelmsford Proposal was packed off to parliament as Command 9109 that, among its radical contributions to the future running of India, had the explicit account that whatever appeared, the viceroy was always responsible for the conduct and administration of India.

'The proposals include a great extension of local self-government so as to train the extended electorates; a substantial measure of self-government; the provinces; developments for better representation of Indian needs and desires in the Government of India and the All-India legislature; and means for continuously enlarging, in the light of experience and at regular stages, the element of responsibility to Indian Electorates.'

Chelmsford saw the first question would answer all questions: what authority do I have? Central and provincial councils were getting more authority and the emphasis was on provincial legislative councils and their extended elected members. The outline was in document, Rights of the Central and Provincial Governments ; those rights included for central government defence, railways, postal, foreign affairs and trade. The provincial councils would have control over police, justice, education, public works etc. The divisions between what central government had and what provincial government took over were in line with all divisions of powers when a colony without becoming independent assumed self-government. India was still a British colony with a governor, but running the colony to its liking with the exception of anything that had British and international implications, such as defence.

The importance of the Chelmsford–Montagu Proposal is obvious – moving government into the hands of more people in areas where they could see the result of local decisions in which most Indians had some say. The document was proud of this in such a way that government had to defy it rather than express an indifference:

'. . . the Government will have the advantage of considering any suggestions to which its publication may give rise . . . proposals can only benefit by reasoned criticism both in England and India, official and non-official alike.'

Chelmsford's experience was that the proposal would be seen as too radical by many in London. The persuasion of Montagu and his India Office would be all important because he understood the politics of government. He knew when to strike, when not to push for debate and when to time a public announcement to India without government being ready for it, but reluctant to be seen dismissing it. Here was a political gymnasium Chelmsford, for all his experience and friendships, did not always understand. What he did understand that too many in government failed to was that although the proposals were designed to make India easier to administer, to demonstrate greater opportunities for the Indians (while recognising that the viceroy's word was always final in dispute), not all Indians would jump at the opportunities. In a caste-based society, with religious as well as social divides deeper than ever, there would as a consequence of the proposals be suspicions among Indians that already-too-powerful groups in Indian society would get even more power. Others very simply did not want change. Chelmsford insisted that Britain should make it clear that she was proud to be 'in

India'. The India Office commentary of the proposal text
made that clear as could be:

> 'In writing of the gravity of the task they have attempted, the
> Secretary of State and the viceroy observe that England may
> be proud of her record in India. Because the work already done
> has called forth in India a new life, we must found her
> Government on the co-operation of the people, and make
> such changes in the existing order as will meet the more
> spacious days to come.'

With the India Office writing about 'the spacious days to
come' we have the inspiration of Chelmsford and Montagu
attempting something of a diplomatic and constitutional coup.
The government had urged a solution on the future of India.
The secretary of state and the serving viceroy were proposing
that anything was possible, but to give British dissenters an opt-
out from full independence. This is what the viceroy's final
decision meant.

There was a further distraction for the British government:
this was 1918. The First World War, although winding down,
remained the British government's foremost subject for consideration and had a considerable impact in India. Some would
have hoped the proposal could gather dust and little consideration. Montagu suggested that the government had not read
any of the 300 words because of the war, but would do.

> 'owing to their heavy preoccupation with the immediate work
> of the war, His Majesty's Government have not yet been able
> to consider the Report and to formulate their conclusions upon
> the proposals contained in it.'

The Chelmsford–Montagu Proposal was, designed to introduce self-government, but not immediately. There was, considering other events including the Great War, little hurry to tussle with the extraordinary document, particularly the thus far little-examined subject of protecting the rights of minorities. There was an acceptance that a new Government of India Bill would go on the statute book (it did in 1919) but for the moment the execution of war was of prime importance to lawmakers. Considering the high numbers of Indians who had fought alongside the British in the 1914–18 war, it was unsurprising that in India there was a greater expectation of the legislation going forward and importantly, greater expectations for concessions in that Bill. Thus, the political leadership in India were never expected to give the proposals a warm welcome and the ways in which the British limited discussion, including curbs on the press, confirmed the British view that they could go no further and the largely Indian (Muslim and Hindu) view that they felt short-changed.

'. . . It is there and not in Delhi or Whitehall that the ultimate decision of India's future will be taken. The liberty of the world must be won before our deliberations over the liberalizing of Indian political institutions can acquire any tangible meaning.'

Here then was Chelmsford, saying the war had to be won before India's future could be given full attention. There was too a greater thought: between the 1880s, including the failure of the 1884 Berlin Conference, and 1914 and the start of the First World War, New Imperialism was attempting to rearrange unarranged territory, especially in Africa. The British, German and French argument in this period was an act of supreme political cant when some of them claimed that carving up Africa – a continent ten times the size of India – was a grave responsibility that would bring civilisation to Africans. The real consideration was to asset-strip the land and the people. Taking over a relatively small country with a largely ill-educated people rarely able to defend themselves was straightforward colonialism. India was an increasingly politically aware, industrialised, educated and potentially easily armed society. India was becoming an unstable asset in the Crown's jewel case. Handing more power to India was nothing to do with the British stepping aside from being an imperial power. It was tidying up what it hoped to be the Dominion book. The India Office declaration that Indians better understood the altruism of the British was in its 1918 summary of the proposals:

> 'The people as a whole are in genuine sympathy with the cause of the Allies, and the educated classes have never faltered in their allegiance thereto. It is observed that speeches of English and American statesmen, proclaiming the liberalizing aims of the Allies, have had much effect upon political opinion in India, and have contributed to give new force and vitality to the demand for self-government, which was making itself more widely heard among the progressive section of the people.'

There is no evidence that the claim that the people 'as a whole' were not sympathetic to the British at war in Europe. However, 'as a whole' suggests a minority view in India and importantly, among some of the millions of Indians outside India, especially in Europe and the United States. An example of the opposition outside India to the British raj was seen in the work of Pandit Ram Chandra, the president of the Ghadar

Party and constant challenger of the writings and speeches of the viceroy.

The Ghadar Party was an anti-British movement of Punjabi Sikhs in the United States and Canada active before the First World War and then afterwards until 1948, by which time many senior members had between the wars become patriotic and even pro-British. Members of Ghadar produced plans during the First World War with help from the German Foreign Ministry and its consulate in San Francisco and the nascent IRA to overthrow the British in India while they were concentrating on the war with Germany. The thrust of the movement was to inspire mutiny in the British Indian Army that extended from Punjab to the Singaporean Strait. They dreamed of 1857, this time with German help. The trigger date for the new mutiny was February 1915 as the British went into something close to meltdown over their political and military failures. The Liberal government was replaced by a coalition. Winston Churchill left the Cabinet. The assault on Gallipoli was launched, the Second Battle of Ypres began, the liner *Lusitania* was sunk by a German u-boat, the Zeppelin raids on British cities started and there was a mutiny in Singapore. However, British intelligence was not entirely at a loose end. The Ghadar Party and what became known as the Hindu–Germany conspiracy were too widespread and the conspirators too obvious in their public feelings for even newly formed British intelligence to ignore reports coming into London from agents among their governors and the viceroy's office and, most convincingly, from British planters and patriotic Indians, whose temperament was totally opposite to the Sikhs, especially those in America. The anti-raj movement was not to be ignored nor its leaders dismissed as of no consequence. These rebels included hard personalities such as Subhas Chandra

Bose, who was instrumental in forming *Legion Freies Indien,* the Indian Volunteers Legion of the German Waffen-SS originally to be part of the Second World War German–Indian operation of western British India. The ferocious ambitions of the Sikhs in the group knew few bounds. Ram Chandra, by this time the editor of the American-based newspaper *Hindustan Ghadar,* was assassinated in April 1918 (the time of the Montagu–Chelmsford Proposal) by a fellow Ghadar Party leader, Ram Singh, who believed he was a British agent – which he was not. Ram Chandra saw his role as ridding India of the British raj. He challenged misinformation by the viceroy and secretary of state – information the British thought to be true but he thought otherwise. It was a typical revolutionary's role but it had credibility during the pre-war instability of India, where each viceroy after Curzon understood the vulnerability of the command and the understanding that, as in 1857, should there be a true crisis, no help could be expected from England. Ram Chandra exploited the apparent arrogance from the office of the viceroy and in particular the London-based secretary of state for India, Austin Chamberlain.

Ram Chandra was, long after his death, dismissed even by many Indians as a troublemaker. He never commanded the admiration of a Gandhi or a Jinnah and was seen as a a dangerous man at a time when India wanted stability. This was a period in which the raj rang with enormous achievements in most of the provinces. There was a sense of stability with true achievements for millions of Indians such as the building of new libraries, hospitals, clinics, schools and transport. Such advances had accelerated during the previous decade following Lansdowne's time as viceroy. But these were not the end of the golden Victorian years. This was India, whose masters were fighting for the lives of non-Prussian Europe. Ram Chandra

saw suppression and cruelty in his country and that the consequences of the war had spread to India, hardly showing a quiet
government or a confident viceroy.

'The India described in the British official dispatches is not the
real India. She is neither "loyal" nor "tranquil." India is seeking
its way to complete independence, even though that way lies
through bloodshed and insurrection. The agitation against the
British Government has grown tremendously since the
outbreak of the European war. The authorities took steps
immediately the war began, which resulted in the suppression
of nearly 350 newspapers ... the Government began a
campaign of house to house searches ... The residence of
Hans Raj, the saintly principal and president of the University
of Lahore was overhauled by the police in the most thorough-
going fashion. His entire library – one of the most noted collec-
tions – was ransacked ... How the common people fared at the
high hands of the police when "bigmen" were thus treated,
may be better imagined than described.'

The *Amrita Bazar Patrika*, the most famous and one of the
oldest English-language newspapers (still) of Calcutta, noted:

'We have been crying and crying till our voice has become
hoarse for putting a check to the indiscriminate search of
houses by the police. But they come, they come, still they
come.'

The people of the district feared more than police raids.
There were what local newspapers in their English-language
versions described as 'reigns of terror', not from the authorities
but the people. Looting, atrocities, riots, minor mutinies in the

native army, murders of policemen, British army officers, English clerks and Hindus loyal to the British. In America, readers beyond activist Sikhs read Ram Chandra editorials.

'The regular judicial procedure was suspended. [March 1915]. Anyone towards whom the Government entertained the slightest suspicion was interned. No appeal was possible from these courts which held their proceedings in camera. That these special tribunals were kept busy may be understood from the fact than in less than a year some 400 men were sent to the gallows, about 800 imprisoned for life with hard labor and some ten thousand interned . . . without any judicial procedure whatever.'

The information was essentially accurate. These were the times in which to speak or write even the documented truth could be interpreted as sedition. Ram Chandra reached Americans through US newspapers that were sympathetic without being activists. He had a basic assumption that he shared with the American and European press, including influential papers such as the *New York Times* and the *New York Sun*. His theme in the *New York Times* was simple: 'Ghadar seeks total autonomy and absolute freedom through revolution. The Hindus detest the British rule and will never be satisfied until British rule is destroyed and India is free forever.'

In the twentieth century, Ram Chandra and Ghadar would be seen as a dangerous but predictable protest group, maybe a terrorist organisation but not one that had any chance of pulling off a mutiny or dominating the day-to-day security duty of the British. Considering the plot with the Germans to bring the Indians into the Great War, Ghadar was successful enough that the movement had to be considered a real threat. Yet there was ever a sense that the threat would come to nothing, which was true. But Ghadar was certainly important enough midway through the First World War for the former and not overly successful viceroy Lord Hardinge in a speech to make it clear that the British still did not understand the possibilities of rebellion and saw Ghadar as a youth movement. The Germans were not so naive as Hardinge appeared to be. He clearly believed that Ghadar should be dismissed.

'Of course there is a certain amount, though small comparatively, of dissatisfaction and disloyalty in India. But even so, this discontent is anarchistic rather than revolutionary. It has not a constructive programme. It represents a desire to tear down authority, not a plan to set up a new authority.'

There are few ways more likely to ring out with truths than dismissal. Ram Chandra and his followers wanted above all to be accepted as republicans. Certainly the Crown Prosecutor, Bevan Petman, made this very clear when he delivered his opening address at the Lahore Special Tribunal in April 1915.

'The aim and object of this formidable conspiracy was to wage war on his Majesty, the King-Emperor, to overthrow by force the Government as by law established in India, to expel the British and to establish *Swedeshi* or independent national government in the country.'

The British at war had long memories. So too did another group that, although a minority, was seen by members of Hindu and Muslim India as a threat. The Christian communities were, obviously linked as special friends of the rulers of

India who were, of course, Christians or who expressed the Christian faith. The sometimes forgotten but all-important Christian intention was not subversive. It was in the open. British officers, some in perfect Hindustani, told Hindu and Muslim soldiers of the coming Christian conversion. This was not the African biblical trek with a rifle in the other hand. But the Indians had seen it before and knew that it did happen. The Portuguese Inquisition in sixteenth- to early-nineteenth-century Portuguese India brought more than 16,000 Indians to trial by the Catholic Church of Portugal, because they believed that the accused were Hindus or Muslims who had publicly converted to Catholicism but were living secretly still as Muslims. Muslims who tried to stop the conversion of non-Christians to the Church of Rome were also prosecuted. The Inquisition was in talking memory, thus the fear was believed. The raj was not a crusade and no viceroy ever thought it was, but at times there was a greater fear of Christianity than of animal fat cartridges.

Indians would never, even into the twenty-first century, allow themselves to forget what they might see as the Christian threat to themselves. Violence against Christians would be a feature of almost every decade of post-1947 India. It was always a strong theme for any viceroy and most saw that they needed to defend their religion as it formed part of the ethos of British India, which was ruled by an Emperor who was a defender of the faith and head of the Church of England. When Lord Chelmsford went to the 1918 gathering of the All-India Christian Conference he found in the Conference's opening address of welcome to him much reference to his position as representing the Christian King in England. It was even more remarkable that the Conference theme, as it did every year, fell back on the events sixty years earlier: the Indian Mutiny and a direct belief that the war with Germany was about the destruction of the Christian kingdoms:

'The Indian Christian community was threatened with extinction during the days of the Indian Mutiny, but through the Grace of God it has more than doubled since 1881 . . . its percentage of literate men and women is higher than is to be found among our Hindu and Mahomedan [sic] brethren; it stands foremost in its appreciation of the noble aims of the British Indian administration and in measures necessary for the defence of the Empire it has a common interest with the ruling race. In the light of these facts the Indian Christians acknowledge with gratitude the recent decision of the Government to recruit an Indian Christian battalion in the Punjab.'

The Christian community saw the Punjab battalion as more than a military offering for the Great War. It was too late for that confrontation anyway. The announcement was symbolic. Punjab was not a private army for the Christians but it was a tough reminder that the Christians were supported in the name of the viceroy and monarch. The other religions that felt threatened by attempts at conversion to Christianity since the sixteenth century saw themselves as defenders of their own faiths and their individual households. Christianity was more than a religious chess-piece. It was a political assumption. India's politics hid little. They were still in an infancy that could have figureheads but rarely policies that would sway one side or the other outside their religious persuasions.

A decade earlier, the Minto–Morley reforms of 1909 did nothing to answer questions over India's political assumptions.

Certainly the system of narrowing votes in the legislatures had failed to persuade members of the ruling groups, the provincial and local legislatures, that they should have a greater responsibility towards the people they were representing. Most if not all those Indians on the legislatures never had to answer questions from the electorate at voting time, as did the parliamentary members in London. Moreover, the viceroy's council was the only body with real power. The India Office was sponsoring the Montagu–Chelmsford Proposal because the Minto–Morley reforms were the final outcome of the old concept of the the Indian government as a benevolent despotism tempered by a remote and only occasionally vigilant democracy in London that might as it saw fit consult the wishes of its subjects.

Minto–Morley had outlived its usefulness. India was being governed by the worst of systems. Chelmsford, the viceroy and his secretary of state Montagu had a single view, which was not always the case. The India Office was promoting the two as holders of one view that believed that the time had come when the sheltered existence that had been given to India could not be prolonged without damaging national life. However, even then there had to be a limit to the freedoms that the British were willing to concede. The British made it clear in 1918 that the improved nation had to be within the empire; in other words, self-government was not independence. India had to remain within the empire, probably as a Dominion in the style of Australia and Canada: monarch as head of state, governor general as a sort of viceroy but as a constitutional reference and without powers of rule and a prime minister to be elected along party lines to rule. Moreover, the British claimed this was for everyone's good and an India within the empire meant much better than anything else

Indians were talking about or could ever have under another system.

Setting the direction towards self-government was more than a question of language. Montagu's draughtsmen had produced what they called a formula. If everything was to be agreed by this equation it would be along the lines of responsibility plus time-frame equals a form of independence:

'The provinces are the domain in which the earlier steps towards the progressive realization of responsible government should be taken. Some measure of responsibility should be given at once, and our aim is to give complete responsibility as soon as conditions permit. This involves at once giving the provinces the largest measure of independence, legislative, administrative and financial, of the Government of India which is incompatible with the due discharge by the latter of its own responsibilities.'

Here was the original concept: a United States of India.

However, the British had to get the India Act through parliament in London. That was not impossible. To do so, the viceroy had to make sure India looked good about it all. The way of doing this was an example of the imperial mind still at work: through legislation called the Rowlatt Acts[8] the government could put in jail anyone suspected of terrorism, for two years without trial. This legislation effectively controlled the press and activists if they produced anything the viceroy thought to be anti-government.

No person and no organisation could speak against the British plans without falling foul of the Anarchical and Revolutionary Crimes Act of 1919. Apart from the specific targets in the Montagu–Chelmsford Proposal, the Act supposedly suppressed the growth of nationalism. It failed in that Gandhi and others spoke (reasonably) against the Rowlatt Acts; furthermore, for the British to produce a plan for self-government would necessarily inspire nationalism. However, what would happen if protesters did nothing? What would happen if protesters closed their work and fasted? This was the beginning for Chelmsford of the protest of civil disobedience.

As with everything in India, a national response was never possible. In Punjab, opposition was violent. Gandhi had to abandon the tactic of non-violent protest. Chelmsford hoped that this was little more than an expected phase of implementing the Rowlatt Act. It was not. The Act was published in March 1919. The Punjab protest intensified. There is no doubt that, in spite of soft-diplomacy of the time and the work from the viceroy down, it was on the cards that an Indian attempt would be made to at least bring British rule in Punjab to a standstill. If, as as expected, the British were not able to coordinate reinforcements, India would take over Punjab and effectively British rule. This was the background to what followed – the single event 'which would change the whole course of British imperial history'9. Protest turned into the Jallianwala Bagh massacre (the Amritsar massacre), a tragedy and a stain on Chelmsford's watch and an atrocity commanded by a British officer that meant relations between British and Indians were deeply harmed for ever; moreover, the officer who led the massacre was praised in the House of Lords as the saviour of Punjab. He was castigated in the House of Commons.

A hartal, a strike, was called on 30 March. The response was spontaneous and for the British a worrying factor was the apparent coming together of Hindu and Muslim factions. With some irony, on 9 April two activists, a Hindu, Doctor Satyapal, and a Muslim, Saifuddin Kitchlew, were arrested – the irony being that both men advocated strictly non-violent demonstrations. Satyapal also worked for the British army. The magistrate had received instructions from the lieutenant governor of Punjab, Michael O'Dwyer, that leading agitators should be deported from Punjab. Followers of the two men protested and the protest grew. On 9 April, the protest moved into the British quarter of Amritsar. What followed was predictable. Houses were pillaged and burned. Troops fired on the crowd. Some were killed. Three British bank workers were beaten to death. Marcella Sherwood, a British teacher at the Mission School for Girls, was dragged from her bicycle, assaulted and left for dead. She was rescued by Indians who managed to get her to the British fort. Others were unlucky. Acting Brigadier Reginald Dyer was in temporary command of the British Infantry Brigade in Jalandhar and gave the order to move on Amritsar, arriving on 11 April 1919 with intent to restore order. Dyer ordered that any Indian passing the spot where Marcella Sherwood was attacked should crawl the length of the street on their bellies. It was not an unusual public punishment during colonial rule. Dyer's mood also was to take revenge on the crowd of protesters. The fear of a take-over of Punjab had never been higher. Dyer, before the massacre, ordered every Indian man to crawl the length of the street on hands and knees. Here, then, was an example of the tensions. On the Sunday, with most of Punjab under martial law, Dyer was warned of the gathering crowd and, believing surely this time that his initial fear of an uprising was coming true, put troops to the streets and announced a curfew. The soldiers were limited in what they could do. A small force could only make a threatening impression, and certainly not inspire the martial capability of a full battalion.

On Sunday 13 April, the day of the Sikh festival of Baisakhi, Amritsar witnessed thousands more taking to the streets. Houses were pillaged and burned; many were injured and five Europeans were killed. Thousands went to the Jallianwala Bagh public gardens. Colonel Reginald Dyer had arrived with a section of twenty-five Gurkhas of 1st Battalion 9th Gurkha Rifles and twenty-five from the Sindh Rifles, still believing that this could have the makings of an insurrection. Dyer's intelligence was not good, mostly second-hand, but later in the afternoon he had good reports that the main gathering was in the Jallianwala Bagh, which at the time had restricted access and exit along two small streets. That afternoon it was mainly crammed with people celebrating harvest day. He ordered his covering force to fire on the crowd trying to get through the gates, thus blocking those exits. They fired for ten minutes and their ammunition then ran out. The Indian National Congress afterwards estimated that some one thousand people were killed. Those whom Dyer believed to be ringleaders were flogged publicly and some sort of blackout on the day was ordered. There was no way Dyer or anyone else could control the spread of news, accurate or not.

The following day, 14 April, Dyer, in Urdu, gave the people an ultimatum.

'Do you want war or peace? If you wish for a war, the Government is prepared for it, and if you want peace, then obey my orders and open all your shops; else I will shoot. For me the battlefield of France or Amritsar is the same. I am a military man and I will go straight. Neither shall I move to

the right nor to the left. Speak up, if you want war? In case
there is to be peace, my order is to open all shops at once. You
people talk against the Government and persons educated in
Germany and Bengal talk sedition. I shall report all these.
Obey my orders. I do not wish to have anything else. I have
served in the military for over thirty years. I understand the
Indian sepoy and Sikh people very well. You will have to obey
my orders and observe peace. Otherwise the shops will be
opened by force and Rifles. You will have to report to me of
the Badmash. I will shoot them. Obey my orders and open
shops. Speak up if you want war? You have committed a bad
act in killing the English. The revenge will be taken upon
you and upon your children.'

This is the skimpiest account of what happened. Its purpose
was to show the sort of pressures that the British were under,
perhaps through incompetence and the army being
commanded by British officers who were not always of the
highest quality. Whatever anyone said later, the British still
suffered from being and commanding in an environment they
secretly feared and had never forgotten the accounts of the
worst battles with Indians, especially the Indian Mutiny more
than sixty years earlier.

Dyer committed what today would be called, if not proven, a
war crime. In 1919 India where every British resident could
recite in some detail the events that began in Meerut sixty-two
years before, Dyer was not a criminal. 'I thought I would be
doing a jolly lot of good,' said Dyer.[10] Many others thought the
same, including the Sikhs who made Dyer an honorary Sikh,
but even this was not what it seemed. The Sikhs could be
persuaded to use their influence and openly support Dyer, but
in reality when they 'crowned' him with turban and sword, they

were supporting the need of government rather than admiring what Dyer had ordered to be done. The Sikh Punjab, so the propaganda and belief went, had been saved. The House of Lords supported his action. Dyer had, the Lordships supposed, saved a mutiny. What of the most influential single Indian voice, Gandhi? Gandhi's view was that civil disobedience had failed and that those who had died were not heroes and certainly not martyrs. Moreover Gandhi, a champion of the British Empire, it might always be remembered, said he was certain that the British themselves searched for justice over the killings.

Gandhi's view in 1919 was his idea of what it meant to be part of the empire. He wanted national identity but he wanted India to have national equality and that would mean being treated exactly the way the British would be in similar circumstances. The general view of the British in India was that the affair could have turned into the nightmare that they had feared for six decades. Sir Michael O'Dwyer thought there was enough evidence to accept Dyer had been right. The commander-in-chief was not of that opinion. In India, General Sir Charles Monro told Dyer to pack his bags and not come back. It could have turned into a full insurrection. Dyer's action had made certain that it did not. There was a deeper question to be asked once the circumstances were debated. This was not the action of a single officer. There was something far more disturbing for the British to understand, or certainly ask themselves in 1919. It was left to the secretary of state at the India Office, Edwin Montagu, who thought Dyer's command 'a grave error in judgement', to ask the Commons:

'Are you going to keep your hold on India by terrorism, racial humiliation, subordination and frightfulness, or are you going

to rest it upon the goodwill and the growing goodwill of the
people of your Indian Empire?'

It was a difficult point to make when Winston Churchill was
saying 'My opinion is that the offence amounted to murder or
alternatively manslaughter.' And H.H. Asquith, the former
prime minister, supported him, 'There has never been such an
incident in the whole annals of Anglo-Indian history nor I
believe in the history of our empire . . . it is one of the worst
outrages in the whole of our history.'

The viceroy Chelmsford was, as the man in charge of India,
in theory to blame for the whole affair. There was a harsh
demand in London that he should be withdrawn. Here surely
was the empire in full creaking and the future of the British in
India unlikely to run far. The immediate task was to make it
clear to India that the British were not still (if they ever had
been) in some colonial blimp. Dyer had support for his position. Dyer had critics of his position. Lord William Hunter,
the Scottish advocate, would chair the inquiry and it would
report as soon as might be possible. What was entirely different
from past misdemeanours upheld or otherwise was the coming
of age of Indian politics. Mahatma Gandhi was appointed to
lead a Punjab committee of inquiry within the Indian National
Congress. Hunter started a month ahead, in October, with
tacit instructions to get it right and not leave anything out that
Gandhi would disclose.

The mood was not simply about what went on in Amritsar
that day in April 1919, but the potential for the British to tear
itself apart in the moral debate about its empire. The unwrit-
ten statement was whether or not Britain could possibly stay in
India and, more, if it wanted to stay.

Hunter started six months after the massacre. Dyer could

easily have changed his story. Dyer did not. He told Hunter that he had, before he got to the crowd, decided to open fire. He was determined to do more than just take control. He intended to produce what Hunter interpreted as a 'moral impact' with the sole purpose of preventing another mutiny. For Dyer and his generation, the Sepoy Rebellion of 1857 was in moral earshot.

There was too a general impression, in the evidence from Dyer, that if he had been equipped with more than basic 303 Lee Enfield rifles then more powerful weapons would have been used. No compromise. The following March, 1920, Hunter with a majority judgement announced that Dyer's was a mistaken concept of duty and his was not the only failing. That suggested that the Hunter Commission view was not unanimous but strongly enough worded that Dyer's career should be ended. Two months later, the full report appeared. Again, it was a split report. Hunter now said Dyer was justified in giving the order to fire although notice to fire should have been broadcast and the firing went on for too long. Dyer's career was at an end and a pension fund for him was started with public support. The relatives of those killed were given compensation payments.

The army's tactical decision making, rules of engagement and procedures were reviewed. This action, although welcomed, was never going to bring about a renewal of any trust between army and civilians that may have existed. The Amritsar massacre did not bring about the end of the British in India but it changed so much that what might have been a reasonable negotiation towards home rule could never be now.

As for the viceroy, Chelmsford was part of the British and Indian government responsible, one that made no credible attempt to win back whatever trust had existed. He was due to go in the spring of 1921 and in his time remaining took command to smooth out all the doubtful contingencies that were imagined to come with the launching of Gandhi as India's enigmatic hope for the future of nationalism. By that time, Chelmsford would be gone. His role in the end game of the British in India and therefore the British Empire is rarely remembered. After Chelmsford's going, the League of Viceroys took on the role of steadying India for the inevitable, although that was not how it was officially seen. There were five viceroys until the arrival of the imperial undertaker in February 1947.

Lord Reading was Rufus Isaacs. There were nine brothers and sisters in the Isaacs family, which got its money from market trading in Spitalfields Market in London, an old selling place of silks and cloths through Jewish tailors and known as the haunt of Jack the Ripper. Isaacs did not fit the pattern of yet another aristocrat going out to govern somewhere; from these beginnings his political and legal reputation went before him.

In a bundle of tutors and schools, Isaacs was a precocious and clever youth who could find no place for more than a few months in the markets so signed on as a sixteen-year-old deck hand on a sailing ship, the *Blair Athole*, out of London. It was a brutal existence and he jumped ship in South America, was captured and returned to London via Calcutta. This is why, after a series of other jobs that Isaacs could not do, he read for the bar, took silk in ten years and was earning £10 million a year by 2017 values. In 1910, he became Liberal Imperialist MP for Reading, solicitor general and, within six months, attorney general and a knight. Four years on he was Lord Reading – a good rate of improvement considering his name

had been linked to insider trading involving Marconi shares. It
was a spectacular rise from grubby bunk in the fo'c's'le to lord
chief justice by 1913. Afterwards, boredom set in so Reading
made a significant return to the bar, just for the fun of it. Not
so bad for a classy market trader's boy. Then came India in
1921 and his and his government's thought that a viceroy was
needed who could put India on the right road for self-government under the 1919 India Act.

Reading's starting point was that there was a fundamental
distinction between colonial rule in, say, a Dominion where
white ruled white and India; that was imperialism where white,
fundamentally, ruled Indians. That Indians were in government too was not going to move the beliefs of much of the rest
of India. Whatever was promised in terms of self-government,
the instinct of generations of governors general and viceroys
was to vote for prejudice, however reluctantly discussed.

Montagu, still at the India Office in London, knew exactly
the sort of man they had sent to India and he was in no doubt
of Reading's starting point:

'. . . the British could not expect to persuade the Indian of the
justice [sic] of our rule until we have overcome racial difficulties.'

The British tried to convince Indians – including many
normally on the British side – that the Amritsar massacre was
a one-off and a very bad mistake for which those responsible
had been punished. Considering the circumstances and the
consequences, why should the Indians have believed anything
the British said? They had for a couple of centuries been told
what to think by the British. Where had that got them? There
is no evidence the Indians were convinced of the British plea.

For all the obvious difficulties and Reading's inexperience

in India, the first year was moderately successful. On the risk side, there was a firmness that many had not expected, particularly in the order from Reading to arrest agitators. The fine line between agitator and seditious hero was very fine. That Reading was successful had much to do with his boldness as a boy; he was a good scrapper on the lower decks and prized fighter of the law. Above all, he was ambitious.

As solicitor general, attorney general and lord chief justice, he was admired by patrons who became friends: Lloyd George would have been one, Asquith another. Ability, drive, stamina and an exciting mind presented the formidable character India needed during this period. First, he believed in the reforms. He believed in self-government and more for the Indians. His principal task was to show Indians he sincerely believed they would profit Indians. He assumed that the general tactic others before him had tried – playing Hindu off against Muslim – would not work while Gandhi was leading both against the British plans.

When, in 1922, Reading had Gandhi arrested for sedition, he had to weigh the consequences for security with the certainty that Gandhi would be a hero in prison. In the 1920s, not enough was made of the prices. Reading, like many of his own people, saw Gandhi as the agitator and the villain of the piece, but he was too aware that one third of the subcontinent was directly in the control of the princes.

The princes never wanted to be seen by their peers as being the first to go along with what the British asked or demanded. At the same time princes were protected by the British, who for half a century said openly that nothing could be advanced in India without bringing all the states, presidencies, principalities, even townships together. Historically, princes were vulnerable to criticism that they treated their own in a manner that would have led to serious investigation and likely charges had the masters been British. Reading brought about the removal of two senior princes because of their cruelty. It was a delicate balance by the viceroy to keep a firm foot in each company and so to come to a reasonable universal conclusion.

For Reading and for the remainder of the British viceroys, including Mountbatten, the conundrum of what Gandhi might next do and how to react remained the single issue they never really resolved.

In the process of handing over considerable power, Gandhi was the most impenetrable opponent any imperial British governor had confronted. There was a side to the Gandhi versus the British confrontation that neither the viceroys nor the India Office secretaries in London ever properly fathomed and which would, even during the twenty-first century, be something of an anxious study: the spectre for some, the refuge for others, the caliphate.

Gandhi had returned to India in 1915; he was, as Gokhale remarked, a man who had in him the marvellous spiritual power to turn ordinary men around him into heroes and martyrs. Historically, the British had thrived on heroes (theirs) and avoided martyrs (foreign). Gandhi had thrived not in India but in South Africa as a lawyer. He was known as a pacifist. The British thought pacifists dangerous. It was remembered that Gandhi supported both major religions. He needed the volume of protest of Hindu and Muslim. He needed also a continual cause and it would not always be a challenge to the British government. It should also have a unifying effect for his followers. He found it in the First World War with the defeat and collapse of the Ottoman (Turkish) Empire. An Islamic movement, the 'Kaliphat', was established by Indian

Muslims in 1920 with the single purpose to protect the Muslim caliphate that had stretched from Turkey in the north to the Sahara and Gulf. This was not two decades into the twentieth century. Most Middle East countries did not exist in the way they are understood in the twenty-first century. The spread of Wahabiism was in its modern infancy. The forces of Abdul Aziz bin Saud had not established their vast homeland that had yet to be called Saudi Arabia (September 1932). India, as well as others in the region, recognised that the collapse of the Ottoman Empire could mean that the holiest shrines would no longer be protected and that Islam would suffer.

Gandhi joined Kaliphat and was a member of its central committee. Arrests disrupted the movement but Gandhi's connection was enough to identify the people and potential that he would need to combine with Hindus against the British. No one in Congress had publicly attempted to join the Hindu and Muslim opposition to the British and thus, for the first time, taken a radical step towards enlarging the support for Congress right across India. When Gandhi was found guilty of sedition he had made a stern statement that non-violence was a cornerstone in what he was attempting. He told the court that he, as a leader, had to accept that if people who followed him committed terrible crimes then even though he deplored those crimes and had nothing directly to do with them, he had to suffer serious punishment under the law.[11]

The judge said that in the eyes of millions of Indians, Gandhi was a great patriot and even the opposition (that would include the British) admired Gandhi's high ideals and 'even saintly life'. He was jailed for six years and came out after two years. Albert Einstein said there would be generations who never believed that someone like Gandhi ever existed. Einstein did not add that a generation also detested him. Those who ruled from London and for London included a strong British caste including Churchill, who treated the subject of India's future as they might have regarded White's Dundee cake – something precious and British without which they could not imagine every day.

Reading went from triumph to triumph including becoming foreign secretary (the last Liberal to sit in that place) and leader of the Lords. He believed he had never met anyone as remarkable as Gandhi and never thought he could really influence the Indian leader. You could argue with Gandhi, even send him to prison. But when Einstein said Gandhi was remarkable then British imperialism knew it was living in rich times that could cause ruin. Reading died in 1935, as he would have put it, in harness with his much younger second wife, his former secretary in India. Gandhi was assassinated. A hero *and* a martyr.

CHAPTER XIII

THE LAST GRANDEES

Halifax, who followed Reading, brought the viceroyal stable back to good breeding stock although he was not so good as painted. Halifax was Edward Wood, a child of one of the huge hunting landowning families of the north country. He was born in his grandfather's castle, Powderham in Devon. His grandfather was the eleventh earl of Devon. His great-grandfather was Grey, who steered the 1832 Reform Bill. After a first (modern history Oxford) and a fellowship at All Souls he travelled the Dominions, returned to All Souls, wrote a book and married well, to Lady Dorothy Onslow, the fourth earl of Onslow's daughter. He then got a Conservative seat when others were falling to Liberals.

It was a steady time, with no one in particular taking to him, but he progressed all the same, although he was turned down as governor general of South Africa because the South Africans expected someone a little more important: a royal would have been acceptable. The South Africans, even with their constitutional temper, were making a soft demand for their own

recognition, their own status maybe, as the Indian princes had
when liking the idea of a viceroy rather than continuing with
governors.

After delay, then standing down from the Commons to be given
a seat in the Lords as Irwin of Kirkby, Irwin, as now he was, was
given India in 1926. He was the ideal man and thought so. At
6'5" with a slight stoop, Irwin cut a fine imperial figure. Yet he
did far more than look the part. Irwin liked India; his father, who
encouraged him to take the post, had been secretary of state
and he was considerably more sympathetic to the Indian cause
than any of those who had gone before, with perhaps the exception of Chelmsford. Indians were not always grateful for his
sympathies and some tried a few times to kill him.

Viceroys were in India to advance the way it was governed,
not to be original. Irwin repeated Reading's caution that Anglo-
Indian relations had to be better and Hindu–Muslim relations
had also to be improved if the 1919 plan were to succeed. He
also worked and explained that the proper aim would be
beyond 1919 India remaining in what would become a
Commonwealth of Nations. The first step had to be to recognise that whatever work Reading had managed on inter-Indian
understanding of what was being attempted, there was still far
to go. Gandhi's personality is perhaps over-portrayed in modern
images of his. He could, with just one interpretation of a smile
or word or silence, send diplomats into furies because he had
the power to lie down to sleep while India smouldered. All he
had to do was to stand and say everything we hear is good. He
did not because everything was not good seen from his or any
other way. Irwin, in his first speech, said the obvious: the inter-
communal violence had to be stopped if India were to succeed
under the 1919 Act. He repeated this message.

Irwin's logic was at its most acceptable when he pointed out that he agreed with many of the points and wishes Indians put forward but while India remained divided surely everyone, Muslim or Hindu, could see that little could be achieved. Perhaps more could have been achieved if the British had not been so insensitive.

The viceroy was not best informed. Irwin might have been wiser, certainly might have been expected to be wiser on how London was proposing to review what had been put forward, how it was working and if it needed reforming. This was the Simon Commission role under Sir John Simon (1873–1954).

Simon was one of the least remembered influential British politicians of the post-First World War twentieth century, whose political view began as a Liberal and who ended as a Conservative. He was one of the few men to hold all three senior Cabinet posts: Home Secretary, Foreign Secretary and Chancellor and, then, Lord Chancellor. In 1921 he chaired what became known as the Simon Commission of seven MPs. The future Labour prime minister Clement Attlee was deputy chairman. There was no Indian representative on the inquiry. Irwin, the man on the spot who felt that he understood Indian aspirations better than most, advised the British government that the commission should be all-white and British Members of Parliament. Irwin had made the recommendation on the assumption that a mixed Indian–British commission would not agree on anything but an all-white commission would get on with the job, and that after set-piece protests the Indians would be made to see sense. This was the way people thought in those times. The most powerful authority in the debate on independence for India was not the government in London, certainly not the viceroy, and there was no government in India; that, of course, was the whole point of the debate. The focal point after the Great War and the point when independence was never a euphemism was Gandhi. Jinnah sadly never encouraged the way in which a minority leader should have been. And the authority of Gandhi lay not in his mysticism and his own mystery nor even the intellectual dishevelment that when whispered appeared as wisdom. The eight viceroys who knew Gandhi, and all who hung on their imperial tails, feared him. They did so not as they might have imagined fearing a tiger – which not one of them would – but because they did not understand him. They did not easily know what he was. In the way that a monarch represents the identity of the nation, so the instinct of the viceroy was that Gandhi must be the nation. There were too many of his own people, people who had his ear, who were as uncertain as British India of the identity of this loin-clothed man dressed as a spectral guru. To know what they feared tells us something of who they were. The Inner Temple lawyer who had worked the streets and late courts of South Africa was not the lawyer disguised as a scrawny figure from central casting. Lord Irwin, in a letter Gandhi sent him on 2 March 1930, had the clue set anyone would need. In it is what he wanted Irwin to think he was like and what he wanted of the British. In short, Gandhi, never motiveless, would, when he had finished the latter, know a little more of himself.

'Dear Friend, Before embarking on Civil Disobedience and taking the risk I have dreaded to take all these years, I would fain approach you and find a way out.

My personal faith is absolutely clear. I cannot intentionally hurt anyone that lives, much less fellow human beings, even though they may do the greatest wrong to me and mine. Whilst therefore, I hold the British rule to be a curse, I do not intend harm to a single Englishman or to any legitimate interest he may have in India.

I must not be misunderstood. Though I hold the British rule in India to be a curse, I do not, therefore, consider Englishmen in general to be worse than any other people on earth. I have the privilege of claiming many Englishmen as dearest friends. Indeed much that I have learnt of the evil of British rule is due to the writings of frank and courageous Englishmen who have not hesitated to tell the unpalatable truth about that rule.

And why do I regard the British rule as a curse?

It has impoverished the dumb millions by a system of progressive exploitation and by a ruinously expensive military and civil administration which the country can never afford.

It has reduced us politically . . . It has raped the foundations of our culture . . .'[1]

In India, the tempo of political ambition had speeded up since the turn of the century; Irwin's judgement may have been poor but, more importantly in the eyes of the new generation of Indian leaders, the viceroy was no longer so grand. What he represented was vulnerable to fundamental change.

When the Simon Commission was announced in November 1927 (just twenty years before independence), Irwin's judgement proved pitifully wrong and the government in London transparently inept in its understanding of what the British were up against in India.

Every political party, including Congress, that would be needed by the British, refused to have anything to do with Simon. The commission arrived in India during February the following year and was boycotted. Irwin had never made such a mistake. Some contacts were made but there was no real progress. Irwin returned to London after the spring 1929

general election and Prime Minister Ramsay MacDonald sent
William Wedgwood Benn to the India Office. Irwin's next idea
was that Simon should propose a round table conference
to discuss anticipated outcomes and remind all parties of
Montagu's 1917 declaration that India should eventually have
Dominion status. Irwin had said at the beginning of this process that an all-British commission would agree terms. No such
thing happened when the draft letter was put before the
commission. Simon did not tell Irwin how opposed were other
members of the inquiry.

Irwin was very slow in understanding that by declaring in
letters between Simon and MacDonald or anyone else in
government that Dominion status was the end game, then
Dominion status would become a promise and therefore a
starting point. Irwin made a statement in India that the British
saw Dominionship as a given, which it had been since Montagu
in 1917. Irwin's declaration should, he thought, have agreement from all sides. It did not. The Conservatives in London
said No. Reading, the previous viceroy, condemned Irwin's
statement. Simon himself then said he did not agree. Hopes
had been raised in India. Now there were none.

After a meeting in Delhi in December 1929 between
Irwin and Indian politicians, Gandhi washed his hands of it
all and started to plan for full independence. He then
proceeded on his twenty-four-day trek to the sea and picked
up a handful of salt, thus breaking the law that Indians were
not allowed to own salt unless it had been bought from the
government – so shabby was the intellect that still contrived
to govern India.

Irwin had Gandhi arrested as the law obliged him to, which
was all nonsense as the 1930–31 peace conference with Indians
and the British had opened in London and there was no way it

could progress without Gandhi there. Irwin, increasingly the wrong viceroy for the times, had Gandhi released and he then proposed eight meetings with Irwin. Irwin, for all his sincerity and his belief that he could bring India together, could not keep up with Gandhi. 'It was,' wrote Irwin to his father, 'like talking to someone who had stepped off another planet.'[2] Irwin was not really talking about Gandhi; he was, without realising it, showing that he had never understood the Indian people he ruled on behalf of the monarch. This was a man who would become the most famous of pre-Second World War British foreign secretaries and saw himself as Britain's wartime leader instead of Churchill. But Irwin was not entirely ineffectual.

The record of misjudgement is sometimes unfair, although entirely just. Irwin may have never understood the Indian mystic side to Gandhi that was sometimes more theatrical than intuitive. The two men may not have admired each other, but they each showed respect for the other's position; if it can be noted as a triumph, in the 1931 Delhi Pact, Gandhi promised to abandon the protest of civil disobedience. The Gandhi–Irwin Pact was an example of two men with obligations of their own putting together a pact that would, if not satisfy their obligations and the people who created them, do for the moment. Moreover, it would convince both that some agreement was always possible, even though this pact could never be seen as ideal. The Pact had twenty clauses and a preamble, unusually brief for modern Asian diplomacy, that went far towards achieving Irwin's ambitions. His weakness in any negotiation was mistrust, not so much of Gandhi but of his own people in London.

We might remember that this was 1931. To modern west European minds, Gandhi is often seen as the loin-clothed saint assassinated by his own people. The Gandhi–Irwin Pact

was negotiated by a very different Gandhi who believed Irwin
more than Irwin believed Gandhi. The fact that Irwin got
more from the Pact than did Gandhi emphasises the puzzle:
what was the Pact really about? Irwin got the cancellation of
the Gandhi-led civil disobedience movement and an agreement that Congress would take part in the London round table
conference. There was more for Irwin, but that was enough to
call it a success. Gandhi did not get everything he wanted but
he could go back to his people with a British pledge to
withdraw outstanding prosecutions, prisoner releases and
restrictions of Indian National Congress and, symbolically
most of all, the lifting of restrictions on Indians collecting
salt.

Churchill, in the House of Commons, saw the whole thing
as an act of utter contempt. 'It is alarming and also nauseating
to see Mr. Gandhi, a seditious Middle Temple[3] lawyer, now
posing as a fakir, striding half-naked up the steps of the Viceroy's
palace, there to negotiate and to parley on equal terms with
the representative of the King-Emperor.' This was not simply a
rightwing reaction. Baldwin was close to being forced to resign.
The Pact was, on the one hand, some form of progress, particularly the agreement of Congress to get to the round table meeting. Irwin may have just saved Baldwin's political bacon before
he appeared in the House to call the Pact common sense and
give every indication that India was too big and complex a
subject to be tossed around in the political arena of Westminster.
Baldwin at his best made Churchill a headline writer beneath
which there was little substance. Within the week Baldwin
had taken the debate a stage further and perhaps never to be
repeated until his cool management of the Abdication debate
in December 1936. It was now that Baldwin made his remarks
about the newspapers and power without responsibility.

In India, Irwin had raised Gandhi's stock because he may not have got all he wanted but he gained more than he or his followers had expected. This was an official agreement and that gave Congress considerable prestige. Concluding an official agreement, even an interim truce, meant to them that Congress was considered on equal terms and, for the Indians, suggested that the viceroy and the guardians of British India were not so invincible as once thought. Gandhi's stock had risen. British India's had fallen. The British had proved vulnerable. Irwin's time was almost up. Before he left for England, Irwin made what was heard as a speech at the Anglo-Indian Chelmsford Club that could be seen as the grounding of the view that he would hold on India during his time as foreign secretary. In his thoughtful biography, *The Holy Fox*, of Irwin, Andrew Roberts writes that the speech 'was a candid reflection of his time in India as well as a warm defence of his policy'. It also threw light on his underlying beliefs regarding India's future. On British action to his declaration he complained:

'Instead of saying "Dominion Status? Of course it's our intention to give India Dominion Status. What other purpose could we have in view as the goal of our growth?" . . . the general note was that anyone who talked about Dominion Status in connection with India must be mentally afflicted . . . What wonder that Indian feeling was offended, and a real chance of approach thrown away!'[4]

It was a simple statement that came from Irwin's belief that, given British history and its direction, then it was impossible but to feel that it was right for people to wish to have what Irwin liked to call political liberty. Irwin was leaving India with a warning to his own people in London and all his successors to independence that it was part of the British responsibility to safeguard and watch for the future of the minorities. Congress and Jinnah's Muslims would have their way (they would not, but Irwin did not then know that), but the many minorities had no strengths they could use to protect their future. Irwin, speaking clearly and without coded language, argued that political freedom was an honourable and hopeful ambition. He was still viceroy and governor general and thus represented the landlords of a British Empire that had for 400 years stood firmly against others who would have shifted it. He was also saying that the British had the obligation to protect the minorities that would be left – and not just the obligation. Britain had the right to protect the minorities because, of the British who stayed behind, some of the fourth- and fifth-generation expatriates were part of the minority class and who would protect them? Within two months Irwin had gone. Perhaps he should never have been sent to India. Yet no one should doubt his toughness at the right moment; for example, his difficult decision not to reprieve a political murderer, Bhagat Singh, from a death sentence. It would have been a popular move among some in India and one that would have been recorded above other and less popular decisions by Irwin. He did not do it. The man was hanged. Irwin left India for a 'bigger' career but was yet another viceregal hopeful who failed to become prime minister. Irwin retreated to the Yorkshire estates. He went back to government as president of the Education Board, although his old-style education policies were clearly of another time – in a speech he announced that Britain should have good enough schooling to train boys to one day become butlers.

In 1931 Britain had for the first time a national government formed by Ramsay MacDonald's National Labour Party with

Conservatives and Liberals. There was an economic crisis and no other form of government could survive. For good measure Royal Navy ratings in the Atlantic Fleet at Invergordon mutinied against threatened pay cuts. The Admiralty promised to cancel the plan to cut pay but not before the international surprise was so dramatic that the government had to take sterling off the gold standard. The national government would survive until May 1940, when it was replaced by Churchill's wartime coalition. In the same year, the new government was to introduce the Statute of Westminster. This was an instrument where the self-governing Dominions had legislative independence from the United Kingdom. India was not part of this but the government wanted it to understand what level of autonomy it would have as a Dominion. It was into this questionable governing of India that Willingdon, a fine cricketer, stepped. Willingdon was a good man. Most if not all liked him. He was not, though, the best man to send to India at that time. The editor of *The Times* newspaper, Geoffrey Dawson (1874–1944), wrote to Irwin, whom Willingdon was replacing, saying so:

'Between ourselves I regard Willingdon as a thoroughly bad choice. He is a most delightful person; as we all agree; but he never had very much stuff in him and was thoroughly tired by the time he left India before. Of course he has had an excellent press; but I laugh when I see references to the "courage and self-sacrifice" of *Lady* Willingdon in allowing him to undertake these new responsibilities!'[5]

As Dawson emphasises, Willingdon was a thoroughly good man if not a thoroughly good viceroy. Dawson does not mention that Willingdon was a thoroughly good cricketer.

Willingdon, captained Eton and Cambridge and then turned out for Sussex and I Zingari – some would say the finest of the four distinctions[6]. As a pastime, he was King George V's favourite tennis partner. Eastbourne Authority named mock-Tudor roads after him. Here was the ideal viceroy in *reasonable* times. These were *unreasonable* times. Willingdon cut his teeth in Indian affairs when in 1913 he was appointed govern-or of Bombay. When Britain went to war, she took India with her. The wounded and displaced passed through and the Willingdons (this was very much a viceroy and vicereine reign) looked after them as best they could. In 1892, Willingdon, as Freeman Freeman-Thomas as then he was, married into a celebrated Sussex family, the Brasseys – railway builders and global travellers in their fine cruising yacht, the *Sunbeam*. Freeman-Thomas married Marie, the fourth daughter of Lord Brassey, who too played cricket and who also had roads in his name and had been sent out to govern Victoria. Marie Willingdon was considered eccentric in a cheerful way. She is remembered for an obsession for the colour mauve and as the vicereine who redecorated the residences, including Shimla, into the post-war twentieth century.

Marie Willingdon had longed for the power of vicereine – they had been considered for an earlier appointment, but London politics can so easily raise hope then let go when so many favours were being called in and there were so few places in the empire to be governed. The Willingdons were not the first viceroy and vicereine to witness the contrast with govern-ing that other sometimes divided piece of the empire – Canada. Canada was a Dominion with its political status and constitu-tional arrangements all settled. The monarch was head of state and sent a high commissioner, a role similar to that of an ambassador in the Commonwealth.

Willingdon was often considered nice enough to be acceptably naive but never naive enough to believe the Canadian example could be easily transferred to India – yet this is what he was trying to do. There was never much chance of Willingdon getting far in his five years once he found himself, like every other viceroy of the period, in conflict with Gandhi, with neither seeing or choosing to see a reason that suited them both. From the summer of 1931 to 1933 there was no agreement and nor could there be when in January 1932, after Gandhi restarted his civil disobedience campaign and 30,000 members of Congress were sent to jail, Willingdon introduced the Emergency Powers Ordinance. They understood also that if they were to bargain with Gandhi the wrong way, then this single man could set the land politically on fire and the chances of recovery could be slim indeed. Moreover, the events that could become a crisis were too often inspired in London, not India. It was not a good start especially when he had to think every day of the week about how he could continue to maintain his own role and the authority as well as dignity, while all the time reshaping the very constitutional possession for the Crown and India that he had been sent to protect.

No viceroy, with the exceptions of Curzon and Mountbatten, ever appeared bred for the role. Willingdon was no exception. They all had high and honoured backgrounds, but the job could easily have gone to any one of half a dozen candidates. Willingdon, in racing parlance, looked likely to be good over six furlongs but was possibly a very good miler and his trainer (doubling as prime minister) had brought him out at exactly the right time for the richer pickings of diplomacy in the India of 1930s militancy. ADC in Australia, popular MP and governor in two presidencies, Bombay and Madras. With that background he could charm in any language and an attractive wife ran well.

When Willingdon was governor of Madras he had to handle the Moplah rebellion during which thousands died. By using a committee of inquiry that reported well within a year and was accepted by the governor, Willingdon restored some form of order that eventually regained the respect of Indians including many who had been in the rebellion. He was then sent to rest in Canada as governor general and in 1931 returned to an India teetering under the weight of social, economic and political crises. The crucial test was how to persuade Gandhi to go to the London conference that year, 1931. Willingdon and Gandhi now started on a game of diplomatic pretence that Willingdon simply kept his nerve and Gandhi, as usual, kept everyone waiting. Would he go? Would he not go? He was delayed. He was not delayed. The other delegates to the Westminster conference had left on the last boat train. Gandhi, Willingdon really knew, would not go on that train. It was not a question of arguments unresolved. It was Gandhi not wanting to be seen travelling with the herd. There was a question of Gandhi's leadership among certain ambitious Indians. Gandhi chose to play the star, which he was. No Gandhi. No conference. When all had waited for the impossible time to approach, Gandhi said graciously that he would go. A special train, for Gandhi alone as it should be, went full speed and the objects were achieved: Gandhi played his game, viceroy let him, ship waiting just the right amount of time. There was more unrehearsed political drama to come in London with a new prime minister (Ramsay MacDonald), a new secretary of state for the India Office (Sir Samuel Hoare) and the new government, now a coalition national government uncertain with domestic and foreign policy crises every day of the parliamentary week, experimenting with a coalition of power, ostensibly still running their British Empire when they had difficulty holding together their tiny part of it all. Even the wisest of the Indian delegates failed to see the comedy before them as they pushed themselves to find yet another solution without the leading players truly understanding the differences and the options to resolve them.

Gandhi was centre stage as Congress's only representative and the Indian government's team (among which were Mrs Sarojini Naidu and Madan Mohan) being as important as they could be as self-appointed observers of the Indian government. It amounted to more than it looked. Willingdon was patted on the back but nothing was achieved, partly because MacDonald handled the whole thing badly. There was an attempt to isolate Gandhi by the Muslims having a pact with the British and Gandhi sat alone – a pathetic figure who did not understand what was going on and had no real idea how far the legal aspects of the conference had got and how much further, if at all, they had to go. Gandhi looked the holy figure in his home spun sheets, but no one quite knew what he was about, only that he was not quite sure what was going on. Willingdon was regarded as a good pair of hands who knew the end game and could play it as well as Gandhi. The criticism came from one of the government of India delegates, Pandit Madan Malaviya.

Mahamana Malaviya was born in 1861, the year Canning was attempting to put India back together after the Mutiny. He understood his identity represented something he aimed for, longed for rather than assumed was for ever because of his caste. It was a philosophy that might reject the popular view that the Mutiny failed. The Mutiny did not fail because it lived on the consciousness of a British raj that was forever uncertain what caused it – the impossibility for the British in the mid-nineteenth century to understand what they created and how much was left of the original source material, an Indian identity stretched across castes, religious and regional identities. He wanted to be a dreamer perhaps, a Kathavacak, a storyteller from the Bhagawat. Within that epic story was identity. But the family was poor and he became a successful lawyer, a millionaire by twenty-first-century reckoning. In 1913 he gave it all up and became an activist, demanding that India and not the British Empire should decide its own future. The father of the Congress movement, Gopala Krishna Gokhale, said 'Malaviyaji's sacrifice is a real one. Born in a poor family, he started earning thousands monthly. He tasted luxury and wealth but giving heed to the call of the nation, renouncing all he again embraced poverty.' There was no real sacrifice. Mahamana Malaviya was a success. He led Congress four times (no one else had done this nor would). Gandhi called him *pratah smaraniyaì*, a pious person. He was seen as a gentle person of sublime blameless grace. He was, also, no one's fool as Willingdon witnessed after the London conference. Moreover, Mahamana Malaviya had made a fortune as a brilliant advocate and with distinction because he was also an incisive academical lawyer – a surly combination when faced with a well-meaning and therefore patronising officer of the viceroy. He had once been described as more than a Hindu. He was the soul of Hinduism. When Gandhi had demanded audience with the viceroy, Willingdon had said 'No'. When Gandhi called a civil disobedience a demonstration, Willingdon arrested him and perhaps twenty thousand of his followers went to jail. This, said Mahamana Malaviya, was not the way to treat someone followed by millions. It was not the way to treat someone who everyone assumed or knew would become leader of a free India.

'Allow me very respectfully to say . . . that it was not Mahatma Gandhi or the Congress but Your Excellency's Government who forced a conflict. Your Excellency knew that Mr Gandhi is the greatest Indian living, that for the purity and unselfishness of his life and his high-souled devotion to the cause of his country and of humanity, he is adored by countless millions in India and widely respected in all parts of the world. You knew that for ten years he has been the recognized leader of the greatest political organization in India . . . You could imagine that whether it be this year or next year, when a new constitution is introduced in India, in all human probability, Your Excellency will have to hand over charge of the country's affairs to Mr Gandhi.'

Did Willingdon believe that? In 1932, he did not know what to believe. The viceroy understood better than Mahamana Malaviya that the British government, a national government, did not have a plan that included anything more than Dominion status and although assumptions were made about Gandhi, there remained those who saw Jinnah as a future leader of India, not a separated state. Willingdon's better assessment was that Gandhi would never want to be India's leader and would put aside any calling from Indians and the British. Willingdon imagined Gandhi would want to carry on being the mystical figure that would sleep while India burned. Mahamana Malaviya's view was based on his assumption that there was no one other than Gandhi who could dominate play-politics and enchant his nation. He could, though, never lead his country in the day-by-day powerplay of *real politik*.

'You also knew that your refusal to see him might lead to a terrible situation arising in the country. It is a calamity that Your

Excellency did not realize that such a man had a right to expect
the courtesy of an interview from Your Excellency as the head
for the time being of the Government of the country. The
refusal of that courtesy was a flagrant departure from the path of
conciliation . . . it was a national affront to India . . . You have
virtually substituted a reign of ordinances for a reign of law.'

Willingdon was not insensitive to this criticism. He was also
right in feeling some of the blame had to be laid at Gandhi's
door. Gandhi was sometimes seen as a devious figure corner-
ing the British by simply saying No (or nothing) to a proposal
or even a meeting in order to sow confusion. He was usually
successful. Government House had long departed from the
days of balancing ghosts, a commonplace pastime in India.
The British token was memories of the Mutiny with the
transformation brought to India by Curzon and now the uncertainties that would mean a Second World War soon. In other
words, the Indians, mainly through the inspiration of Gandhi
(inspiration not leadership) and the confusions from the political house of Jinnah, were reaching into the practical rather
than protest positions of challenging for freedoms. A large part
of the challenge being for self-government and the more
unwilling challenging for full independence. The events in
India and in London had precluded much chance of the one
thing necessary to sort the differences: a policy. This was the
issue Willingdon addressed at Calcutta on 30 December 1931.

'I have fully realized since I have been the head of the
Government of India, the feeling of doubt and bewilderment
that have risen in the minds of both officials and non-officials,
on account of the fact that they found it difficult to understand
what the policy of Government has been during recent months.'

This was an admission of two proportions. Firstly, the viceroy did not have a form of words to disguise the situation because the people he was apologising to were better informed than he. Secondly, this was one of the few times any viceroy had been on the defensive. India had changed and there was no going back. From December 1931, India was on the road to independence. It might not happen for sixteen years, but happen it would. Willingdon spoke with authority, but he sounded more convincing than he was.

'Let there be no doubt about our policy now. We are determined to move on as rapidly as possible with our work on constitutional reforms. But I wish to make it perfectly clear, that while non-cooperation or any other subversive activities will not be allowed to impede the constitutional programme, every measure will be taken to maintain law and order throughout the country and to prevent any party who attempts to do so from paralyzing the administration whether their activities take the form of no-rent or no-revenue campaign or boycott of British goods and institutions as political measures, or defiance of the laws of the country. Any measure which Government may take will be particularly directed against organizations which deliberately attempt to create chaos and destroy any chance of any economic improvement in the country and there will be no hesitation on the part of the Government in giving local Governments all reasonable powers to deal with the situation that may arise.'

Again, was Willingdon right abut Gandhi's image? Was he out somewhere on another planet, ill-prepared, ill-informed and dressed as a symbol that could never be of any practical value other than inspiring followers who had no one else to

look to their interests? Yes. Gandhi could have made a proper
contribution and therefore a difference to the outcome of the
London conference. He frustrated those who were looking for
a solution and when the meeting ended did nothing more
than recite a clever goodbye that he expected would make
everyone think it was everyone other than Gandhi who failed
at Westminster; in fact, there was a case that it was the other
way round. Gandhi gave a vote of thanks to MacDonald –
hardly the moralising chairman needed in the conference –
and said he was sorry that they had come to a parting of the
ways. The conference was a second-rate affair and showed
that, in spite of title and responsibility, none had gone to
Westminster with any plans that would move forward the
debate. The British did not want it moved on in this forum;
the Indians – split as ever – had no idea how to get anything
but a trip to London out of it. Gandhi was the biggest disappointment because he had nothing to offer other than his
image. Too many of the India delegates, as Pandit Nehru
observed, were looking for jobs. 'It was all jobbery,' is how
Nehru described the occasion, 'big, jobs, little jobs and seats
for the Hindus, for the Muslims, for the Sikhs, for the Anglo-
Indians, for the Europeans, but all jobs for the upper classes,
the masses had no look-in. Opportunism was rampant and
different groups seemed to prowl about like hungry wolves
waiting for their prey – the spoils under the new Constitution.
The very conception of freedom has taken the form of large-
scale Jobbery.'[7]

Gandhi's view was that as Congress was representing 85
per cent of India it should have a special position. His second
point was that India did not need the British to resolve communal issues. It was as if no one listened, only to themselves. Here
again the purpose of the viceroy was to rule, to be head of

government in India. The talks in London at official level and subsequent discussion in India appeared to see the viceroy as almost a bystander. It was as if the three centuries of British authority and experience in India were forgotten; not much more than a ceremonial status that had brought nothing of interest to the discussion. The London talks were very much about India's present state and how it might be brought perhaps to independence through self-government and whether or not that difference was understood.

Gandhi could have got so much from the London conference. Instead he returned to India demoralised and that was mostly his fault. He had gone to London without any advisors and knew little of what was going on. London, Paris and Geneva were next on his itinerary. He never spoke to the people who could have helped the cause. Willingdon's expressed disappointment was real enough. He did not want empty conferences, nor did he want a disgruntled Gandhi in jail along with thousands of his followers. Furthermore there was his own promise that the government would stand firm but at the same time he wanted the discussions to see the logic and get rid of Nehru's 'jobbery.' Mahamana Malaviya would not let go of Willingdon.

' Let me assure Your Excellency that the determination to win freedom [this is 1932] is stronger now and that oppressive and unjust orders and ordinances will be defied to a greater extent than even before. Since the present policy was adopted, within the short period of a few weeks, the total number of persons who have been arrested and imprisoned has already gone up to over 20,000. If the Government will continue their present policy it may be taken as certain that the number will go even higher. And what will you have achieved? Far from having

been crushed, the Civil Disobedience movement will have
been fed and made stronger by reason of the suffering people
will undergo. Their determination to obtain full freedom will
have become stronger . . . Is it wise, is it statesmanlike to create
all the loss, all the suffering, all the trouble that is staring us in
the face, when it is certain that you will have to retrace the
steps you are taking at present? Equally wrong and futile will be
the effort to kill the Congress. You might as well think of killing
the political soul of India . . . I very respectfully call upon Your
Excellency to undo the great wrong you have committed . . .
And when you have thus created a calm and peaceful atmosphere, invite Mahatma Gandhi and others to discuss the larger
question of constitutional reforms and enable them to tender
their co-operation in framing a constitution for India which
will place her on a footing of absolute equality with Great
Britain and thereby establish a friendship between England
and India honourable and beneficial to both countries.'

The importance of this edited letter to Willingdon is to give
some idea of how the role of the viceroy was handling the other
end of Indian dissatisfaction. This was the quiet intellectual
approach that contained enough truth, certainly impressions
of reality if that is what truth is, to wonder how much of what
was proposed could be delivered. Equally important, was this
the point when the India Office and therefore the national
government would want to move on policy and if so, how far
and in what direction? One thing Willingdon knew without
asking was that there was enough opposition to changing
policy on India if change at all hinted that independence was
remotely possible. He, for one, understood that the cross-mix
of Indian leadership had not yet understood the terrible possibilities for the whole of the subcontinent at that moment if the

British went. Mahamana Malaviya's voice was faint. What of Gandhi?

In the spring of 1933, Gandhi was let out of the Yervada jail having led another disobedience demonstration and started a twenty-one-day fast. Willingdon's policy was to discharge Gandhi when he went on any fast to forestall the consequences. Gandhi immediately asked Willingdon to release the rest of his followers. Willingdon would not. A further threat from Gandhi followed and back he went to Yervada, back he went on a fast, back he went to the gates and was sent on his way. Willingdon, while not losing sight of Gandhi's potential for trouble, was demonstrating to him that his movement was seen as less and less powerful. It was as if he were treated as a vagrant. Willingdon was wrong. In the 1934 elections, Congress triumphed and the civil disobedience movement was seen as all but finished. Gandhi was a single emblem. The movement itself was about to become an outsider, an all but secret society. Congress could not hide its disappointment. Gandhi after all only had to say he was fasting and most of India watched anxiously for news. As for Willingdon, the viceroy had excelled. Yet his judgement could be awry on important and established issues, such as how far the princes wanted to go with changes. One mood of the princes entirely escaped Willingdon: some did not want constitutional change because they rightly believed their positions would be usurped as independence approached. There certainly were those among the new leadership who saw the princes as worse than the imperial rulers. Where Willingdon could never be faulted was in his sense that times were indeed in change and the indignity of being denied because you were black, brown or whatever was beyond his patience. The opportunity for protest came as governor when he was banned from Bombay's exclusively

white combined clubs – Byculla, Bombay Gymkhana and
Royal Bombay Yacht Club – because he insisted on taking in
Indian friends.

Willingdon's response was very Willingdon: he started his
own club open to all and it still exists as the Royal Willingdon
Sports Club and is considered to be the most exclusive club
in India, where membership is closed to outsiders and only
sons of members may go on the club waiting list. A very
different exclusivity. No viceroy has his name on anything
that reminds one so much of the raj, but it is in memory of a
man who by challenging such a social distinction was digging
at the fabric that made peaceful change so impossible. An aristocrat may have thought the same but may not have challenged the social distinction that Willingdon quietly ignored.
He went in 1936, was made a marquess, constable of Dover
Castle, lord warden of the Cinque Ports and watched some
cricket.

No one could have been better turned out by Scottish aristocracy to be viceroy of India than the second marquess of
Linlithgow (1887–1952). His pedigree was impeccable. He
was to make the most arrogant of howlers, but when he did
Britain was once more at war with Germany and few bothered
with the preciousness of protocols. Anyway, as far as the British
were concerned, only the Indians were upset, which was a
good enough reading of the situation.

Linlithgow was one of the Linlithgowshire Hopes, in his
case Victor Alexander John Hope of Hopetoun House where
he was born on 24 September 1887, the year of Queen
Victoria's Golden Jubilee and coincidentally the year of the
first colonial conferences, the forerunner of the still existing
Commonwealth Heads of Government Conferences. He

married Doreen Milner, daughter of a baronet. Life was straightforward. In the Great War he was a colonel in the Lothian and Border horse and had a battalion of Royal Scots. He was an ideal candidate for a chairmanship in Whitehall and so he was chosen as Lord of the Admiralty, deputy chairman of the Unionist Party, president of the Navy League, the Medical Research Council and the Imperial College of Science and Technology. Importantly for his later role, Linlithgow, having turned down the governorship of Madras (it was no great appointment if a man with a castle to keep had to have a sound income), became chairman of the Royal Commission on Agriculture in India for two years (1926–28) and from 1933, two years as chairman of the joint parliamentary select committee on Indian constitutional reform.

When Willingdon returned to Lord's, Linlithgow was the obvious choice to go to India. He was to become the longest-serving viceroy (seven and a half years). His were the most trying times: constitutional failure; insurrection; the Second World War. No sign of a sinecure for this marquess. When Linlithgow went to Calcutta, India was still living by its 1919 constitution and there had been in just seven years six attempts to bring all sides together: the 1928 Simon Commission, the three round tables of 1930/31/32, 1931 the parliamentary joint select committee to set up the 1935 India Act. Linlithgow had been the chairman of the select committee, which is why either he or Lord Zetland, both with India experience, should succeed Willingdon.

The way of the 1930s was generous to appointees. With his administrative experience, especially on the committee, Linlithgow should have stayed in England to be secretary of state in the India Office. Instead he was allowed to take his pick and chose the harder job, viceroy. Zetland would have been a better choice for everyone, certainly for Linlithgow. The government in London's objective before Linlithgow went to India was Dominion status – self-government under the Crown. The Conservative Party majority accepted this attempt, with the right wing of the party voting for it but very reluctantly. There were four principles in the India Act. Each one was a challenge for any viceroy. The provinces would have parliamentary government but the governors could take over if the system broke down. The governors were also expected to protect minorities. Voting was for about thirty million selected Indians and there would be separate voting rights for Muslims and Hindus. Thirdly the princely states and British India would be represented in a federal government. This was opposed by Churchill and the Conservative right wing in the Commons and by Salisbury in the Lords; it was an almost impossible task for the viceroy to establish, certainly one with unknown hazards. Linlithgow would be the keystone; if he failed then the whole apparatus of Indian government could easily collapse. It would be, said sometime chancellor Sir Robert Horne (a ladies' man of considerable record), the most exacting duty laid upon one man in the history of parliament. In his book on his father, John Glendevon records that, such was the belief in what Horne had said, John Fergusson the estate manager had cut the grass of the mausoleum at the family seat, Hopetoun, on the grounds that one never knew what might happen in these circumstances. Given the record of viceroys and vicereines in similar circumstances, that was probably a seamanlike precaution.[8] Linlithgow was a strong man with a sensitive nature. If that should sound unlikely or too forgiving, it was an observation for many who knew him and saw him attempt to deliver on his terms of reference when he arrived in India in 1936.

This was apparent in what was something of a novelty, a public radio broadcast that year in India in which he immediately swore his viceregal oaths. Strength in any such society must work from all sides and be protected by law and, in that case, most easily by order. Note the opening sentence, we may not always think that possible.

'Now speaking to you in your homes with those you love about you, I wish you to know that as I promised my true allegiance to His Majesty [broadcast in April, so Edward VIII who abdicated in December 1936] and dedicated myself to the service of India, I was conscious that I spoke not only for myself but also for you all . . . Among the manifold duties of viceroy, none is more vital than that of the maintenance of peace and good order throughout India. Believe me my friends, that I can do you no greater service than by the vigilance and effective discharge of this duty. The long story of progress and political evolution throughout the world proves beyond all question that of all the factors that may make for retrogression and reaction, none is more powerful than civil disorder to inflict irreparable hurt upon the body-politic. This and all other duties and responsibilities laid upon me . . . I will discharge without fear or favour, affection or ill-will . . .'

This was not a standard speech. Linlithgow was not a stranger in India. He knew the sometimes destructive corruption of law and order in the name of movements and the right to protest. Gandhi's protests were included in his suspicions that for example, civil disobedience was considerable, albeit momentarily hurt in the progress towards self-government that was impossible without self-reform. His message that April day of impartiality within the rule of law brought the reaction of some that the new viceroy would continue the right if uncertain way towards reform and therefore eventually self-government and more. There was also the rumour that Linlithgow was instructed to meet Gandhi, which he had never done, and so that prompted the word to come back to him that Jinnah, the president of the Muslim League, construed impartiality as a means of proportional bad reward for Muslims' loyalty to the government. It was not a good start, although the viceroy had not seen either of the two leaders, Gandhi and Jinnah. If he saw Gandhi it would be confirming what Jinnah imagined. When the Indian industrialist G.D. Birla, a Congress Party funder, tried to get Linlithgow to meet Gandhi it was because Birla, although he was not so influential as he made out to be, knew that if Linlithgow sent for Gandhi (and that was the protocol) then the process would move on. Gandhi would have the authority that comes from successfully defending a position. Linlithgow's position was not as might now be imagined; he was not there to go between the protagonists until an answer that would suit the government in London had been achieved. His response to Birla was that he (the viceroy) could not possibly do anything, meet, write and talk in any manner that would seem to be pro-Congress. Thus, he understood the difficulties between Gandhi and other voices in Congress but Congress had to sort out its own problems.

While the balancing act of who to see, what to see and what to say was going on every day in Linlithgow's routine, his biggest daily difficulty was one that today would be unimaginable. He, the viceroy of India, did not have a secretariat. It was bad enough not to have a proper administration group in his office, but imagine what it would be like if federation were achieved.

When he asked for a secretariat, there were shrugs all round. It was not simply a financial difficulty. India did not have sufficient numbers of young men who either wanted to enter for or could pass the Indian civil servant entrance examinations and the ones that did were not passing at high enough levels to staff top-class departments, such as Department of Finance. The viceroy's secretariat was supposed to be different from other departments. He would take the best graduates and then train them further. At a time when Linlithgow was supposed to be getting on with the most trying job ever asked of an individual he was discovering that no one in any authority had thought ahead. It was more likely that, during the shortages naturally occurring during the First World War as men joined the army and similar shortages after because men went different ways, departments had refused to get involved in a collective search for new recruits and restructuring because they would inevitably have risked losing some in their own departments. The bureaucracy of bureaucracy choked on its own. The viceroy had to succeed if he was going to endless meetings with no expert back-up, never mind file writers. Moreover, for the first time departments were going to find notes from the viceroy in their agendas. The land of bureaucracy was stepping up to a new level of the very same profession.

Linlithgow was being criticised for not getting the pace set towards federation, but he could not rely on the India Office to get on with what he regarded as their end. In September 1936, Linlithgow pressed the India Office for what was happening to get the princes into the federation programme. Federation was all about the native states and the princes or their nominees attending the proposed federal parliament. It was the way to bring the different factions in India towards governing an independent state. That autumn in London, Linlithgow was pressing the secretary of state on whether he realised the need for speed in negotiating with the princes. Everything about setting up the federal system was going well enough for it to be in place by the spring of 1937. Everything, that is, other than the princes. Zetland was slow or not answering. Linlithgow had three men from the Political Department – Sir Arthur Lothian, Sir Francis Wylie and Sir Courtenay Latimer – who could head three small teams to talk the princes through the process, answer their questions and take, where necessary, their suggestions as well as their queries to him and then to London. They were not allowed to try to get the princes to join. It was a good idea in principle but would run into trouble when the princes sometimes together observed that the three appeared to be bypassing the political agents. The princes were hardly an ill-informed and ill-educated bunch. They did what Linlithgow should have expected. They got their lawyers onto the federation brochure that raised what became major issues, such as what would happen to tax revenues, who paid and how much for army protection. Add a simple miscalculation to the major and impossible obstruction to federation like Congress's steadfast object, and Zetland's instruction to Linlithgow to take a rest was probably as good as advice was going to get. Zetland did not want to lose the princes by rushing them. They in turn had a view not expressed but one that went with a sentiment going back to the introduction of the viceroy in 1858. Although the viceroy was subordinate to the secretary of state, in the princes' eyes, the viceroy was the monarch's representative and a prince walked with royalty – or his representative. Whatever their sentiment, Linlithgow was certainly obliged to give in to Zetland. The viceroy was the one setting the pace not the secretary of state, a point to be remembered with a consideration of all above before going along with the historical view that Linlithgow's indecision and progress rate was not what had been expected of him when he was sent to Calcutta.

In 1939, the major princes who had, less than a decade earlier, supported the federal idea gathered in Bombay. Federation? No thank you. What had happened for Linlithgow to lose the princes? Linlithgow blamed the political officers. They blamed Linlithgow. One of them, Wylie, said they should have been allowed to advise the princes to join. But it was unfair to blame Linlithgow for that. It was Zetland in London who had insisted that the political officers sent out by Linlithgow should not be allowed to tell the princes what to do.

The princes were in the odd position of not wanting a federation but not wanting to be seen as the people who spoiled it. They wanted to be in the process – fearful rather than indifferent. The fear included loss of status. They were princes but could be reduced to constitutional rulers. That was not what they expected. Linlithgow could not be seen to help them because he had authority to change the conditions. There was not much he could not do, amend or instigate. A recurring condition of his inability to press on was that Willingdon had not been able, certainly in his closing quarter of his rule, to set any pace that Linlithgow was now attempting to do from scratch. Willingdon was living up to a reputation of being a good man, likeable but surprisingly not as good as most had thought him to be. Linlithgow was paying the price although as he was in office for so long, he had less reason not to put everything in place on his own terms.

The 1937 elections took place for provincial government and Congress won six provinces. Congress refused to take their seats and Jawaharlal Nehru, its president, had never intended to. Linlithgow knew this before the election. London blamed him for Nehru's action. The suggestion was more elections. The viceroy could see no reason to dissolve the Assembly, have another election while knowing full well that Congress would take part in the election but refuse to take office. He did what he could only do under Section 93b of the Act: at no stage leave himself open to any suggestion that he had failed to give the utmost help in working, or trying to work the parliamentary system in India. This, though few appreciated it, was a sign that Linlithgow was going to do nothing. He was waiting to see what the governors would do. Linlithgow had decided it was not time for him to intervene and he would not repeat that even to Lord Halifax the foreign secretary, who seemed to forget times had changed since he was viceroy as Irwin.

This period, the 1935 India Act and the 1937 elections with the predicted Congress attitude, brought the question of federation to a standstill. Linlithgow had been in India not a year, but he knew enough of what the working documents had produced at the London conference to believe at this stage, as often in India, it was best to do nothing unless he could see the opportunity among personalities that would not be there later when they took stock. Now was such a moment, but it was the secretary of state in London, Lord Zetland, who wanted the viceroy to hold back. Zetland in London was under just as much pressure as Linlithgow in India, but of a different kind. His enemy was neither time nor the mysterious Gandhi. It was the group of rightwing Tories who still refused to accept that the British might lose India. Charles Chenevix Trench was in the Indian army at this time and as the title of his memoir, *Viceroy's Agent*[9], suggests was on what he called the front line watching the future of India unfold. He was not a fan of Linlithgow. He was, like Zetland, even less a fan of Churchill.

'The die-hard wing of the Party took its lead from Winston Churchill who was stubbornly hostile to any political concession. As a British cavalry subaltern he had served briefly in India forty years earlier but had spent the long hot afternoons perfecting his prose-style by reading Gibbon rather than increasing his knowledge of India by learning Urdu. He knew nothing of India and did not want to learn. He disliked and distrusted Indians.'

This was a common view of one of the most influential men at Westminster who could so influence the way Cabinet would vote on India. Moreover, was he so uninterested in India? Was it not Churchill who had said that he did not become a member of the British government just to see it given away to India? Irwin had made a strong point on the difference of perception of viceroy and secretary of state. The view of the princes was quite different, as Irwin pointed out to Zetland.

'I don't know where you get the idea that the Government of India is unsympathetic to the idea of the All-India Federation. This is really not the case, for while some of us, including myself, may have thought it very odd and very undesirable for the princes to tumble into a Federation three years ago, having committed themselves to it, we have always felt that it was impossible for them to keep out . . . I spend the greater part of my time canvassing the princes and exhorting them to take the plunge.'

In May, the London political journal, the *New Statesman*, criticised his decision with the theme that Linlithgow's do-nothing policy was at the very least unhelpful. In the Lords, a debate supported Linlithgow's position. He wrote to Zetland

saying he was encouraged by the debate. However, he did
wonder if the time had not come for him to ask Gandhi to
come and see him. His advisors suggested the time was not
right. He accepted that advice. Meanwhile Nehru was attempting to break the stand-together action of the Muslim
population even to the tactic of getting the left wing of the
Muslim League to break away from the League and join
Congress. Congress was trouble in a barrel. There was no rattle
to it. It was doing everything to turn the idea of federation into
a kaleidoscope of crooked promises and direct challenges that
could only frighten off the princes and Muslims alike. Zetland
was wilting. He virtually said as much in a letter to the viceroy.

> 'I have the uncomfortable feeling that the market is at present
> against us. We appear to be dealing with unwilling sellers and
> are tempted to put our offers high in consequence. But so far
> as I can judge the States are unwilling to commit themselves
> until the political and financial future in British India is clearer.
> If they come to see that they will be safer inside the Federation
> than out of it – and otherwise the Federation cannot come into
> existence – then we shall be dealing with people who must sell
> and shall be able to make a better bargain . . .'

There comes a moment when diplomatic code must not be
confused with the cleverness of a secretary of state who could
put forward suggestions but they amount to nothing more than
yet another way of coming to the same failure and so the secretary of state resorts to poor theatre. Linlithgow was not contradicting Zetland; after all, he had few fresh ideas of his own
other than extending the life of the Assembly. Zetland was at a
loss with anything but the theatre of his office playing to an
almost empty theatre. No one was listening to him. He needed

to take more notice of Linlithgow, who had now made clear that he believed the shortest road to independence was to accept the new constitution to work its best pieces because in his view constitutions were to be plundered for the most useful parts and not to be followed line by line. Linlithgow delivered this message then went back to the residence to see what would happen. Linlithgow kept his nerve and all in London praised him. His stock was rising again and he remained calm.

British India was the original East India Company territory solely ruled by the British Crown after 1858. The 562 princely states were ruled by the princes and were in alliance with British India – the princes paid allegiance to the viceroy and so to the monarch. Linlithgow's task was to get British India and the princely states in one federation, so setting both on the road to self-government and perhaps beyond. Linlithgow was expected by the government in London to pull together 390 million Indians, 300 of whom were Hindu and so, if they followed any political party, it would have been Congress and Gandhi and Nehru would have been the political heroes. The rest of India was some ninety million Muslims and in theory they were followers of the Muslim League and Jinnah. The rest of the population were the nine million in the princely states. It was like trying to rule modern Europe with no one agreeing to the rules. And the similarity may be exaggerated. Linlithgow's task was hardened because he was not getting the basic support he needed from London and, for apparently good reasons, he had never met Gandhi, Jinnah nor Nehru – the three men who could swing peace only if the three agreed on whatever the plan and, because the viceroy's plan was a federal state, this was unlikely.

Although this period in the 1930s would decide the future of the empire, the government in London was divided on what would happen, if anything. The different groups in India were not even beginning to work together, even to get what was open to them all. The viceroy had hardly any staff, very few ideas of how to get a set menu of political decisions to come together and did not know how the Indian protagonists would react to anything he and his government in London would propose. Linlithgow himself was not always certain that his supposed friend Lord Zetland, as head of the India Office, was being entirely straight with him. They could never at 5,000 miles' distance always see eye to eye, with Linlithgow suspicious of Zetland's motives and the Indians opposing Linlithgow and each other. In spite of the new communications – and we should have long abandoned the idea of the hopeless pre-First World War system – there was a continuous anxiety that the viceroy was not being kept up to speed. It would take nothing more than Zetland going home early, and therefore the viceroy going two days without direct communications, for his insecurities about not being told everything to surface. Zetland apologised; Linlithgow had every right to be suspicious. Distance was a poor diplomat.

Linlithgow had a harder job as viceroy than any of his predecessors. He was being told to pull the Indians together into a scheme of federations and perhaps more without the slightest hope that the Indians would agree among themselves, never mind with him. He was a hero in London one month and not the next month. It was not the job many people thought.

The 1935 India Act allowed the eleven Indian provinces to assume autonomy and, if the princes unanimously agreed to conditions, an all-India federation. Changes demanded cooperation among India's leaders, particularly from the princes. None of these conditions for transforming the ruling of India could be guaranteed. Congress had a majority of the provinces after the 1936 elections. Linlithgow hoped for progress and he got it but not until after Congress had been promised that the provincial governors would not exert their special powers, a tactic in India used to spoil reasonable decisions taken locally. Moreover and as ever, the viceroy could never truly guarantee the position of the princes who the British had invented (Gandhi's view of them), who kept an ear to who was getting what in the way of concessions and immediately wanted a better arrangement than before – still an echo of who had more gun salutes. In London, the Department of State was asking their viceroy why he had delays and he was mentioning concessions and money and London was refusing to make concessions and give any more money to the princes. Equally, Linlithgow might have acted with sternness towards the princes that would have come naturally to his possession and the ways of Scottish estate owners but once more it was London who warned him off.

The democratic conversion of India was still opposed by those powerful figures in St James's who believed that nothing should happen in India that aroused suspicions that the princes in particular were taking advantage of the limited negotiation powers of the viceroy. Furthermore, true to form, the Muslim League and Congress chose not to agree although they could harmlessly have done so. Then came the Second World War and the bewildering political and diplomatic blunder by Linlithgow. The manner of Linlithgow's announcement of war was tactless and sadly, all that he is remembered for.

On 3 September 1939, Britain with France declared war against Germany. Linlithgow without a single word to the

political leaders in India – the provincial governments including the eight under Congress – announced that India was at
war with Germany. A viceroy had done what no other viceroy
had done, even in 1914; Linlithgow sent 400 million Indians
to war without telling them. Indians generally appear to have
seen this single act of a formal constitution position (the federal
constitution he had been negotiating had not been set up) as
imperial insensitivity at the very least. Taking a country to war
without prior consultations, even a courtesy discussion, would
seem so unlikely as to appear an administrative mistake. It was
not. The viceroy had no intention of asking the Indian political body what would have been seen in his mind as permission
to go to war with Germany. India was British. India was therefore at war. Eighty years on, India was still ruled in the manner
of Curzon and Mayo. The Muslim League supported
Linlithgow in principle but demanded there should never be
a constitutional shift without the League's prior notice and
approval. Congress provocatively but reasonably demanded
that Linlithgow explain in considerable detail what were the
details and demanded independence. Congress then organised the Quit India campaign and its leaders were jailed. War
was declared and two and a half million troops were sent to
fight in the four quarters of the war against the Axis. Eighty-
seven thousand were killed.

India was at war and the apparent key to negotiations on
India's future, Gandhi, was the world's most famous pacifist.
He, seemingly as ever, did not react as the diplomatically nervous may have expected. Gandhi distinguished between
Germany who had committed aggression and Britain who had
not. Yet, Gandhi within his persuasion of non-violence could
only give his moral support but no active help in the Allied
effort. Moreover, this was not the British loyalist he had been

in South Africa during the First World War. This second Great
War would demand Indian participation even if Britain in the
European theatre fell. In India, in 1939, the attrition was not
military but political. The Congress ministers resigned and
would never return. Linlithgow needed the support of the
Muslim League and the Hindu Mahasabha, who saw the obvious: any group who supported the British would not be slaves
of the British but would be seen as defenders of India and,
importantly, would be given guns. Linlithgow's mind was also
exercised by what Gandhi might do. He could cause no end of
mischief that in wartime would not be so easy to dismiss. Word
was also coming from all sources that the Congress leadership
expected major pronouncement and action from Gandhi. It
did not happen. Gandhi did not want to use the war to break
whatever unity might come with it. Nor did he call for civil
disobedience, being aware that some would use it as a reason
to call major strikes and so he would be blamed for that. This
would result in nothing more than anarchy and ruin. Congress
as near as anything took action that would make Gandhi's
warning come to something.

Congress's view was that Britain was at war for imperialist
reasons and so it insisted there should be a return to civil
disobedience. Congress did not have the authority to organise
civil disobedience. Only one man had that. He called the war
in Europe 'hourly butchery'. He wanted no part in it and more
perceptively understood that the British had no time to come
to anything like a future agreement while the lights in Europe
were still out. 'Wait till the heat of the battle in the heart of
Allies countries subside . . . we are nearing our goal without
firing a single shot.'

The politics of India had never been simply exercised and
there was nothing in the conduct nor consequences of war that

would change this condition nor push forward a leader who would be heard differently in these times. Now there were. Congress suggested they would support Britain but by doing so would be entitled to independence after the war. Gandhi was out. Congress cut him adrift. He wrote to the viceroy. He told him that Britain was losing the war and that if the British were to send him (Gandhi) to Germany to talk to Hitler (not a bad man, said Gandhi) he would be at the viceroy's disposal. Linlithgow thanked Gandhi for his offer but assured him that the British would win the war. It was Linlithgow's view, however, that Britain could be attacked in areas and from sources she had not anticipated.

When America joined the Second World War, President FD Roosevelt made clear that it was his view that the 1941 Atlantic Charter that declared the right to freedom and democracy applied to all countries. Linlithgow had not picked this up. Churchill had. He made the point that this did not include India and that he (WSC) 'had not become His Majesty's First Minister to preside over the liquidation of the British Empire.'

Churchill sent Stafford Cripps to India in March 1942 with a single purpose: to get the Indians on side in the war effort, particularly as Rangoon and Singapore had fallen to the Japanese and India had to assume it was threatened as it had not been in the First World War. In 1914, under unhampered imperial British rule, India joined the war and were told who they should fight and where they should fight. After Linlithgow's insensitive declaration that India was at war, the politics of India's reaction made the matter totally unmanageable. Cripps, a very close friend of Nehru (but not of Churchill), arrived with a British promise of elections and constitutional changes after the war. Linlithgow read the proposals and took against them. They were in fact written by Cripps, who believed he had what the Indians would accept (Nehru's influence?).

'the creation of a new Indian Union which shall constitute a Dominion associated with the United Kingdom and other Dominions by a common allegiance to the Crown but equal to them in every respect, in no way subordinate in any aspects of its domestic and external affairs.'

What become of the viceroy after the war was left open because no one seemed to know what to do with the post. It would depend on how India got to independence. That was the official line that was not quite the case. Cripps told the Indians that he would make sure that Linlithgow would be recalled immediately and India could have Dominion status so there was no need for a viceroy at all – a governor general, yes but not a viceroy.

Gandhi told Cripps that if that was all the British could manage he may as well get the next plane to London. This was the moment for the Congress to set up the 'Quit India' movement when Gandhi suggested what to him was the obvious: Japan was at war with the British. If the British left India there would be no reason for Japan to invade.

The Cripps mission failed because Gandhi was against it; because Indian power would never be legalised and so was an illusion; because Linlithgow himself schemed against Cripps and had support from the very top in the India Office in London and with Leo Amery, the secretary of state, for so doing. It went higher than that. That the viceroy could be plotting against what was presented as British policy suggests that he must have had tacit support from Churchill even if none spoke directly about it.

When the war was done, Churchill had gone and Cripps's long-term offer of independence remained the only possibility for India. This had to be the case otherwise Congress would not have stood in droves for seats during the immediate post-war elections. Linlithgow was a man of undoubted courage but the wrong viceroy for this time, his colleagues in London decided. Maybe not true. Willingdon had not prepared the ground as he had been expected to do. London had let the viceroy down because too often the national government had been indecisive and at other times totally preoccupied with the road to war. Furthermore, almost no one in London, not even Attlee and Cripps, knew what to do about India and they certainly had to rely entirely on the viceroy to make it happen even when they were not sure what was supposed to happen. As they grew closer to the truth that it was straightforward independence, they were still keeping clear of that reality. Linlithgow did not achieve what could have been achieved. He was there, for more time than most, to prepare India for independence and failed. But was it failure? Was it really, at the time, so easy to make such a judgement? It is worth remembering how the critics, including Linlithgow's own colleagues in the early 1930s, had coped with Gandhi. What had they really understood by the dilemma of Jinnah? Did they really understand the deviousness of Nehru? The answers are plain: they did not cope with Gandhi. They did not understand Jinnah. They found Nehru a mystery when all the time his motives were obvious. He, as others, was mesmerised by Gandhi but never understood the importance of Jawaharlal Nehru, whom he thought something of a dilettante. Nehru saw Linlithgow as slow, not very intelligent and certainly an untouchable. Gandhi had no doubts about Linlithgow. On 27 September he wrote to the escaping viscount and said so:

Dear Lord Linlithgow,

On the eve of your departure from India I would like to send you a word. Of all the high functionaries I have had the honour of knowing, none has been the cause of such deep sorrow to me as you have been. It has cut me to the quick to have to think of you as having countenanced untruth and that regarding one whom at one time, you considered as your friend. I hope and pray that God will some day put it into your heart to realize that you, a representative of a great nation, had been led into a grievous error.

With good wishes, I still remain your friend,
M.K. Gandhi

Linlithgow's reply? Simply what he thought of him:

Dear Mr Gandhi,

I have received your letter of 27th September. I am indeed sorry that your feelings about any deeds or words of mine should be as you describe. But I must be allowed as gently as I may, to make plain to you that I am quite unable to accept your interpretation of the events in question.

As for the corrective virtues of time and reflection, evidently these are ubiquitous in their operation and wisely to be rejected by no man.

Yours sincerely.
Linlithgow

Both men knew the truth of it as important failures – which is what they were – usually do.

No one got it right during the crucial period between 1936 and the middle of the Second World War. At least Linlithgow had understood in 1936 the British guns in Singapore were facing the wrong way and if the Japanese invaded, which he thought they would, then all would be lost. He told the right people. The right people did not believe him. That Linlithgow was extremely tall, 6'5" with a permanent physical infirmity that gave him a stiff posture, was not an easy image to carry. His wife was 6'. They certainly presented a formidable platform at the residence. In truth, they looked a bit like the empire: rock solid and giving little away about its true reasons for behaving as it did. He went in October 1943, the war still on. The British sent a general. A very good general. He too they did not properly listen to.

CHAPTER XIV

IN THE END – THE GENERAL
AND THE ADMIRAL

Archibald Percival Wavell came from a line of soldiers via Winchester College, had a good war and with his hat off and just one eye looked a poet, which is what he was. He knew India from childhood and was commissioned into the Black Watch and sent to India with his regiment. He was a star of army staff college, spent a year with the Russian army and as a liaison officer to Grand Duke Nicholas served on the staff of some of the most brilliant and successful generals of his day including Allenby. His book *Generals and Generalship* is a classic on military leadership and was carried by Rommel in his kit-bag. His war record began in the second Boer War, Bazar Valley, Ypres (Lost his eye. Got an MC). During the Second World War (in spite of some views, Wavell did better than most) he was commander-in-chief of the Middle East and then India and commanded the army against the Japanese – this, a typical story of too much to do with too little to do it, an obvious historical cliché but one enviously made by Adrian Fort in his biography of Wavell[1].

Wavell has all but gone from his nation's memory of the Second World War, yet he was, particularly during the difficult months of 1940 and early 1941, the most successful general in the British army. It was a period of too many reversals in the northern campaign and demands not fulfilled in the Western Desert until Wavell's appointment. In January the Italians surrendered in the Western Desert. Wavell's stock knew no limits. He was rightly a national hero and admired in America and throughout the colonies. For three years, from 1940 to 1943, Wavell commanded successfully in the Middle East and the Far East across imperial and colonial territory on the eve of the period of change that would mean the very territory he was saving from the enemy would begin the process of demanding that Britain would set the people free. The empire was demanding freedoms that could not be denied once the Second World War was over. That Wavell had commanded in the Far East and understood better than any governor, including Mountbatten, what was inevitable, what therefore was impossible and thus possible, makes a bit of a mystery why he was never allowed to stay on and bring about the end of India as part of the empire. He was too, the product of the system that made that entire notion so obvious. He had been good at Winchester, but then probably so was everyone else and so had been the nine earlier Wavell boys tutored at that place. He might have become an academic, but the Wavells were soldiers; he was born when his father's regiment, the Norfolk, was garrisoned at Colchester. Archibald Percival Wavell was weaned on regimental routine and at the age of five the regiment moved to India. Little wonder Wavell became a boy of Kipling's tales. The Wavells were just three years in India, but the impression never left the boy. From the fantasies of Kipling's morning sunrises was an easy step into the old fantasies of

Classics at Winchester. Whatever Wavell's talents and pleasures, the fact that he could easily have disappeared into the university never dawned on his father. Classics would always be there for pleasure, Wavell was sent to Sandhurst.

The structure of troop formations, the thoughts of generals in victory and defeat and the proper scrubbing brightly the ways of discipline and leadership were thought to be a proper Wavell way into adulthood. The empire, a quarter of the world population, was still in place in 1900. Curzon was still in India. The newly commissioned Wavell went too. It is important to see Wavell in this early career and reflect on his class, his classical education and his finest hours of soldiering where he defended and retained all that territory that was mainly British and that within very few years Wavell, possibly the most thoughtful of viceroys, would preside over one of the most disputed periods of British history at a moment when the people, or their leaders, cried Enough. He grew up and then fought in a British society often governed by those who assumed the empire would always be there. India was the foundation stone and the imperial structure fragile; Indian independence, even in the early 1940s, could not be contemplated by people with considerable power who perfectly understood the prospect that democracy in India could only lead to collapse of the raj. Churchill, who was at the forefront of those who could barely contemplate independence but knew it inevitable, would have to decide on whom he should send as possibly the last viceroy. Wavell was not on his list. There were seventeen good names including men who made themselves in other ways, for example Anthony Eden (the front runner), Samuel Hoare, Clement Attlee and R. A. Butler. The list was whittled quickly and some chipped off because their wives were not quite suitable as vicereine while others would be too important for Britain's future to be let free in India.

Wavell, who had left India for an Anglo-American conference, had been held back in England (the rest of the family still in India) by Churchill, who was in two minds how to use his talents. Wavell was a person needed for a Big Job; his military career had proved that. But what big job? Churchill took a lot of persuading that the reduced shortlist for India should include Wavell. If there was a single deciding influence on Churchill's choice of Wavell it came from the departing viceroy, Linlithgow, who had been all but exhausted by the posting he had held since August 1935. Linlithgow could not carry on although a large proportion of India felt he should do so. He had had enough. He saw Wavell as his successor and as the man who could tidy up India after the war and then put it on some sure footing towards becoming a proper industrial power even more superior to its considerably global position in industry. Churchill and Leo Amery, the secretary of state for India, both understood that Wavell had nothing to learn and India was an obvious appointment other than the small matter of Wavell being a candidate for Supreme Commander South-East Asia. The debate was long-winded and would have continued had not Churchill decided that Wavell should, in spite of so many misgivings, give up his job as C-in-C India and become viceroy. This was the first time that a viceroy had been appointed who had a personal belief that his very first task was to convince London he should be allowed to promote the idea that Britain believed India's future started as an independent nation. Wavell's observations of the British in India, from schoolboy to commander-in-chief, allowed him to doubt the nonsense about British brilliance as an imperial administrator. This proposition was not one that is imagined in modern tellings of the story of independence where the British know they are virtually being kicked out of the subcontinent. When Wavell went to India as viceroy there was still a belief among some, even in the India Office, that India could be persuaded to stay as the centre of the empire. This was not so. Moreover, there was no clear plan for how the two religious forces of India could come together and make one ambition work. Neither Jinnah nor Gandhi were allies of the British (nor of each other) but they were the only leaders whose leadership had to be recognised. It was a variation of they may be bastards but they are our bastards. To Wavell therefore, the solution was obvious and practical.

Wavell (basing his thinking on the ideas of Sir Stafford Cripps) wanted to bring leaders of lesser celebrity into a private debate that would produce an all-party government to replace the moribund executive council. Gandhi was anti-British and in jail. He would have to be released. Wavell was not getting off to a good start as King George VI pointed out, Gandhi was discredited at almost any but the street popularity level. Wavell's policy was seen in London as bound to fail. The Muslim League did not represent all Muslims and was also against the British. Wavell, not yet officially in office, was starting out with something of a failed plan. His instructions were simple: defend India and offer it self-government, but that did not mean independence.

Wavell arrived in India for that last time, a man determined to contain his instinct to work until the job was done and to even find time for the crossword puzzle, a couple of hours of golf and travel. During his first twelve months, he travelled some 30,000 miles in reviewing the estate of India. In spite of Wavell's record, the government in London did not see him as a heavyweight administrator. If there was a plan for him it was to hold the fort until the war was done. After the war there would have to be change because there was an inevitability about it all, but still there was a die-hard school that said this was not the time to hand India to the Indians. Self-government perhaps with Dominionship? But at first sight, Wavell was not in the political plan. Indeed his first job in his first week was to solve a famine in Bengal. He used his army to distribute food and, where he could, bring in rationing. These were the sour days of British India. There was no one with any realistic plan. There was always hope and the mantra of the raj based on Nanny's instruction to her charges before the children's party: you will like it when you get there. Wavell's tours as a soldier meant that he 'knew' India. The soldier's view could never do for a viceroy. This time, he was expected to get closer to the heartbreak that was India in the 1940s preparing to run alone.

India was in famine and was a subcontinent with a self-described reputation as a bureaucracy and an experience of being able to cope with almost any disaster – none of which was true. Three million would die in the famine and there was little the administrators of India were able to do about it. They had not settled in properly before the viceroy and vicereine set out by day and by night to see the worst chance could do to the King's people. Calcutta, as ever, where dogs ate at corpses, where hundreds were daily piled into streets and alleys, where destitutes hoped for a few fingers of basic food while others about them never reached such fortune. As for Bengal, where the British supposedly ruled with some clarity, the viceroy wrote to London (and therefore King George VI) of the inability of the British to govern and the Indian administration to survive a crisis. Wavell soldiered through and therefore made a path to reaching some relief better than most could. The states and provincial administrators jealously guarded their domains and so little of value was done. Wavell persuaded Bengal to let the army help distribute food. Such an obvious task would make all the difference. It took an impossible time for the army to get access to stores. Elsewhere he set up refugee camps to better care for the destitute and forced administrators to agree to rationing, an imposition none wanted because the people would see this as punishment.

Wavell, the best viceroy to have been sent by the worst government to send him, understood that the time had come for the key figures to get what they said they had always wanted – independence. The overwhelming difficulty was that as ever those same leaders – particularly Gandhi and Jinnah – had to show their people they had triumphed and that they had got more than the other side. Gandhi was losing a following. Jinnah was ill. The viceregal nanny was in a very stubborn nursery of true power as opposed to protest power.

Neither Jinnah nor Gandhi did their people well. It was not possible for Wavell to avoid the politics that would drive Mountbatten to Partition four years on. Gandhi and the 'Quit India' campaign, Jinnah with the Muslim League and the quivering demand for independence. He brought to India a good general's brain. He sized up the situation, checked the opposition's capabilities and matched them with best-guessed intentions. He looked at his own resources and at how and for how long he might use them and what had to be guarded while he so did. Then, the hard part, he checked to see whether what he had seen and what he could do about what he had seen matched what his political masters wanted – should they know. All good soldiers should get through the first part. It is the last part that is the unknown. Wavell had this in front of him.

Churchill did not agree, even know what he wanted to do because he was dead set against independence and anyone who may consider it. Churchill's successor, the Labour prime minister Clement Attlee, knew something of India, and had been the deputy chairman of the Simon Commission to the subcontinent, but still could not do what was obvious. Wavell took another decision. All the while Gandhi and mostly, the leaders of Congress were still in prison, they would remain martyrs and heroes and so nothing would be accomplished. Wavell's suggestion that they should be released was bad judgement and based on an assessment that Gandhi was long past his best and could never regain his place in India's revolutionary politics. He presented on that basis a case for releasing Gandhi. London, with reluctance, accepted the views of the man on the spot. Gandhi was released and as Churchill had suspected and as Wavell got so very wrong, Gandhi did not go into retirement. Churchill had always thought Wavell never quite understood the man.

Yet even with the sense of the inevitable and with changing social and political ideas at home influenced by nothing in the bank and an understanding of a changed world but little idea what to do with it, India was too big a question. The questions had long been asked but few understood the consequences of the answers.

The historical image of the British refusing to let go and India led by Gandhi forcing them to do so have always been too simple to accept. Wavell, simple soldier, knew this. India had been changed with a decade of anticipating the end of imperial occupation and not self-government but first self-rule and then independence. The British failed to understand that it had no post-colonial history that told it who would have the country and who would know how to keep it running once the British had gone. Furthermore, the British never understood what independence was about. They saw it too simply as being

India without the British. They never understood that India could go to the office and sit down in the British chairs and just carry on being India learning to govern and run the trains. The viceroy establishment no longer had a role other than to say when it was going.

There was nothing in the British rule of India that could see how to move on even when some wanted to. There was no process in British history of giving back a country other than losing at war. Those who understood that the time had come did not know what to do, especially when the viceroy and the understanding of India clashed with what was wanted in London. Reading had been correct all along. There could be no solution until the Indians themselves found a common ground. That they never did was a reason for the tragedy of Partition. Wavell did not have to be a field marshal to know this. The answer had been found in the pocket of Rommel. Leadership at all levels when coming together has to understand how far each can look ahead, remember whence they had come and why. Wavell could have used this simple doctrine to anticipate the collapse of hope brought about by the war and the inevitable vulnerability of those who would see India and everything it had represented as part of the thus far unaccepted end of empire as seen in the raj.

Wavell was certain as early as the summer of 1944 that the raj was finished. If no other reason for the end, there was the way in which the British had failed to devise a workable future within the seemingly impossible framework of the internecine war in India. The main players, Gandhi, Jinnah and Churchill, who had aged into their own reputations, made no concessions, saw no others' reason and hurt so much. Gandhi was facing rejection, Jinnah was dying and Churchill would never understand how he too had been rejected by the nation he had saved. There was a plan and it had a chance. In June 1945 Wavell produced what became known as the Breakdown Plan. The two essential points were:

A new executive council in which only the role of viceroy and the commander-in-chief would be held by the British. The rest of its members would be Indian. All the portfolios and heads of departments other than defence would be held by Indians. If there was to be disagreement in the council then the British would pull back to what now would be the six Pakistan provinces. Most importantly, this council was just a holding government committee. It would be succeeded by a new organisation drawn up and agreed in a permanent consti-tution. It had everything that was immediately needed to run India, which by then was a failed state. The Wavell Plan had two main paragraphs. The first covered withdrawal of the British from India. The second section said the way to avoid partition of India would be to keep it as one geographic unit. No name changing. No borders and this could be done by having people moving.

Wavell's very military withdrawal as opposed to an unstruc-tured retreat had Britain going in stages and would begin with the move from the Hindu provinces (Bombay, Madras, Orissa and the Central Provinces) thus creating space and facilities for the second stage. The general withdrawal would be completed by spring 1948 and there would be no mention of a Muslim state, later called Pakistan.

The next phase would be partitioning Punjab and Bengal. This would prevent, or so Wavell thought, any separate Muslim homeland. It was simple and it would stand a chance, or so it was thought at what became the failed Shimla conference at which Wavell laid it out. London said 'no' and so, perhaps, lit the fuse to carnage and Partition.

Wavell's plan would have more easily established political unity, prevented Begal and Punjab becoming Muslim states and he would have had something that compelled the Muslim League and Congress to agree. Importantly, the constitutional federation that came from the Wavell Plan would encourage Muslims to remain in the federation. In Britain the governing Labour administration did not believe there could be workable compromises:

> 'We are anxious to give India her independence and have put forward plans for achieving it. Unfortunately, the Leaders of the political Parties of India cannot agree among themselves on a plan for independence. We cannot in these circumstances allow a situation to develop in which there will be chaos and famine. Accordingly we must maintain our responsibilities until the Indian leaders can find a basis for accepting our offer.'

India went to war with itself. Wavell continued in his belief that an interim coalition government could avoid conflict. Instead, thousands died (4,400 in Calcutta alone) and on 2 September 1946 the Congress interim government started in power and Jinnah's Muslim League flew black flags in deep mourning. As late as December 1946 Wavell's Breakdown Plan went yet again to the prime minister's office for consideration. It all rested on the fact that rightly everyone believed that one side or another would not accept the detail and then what would happen. No one knew that, so no one wanted to vote 'Yes', especially when Wavell said a date had to be announced for independence and that would concentrate the minds of the Indian leaders.

The India and Burma Committee in Whitehall made alterations to the Plan and pointed out what Wavell had already pointed out – the Government of India Act. Soldiers at the high echelons are always aware of the laws within which they fight their battles. The oils burned for new wording. It never came. The Cabinet in London could never accept a military plan – and that it was – in a post-war world and particularly the image of the raj packing up and leaving India smacked of defeatism. Attlee's objection to effectively 'abandoning Madras and Bombay' left him to conclude that Wavell the soldier saw the operation as a military exercise and he felt reassured in his belief that Wavell was using military thinking when Cripps pointed out that he saw Wavell's plan as inevitably producing something like civil war and that would mean Britain being in the middle of it. Attlee was not looking for a way out of India. He wanted India to take over with a sense of the possible not the impossible.

On 3 January 1947 the India and Burma Committee rejected Wavell.

'. . . It was wrong to press too far the analogy of a military with-drawal. The operation now to be begun was not so much military as a political operation of great delicacy. It must be regarded not as a withdrawal under pressure but as a voluntary transfer of power to a democratic government. To an increas-ing degree the viceroy would assume the position of constitu-tional ruler and he and the British officials would act in conformity with the policy of that Government.'[2]

It would also be wrong to think that blimpism rejected Wavell. The astute Labour foreign secretary Ernest Bevin, the minister who would be the lead European in the campaign to set up NATO in 1949, called both his Cabinet and Wavell defeatists and it was Bevin who put pressure on Attlee to sack

Wavell on the grounds of that defeatism. Attlee needed Bevan and so Wavell would go.

India was ungovernable. Attlee asked Wavell to return to London for more talks. Wavell believed that would be a waste of his time and stayed in Delhi. He had written to London the letter no viceroy, no governor general had ever imagined that he would have to write. Field Marshal Wavell wrote that the British raj could survive no more than a year and a half. No more than that. He wrote that London should accept his judgement and arrange Britain's withdrawal from the subcontinent. Prime Minister Attlee carried out Bevin's wish and sacked him with one month's notice. The man who had listened to what had gone before, who understood at least partly what would be acceptable, was closer to right than any one else and had the courage to tell his masters it was time to go was dismissed as a defeatist. He went. Mountbatten arrived. He was not. He believed that a structured departure could be achieved over eighteen months. There is some evidence that whatever the extended period and Wavell's sure planning for withdrawal then the calamity that was to follow under Mountbatten would not have occurred. He and India suffered because earlier governments held on to India when they were no longer able to govern the subcontinent. The final irony was that when Wavell returned to London the India Committee asked him if he had advice for them as to how the British government should proceed.

Mountbatten became viceroy of India on 21 February 1947. On 15 August 1947 he was gone. It took just seven months to shut down three centuries of British imperial India. It was a botched job. It could not have been anything else.

When Mountbatten arrived he already had an impossibly

short time to do the job, not much more than a year. Within a few weeks he had no more time than the English cricket season. Of all the people the British could have sent none would have aroused so many different opinions; no one other than Mountbatten could have had so many enemies as well as supporters. It is however very likely that no one of the time could have done what Mountbatten did, with the possible exception of Wavell. Mountbatten was royal and lucky and had the most remarkable vicereine at his side – mostly.

Louis Francis Albert Victor Nicholas Mountbatten was born Prince Louis of Battenberg in 1900 at Frogmore House, Windsor. He was related to much of European royalty. At the age of thirteen he went to the Royal Naval College at Osborne on the Isle of Wight (the college moved to Dartmouth the following year). During his time in training, his father, the British first sea lord (head of the Royal Navy) had to resign because of the family's German name. Following the royal family example of changing names, Battenberg became Mountbatten.[3] Anecdotally, the young Dickie Mountbatten was not much put out by the change, announcing that, as one day he too would be first sea lord (and was), the name change mattered.

Mountbatten had more powers as viceroy than others had because India's future had been decided and the country was displaying the saddest and ugliest signs of collapsing under the weight of being ungovernable. Mountbatten was both fireman and undertaker. His specific order from London was to bring about independence along the lines recommended by the Cripps Cabinet Commission the previous year. There the nub of Mountbatten's effort was to create a united not a partitioned India. By the time Mountbatten arrived it was clear that apart from Gandhi, the main political leaders believed that partition was the only way. If the British had given more time to Jinnah during the years between the wars, there just might have been a unity option.

Indian independence has become synonymous with the name Gandhi. Gandhi was the surviving image, that travelled the globe, of the Indian independence movement. Perhaps for that reason, little popular attention has been paid to Mohammed Ali Jinnah.[4] The story of Mountbatten's viceroyalty is at the end also about Jinnah. Jinnah could not have changed the way independence went but his character is very much a lead in the drama Mountbatten faced.

Jinnah was a Muslim from a merchant's family of Karachi. His people had origins that dated back 500 years. In the 1890s, having been sent to a London business house, Jinnah read for the London bar and was called in 1896.

His politics were excited by sitting for hours in the Strangers' Gallery in the House of Commons. When he returned to Bombay to practise law, he had all the opportunities of becoming a magistrate and then a judge. However, Jinnah was a nationalist at heart and it is his political education that reminds us that Gandhi was not the first independence campaigner. Jinnah's hero, the celebrated constitutional expert and campaigner of the Indian National Congress, G. K. Gokhale, came before both Gandhi and Jinnah.[5] Gokhale was an academic who became a legislator and continued under the reforms that were to be introduced by Curzon's successor, Lord Minto.

Jinnah learned well and in 1909 was elected to the legislative council. His legal and constitutional training, and not a little of his merchant family instincts, allowed him to pilot through legislation that might otherwise have disappeared. In 1914, it was Jinnah who led the Indian National Congress delegation to London to lobby British MPs who were then contemplating the Council of India Bill.

Jinnah could see the disaster waiting without an India of absolute unity. He understood nationalism as a dangerous concept, as well as one that had moral might on its side. For example, the All-India Muslim League came about, as its name suggests, winning rights and privileges for Muslims. Jinnah said that radical groups could only destroy the hopes of the whole of India. It was he who brought the All Congress and the Muslim League together. It was Jinnah who negotiated in 1916 the Lucknow Agreement that parcelled up the numbers of reserve seats for Muslims on councils.

Until the end of 1918, if any governor or London politician wondered about the future of India, they had to know exactly what Jinnah was thinking. Jinnah was, during those three years from the beginning of 1916 to the end of 1918, the main figure in Indian politics and the leading advocate of Muslim–Hindu unity. What stopped Jinnah from becoming the first leader of India? Most certainly, the rise and popularity of Gandhi had much to do with it. He and Gandhi differed in one particular aspect: Jinnah believed that, to maintain multi-racial unity, India should have self-government, but beneath an umbrella of British constitutional rule. Gandhi championed non-cooperation. Gandhi had to destroy any advantage there was and to do that meant only independence.

By the end of 1920, Gandhi completely overshadowed Jinnah and the latter felt lonely enough to resign from Congress. Although he remained a senior figure in Indian politics, he was never again a formidable one until the end. He was offered a knighthood, which he turned down. In 1927, when the Simon Commission was established by London to look at the possibilities of constitutional reform, Jinnah once more attempted to bring the Muslim League and the Indian National Congress together. He failed. The provincial organisations, especially the powerful League of the Muslims in Punjab, were not on his side. He did not have control over provincial Muslim opinion. A sign of Jinnah's disillusionment was that in 1930 he saw the hopelessness of his position in India and began practising law in London. He did not go back to India until 1935, when he saw new opportunities through the general elections that would follow that year's Government of India Act.

Both Hindus and Muslims were unhappy about the ways in which the British would still control Indian politics. There was much to fight for, but that could only be done from a sound political base. By 1937, Jinnah did not have that. The Muslim League had not much more than a fifth of the seats that were won at the 1937 elections. A Congress party controlled Indian politics. Gradually, Muslims felt more and more threatened by the single-minded policies of the Indian National Congress. It took the Second World War for the British to realise they had to build up faith in Jinnah as a leader. He was the only person they could expect to counter the policies of Congress.

This was no constitutional morality on the part of the British. Instead – and here we go back to the shadow of the Indian Mutiny almost a century earlier – the British may have been disturbed by Congress, but more importantly during wartime was the fact that Jinnah would have influence over 50 per cent of the Muslim-based Indian army. By 1942, Jinnah's stock had risen over five years of confrontation. The Great Leader, as by now he was commonly called, was the Muslim political head, but he was still not a global figure as was Gandhi, who had an almost mystical reputation. The Muslims more than ever feared the Hindus. While the British government could not bring themselves to resolve the independence in India during wartime (Churchill would later be panicked into promising it quickly because he thought that would allow him to stay in power), Jinnah understood there would be a separate Muslim community.

In 1944, with Gandhi a most uncompromising leader, Jinnah failed to get Muslim states set up within provincial boundaries. In June 1945, there was a conference called at Shimla to bring the Indian National Congress and the All-India League together as an interim government before independence. The irony is that Jinnah, the man who had forty years earlier fought so hard to unite Hindus and Muslims, rejected the British idea because he maintained that each Muslim in the new interim government had to be a member of the Muslim League. In the 1945–6 elections, the Muslim League swept the board in the legislative and provincial assemblies. The confrontation between Jinnah and Gandhi could not resolve itself in unity.

There was a great deal left for Jinnah to do and, observing the cliché, little time. In the summer of 1946, there was a plan that would give most power at independence to combined Muslim and Hindu provinces and the states still governed by the princes. The government itself would be a coalition whose major role would be defence and foreign affairs. Jinnah accepted this, but tried to get the Muslim League on the same level of authority as Congress. Predictably, Congress would have nothing of this. Thus, Jinnah saw no alternative but to have quite separate states in the subcontinent. All his ambitions over decades, for a peaceful union of Hindus and Muslims, had failed. Gandhi had beaten him. Those 1946 elections had shown Lord Mountbatten, whose job it was to bring about independence and whose previous command of the region gave him the experience to understand the politics as well as the people, that the Muslim League, although opposed by Gandhi, was indeed a force to be reckoned with and that there was no possibility of creating anything else but a separate state.

Pakistan was to be created from the majority-Muslim states. Even the name would be artificial and made up from Punjab, Afghanistan, Kashmir, Sind and Baluchistan.

When the new government had arrived in London, led by Clement Attlee, its first foreign policy decision had to be what to do with India. Attlee knew exactly what needed to be done; most of all because the Labour leader had been a member of the pre-war commission led by John Simon. He had known since the thirties, as every politician should have done, that independence was inevitable. As far as Attlee understood the problem, there was no great chance of perfectly satisfying the Muslims of Jinnah and the Hindus led by Gandhi.

There had, during the Second World War, been quite serious explorations of independence plans, but nothing came of this planning. Sir Stafford Cripps, who had joined Winston Churchill's wartime coalition, had gone to India in 1942 to see how self-government might be arranged.[6] He had no success. By 1946, everyone concerned could see the very real possibility of approaching human disaster. In August of that year, direct confrontation between Muslims and Hindus left thousands dead. By October, Jinnah had lost his firm authority over the League, which was now in the interim government with Congress having abandoned Jinnah's demands for parity.

That was the situation when, on his arrival, Mountbatten told Jinnah that the British plan was that there would be a Pakistan, but it could only be made up of more or less Muslim Bengal and Punjab. Jinnah was beaten and had to accept what he described as a moth eaten Pakistan.[7]

Mountbatten was never going to convince Jinnah that unity was the better way and whatever the personal wish, Jinnah could never have carried the radical Muslims. Mountbatten was sworn in as viceroy on 24 March 1947 in the Durbar Hall and even though the urgency was there for all to see, there was among many of the British residents including those in the residence the hope that something 'would turn up'.

For decades there had been a suspicion and then a surprise that many of the expatriates really did not know what was going on in India. Viceroys had come and gone every five years or so with the impression that the white British who came to the parties, the balls, the feasts had little idea of India and that in spite of its geographical vastness, India and the Indians were outreaches of their society. The imagery of smoke where nothing should be burning, the noise of insecurity and uncertainty at street level, the derailed railroad, its travellers, robbed, raped and plundered. Senior Indians, both Muslim and Hindu, said India was burning yet British ladies wore cotton gloves to tea. There was a sense of all this when the new vicereine rang the tea bell.

Edwina Mountbatten's godfather was Edward VII as her name might suggest. Edwina inherited a fortune and the famous Palmerston Hampshire mansion Broadlands and Classiebawn Castle in County Sligo where Mountbatten would be assassinated by the IRA; she married Dickie Mountbatten in 1922. If it were a marriage made in heaven, then many heavenly wills were tested. Dickie had his Royal Navy and ambitions to be first sea lord; she became a globe-trotter and took many lovers – it was even rumoured that Edwina and Jawaharlal Nehru were in love. The Second World War may have saved Dickie and Edwina's marriage.

Edwina knitted for the Navy and Dickie did not go down with his ship. He commanded this and that seemingly by telling the few who had highest authority that he was the best man to do so. Mountbatten's high opinion of himself (often right) and the willingness of so many in high places to give in to him (often sensibly) made everything possible for them. In Asia after the war, where Mountbatten commanded the whole region (his title was Mountbatten of Burma), Edwina put together a rescue team to set off to find thousands of young prisoners of the beaten Japanese army. The story of the young Mountbatten is much more demanding than the one full of grand occasions. But the most publicly memorable moment was on them. When she arrived in India that early spring Edwina gathered her energies and instincts to help those who needed help and not necessarily clean cotton gloves. She was amazed at the gathering that looked blankly at her demands for assessments of who had and did not have.

Decades of vicereines had given much authority to get staff, equipment and fundraising to local nursing, hospitals, schools and what elsewhere would be charity work for those unable to help themselves. Memorials to the work vicereines either did or supported were and in many places remain on the road, building and wall and ward names. Willingdon and Wavell, the Minto Nursing Association, the Dufferin Fund Charities (Hariot Dufferin is still an admired vicereine in modern India for the work she did for children and continued to work at long after leaving India and up to her death in 1936). There too the Hardinge, Reading and Linlithgow rooms. True, some of the duties were inherited obligations. The efforts were no less. Yet when Edwina Mountbatten gave her first tea party for the resident wives she was faced with baffled British ladies who had no idea of the terrible and terrifying conditions of poverty, hardship and fear so many Indians were facing each day. Worse, there was an open anti-Indian sentiment that amounted to a

statement that Indians had brought hard times upon themselves and were spoiling it for the British. It was all too late to
get those involved who would be surprised by the encouragement. Moreover, what was the plan for after the British
flitted?

Edwina Mountbatten seemingly achieved the impossible;
certainly she managed what others had never seen the
importance of. Medical and social facilities were often chari-
table societies and not all had central planning and development. The vicereine, when others might have been bag-pack-
ing, worked every hour to bring together all those people
running medical and welfare groups to find out what they
did, what responsibilities they had and where work crossed.
Using the influence of Nehru, Edwina Mountbatten
managed to persuade the need for a Nurses Council that
would establish and continue nursing standards in India.
The ladies in gloves were not much consulted. Too late to
teach at that level.

In such anxious months Edwina Mountbatten was as well
known and, not unnaturally, partly though her undisguised
anti-colonial tendency, often more popular than her husband.
He preserved the dignity as well as the foresight to manage
security, administration and timescale of his unimagined brief
to be the most important viceroy since Canning; she was the
agitator using every courage and instinct to rescue the greatest
to the insignificant from the trauma that had started and would
only spill more blood and misunderstanding.

Mountbatten had been told 1948 was the time to go. Reality
said there was no chance that India could be governed until
then. Internecine feeling could bring full-scale internal war.
General 'Pug' Ismay on Mountbatten's staff did not, as early as
March 1947, believe India was governable for more than a few

months. His view was that what he called 'the mine' could explode at any moment. The frenetic viceroy's headquarters was something designed by a movie director. No one moved without purpose. Every movement was in response to something anticipated. The assumption was that the enemy was at the stockade gates.

Mountbatten's note to Prime Minister Attlee needed no explanation.

'Each party has its own solution and does not at present show any sign of being prepared to consider another . . . unless I act quickly I may well find the real beginning of a war on my hands'[8]

He did have a war on his hands. It was in India and the sort of confrontation that could last decades. In April, just a few days after his arrival, Mountbatten was being read security reports that promised what he had feared, 'the real beginning of a war.' Three weeks after Mountbatten assuming office Agra, Amritsar, Calcutta, Delhi itself and Peshawar were put under curfew because of rioting. Gandhi and Jinnah joined political hands and issued a statement condemning violence. It was a false declaration. Jinnah did not believe it and neither he nor Gandhi had talked it over, but Jinnah, introspective in ill health perhaps, had given up using violence, he said. Nevertheless he had signed their declaration and so in theory he could not go to war with Hindus or anyone else. Whether that was Jinnah not quite up to his own mark or not, it only suggested that it was another example of him not being in command, but still worth Gandhi's sense of publicity to be seen with him and to be seen getting the better of him. On reflection, Gandhi was less important also. If that were not enough, an increasingly bewildered viceroy had to contend with the Sikhs, who were now demanding an independent state of their own. It could only get worse for Mountbatten and it did. He did not trust any of the main characters, the Muslims, the Hindus, the Sikhs and almost every hour he heard reports of skirmishes and worse across India.

In London, Attlee and his government could hardly believe what they were hearing from the viceroy's summer residence at Shimla. The Mountbattens were actually applauded by a hostile, armed crowd of thousands but probably because he was wearing his jungly greens, uniform that matched their own persuasion. The crowd were Muslims and green was their Islamic colour. This was the point at which the Cabinet talked about the consequence of replacing Mountbatten. The prime minister's private office recognised that the moment was so grim that no politician wanted to get 'India – Failed' on their CV. Attlee listened to his office but when a note came through that a minister should be sent with full powers to wrap up India as quickly as could be no minister was available. Far too busy. Attlee recalled his viceroy. This was May 1947. For the moment as far as the public in the United Kingdom and India understood, independence was not due until the following year. Mountbatten's view was that if handover were to be brought forward then Nehru and some others might well accept Dominion status only. Churchill promised Attlee that his Conservatives would support a bill that had Dominion Status stamped across it.

On Mountbatten, Churchill remained a sceptic and so was cautious about the offer of early conclusion and therefore Dominion status rather than complete independence, which in the background had been the work of Edwina. Nevertheless there was too the Mountbatten enthusiasm for Dominion status as a means of having India in the Commonwealth, which the viceroy believed would be a good vehicle for global settlement of dispute and so peace. What Churchill thought remained important even though he was in opposition. Mountbatten needed Jinnah to give way and Churchill was the only person Jinnah would listen to.

Mountbatten, back in India, called all the Indian leaders together. He had the plan. It was partition with arrangements for which side the states should join and most importantly with Dominion status and membership of the Commonwealth. If at some future date either side wished to leave the Commonwealth and become totally independent then so be it. Mountbatten was straightforward with them:

> 'I have always felt that once it was decided in what way to transfer power, the transfer should take place at the earliest possible moment but the dilemma was that if we waited until a constitutional set up for All-India was agreed, we should have to wait a long time particularly if partition was decided on . . . The solution to this dilemma which I put forward is that His Majesty's Government should transfer power now to one or two Governments of British India each having dominion status as soon as the necessary arrangements can be made. This I hope will be in the next few months.'

Congress and the Muslim League said 'yes' immediately. The Hindus voted for the partition of Bengal and the Punjab Assembly did the same. Even Gandhi had to accept the Congress Working Committee's decision to accept the plan. Jinnah had to accept the plan but it was nothing more than he had rejected earlier. On 3 June 1947 the partition plan was announced. If the people of the Muslim-majority areas so desired they would be allowed to form a separate dominion. A new Constituent Assembly would be constituted for that purpose. In case there was partition, there would be a partition of Bengal and Punjab, if the representatives of the non-Muslim-majority districts of the two provincial legislative assemblies so desired. The Legislative Assembly of Sind would decide as to whether its constitution should be framed by the existing or a new and separate Constituent Assembly. In view of its special position a referendum would be taken in the North-West Frontier Province to ascertain whether it would join Pakistan or remain in India. In case of partition of Bengal there would be a referendum in the district of Sylhet (Assam) to ascertain whether the people would join the new province of East Bengal. In case of partition of Punjab and Bengal a boundary commission would be set up to demarcate the exact boundary line. Legislation would be introduced in the current session of the parliament 'for a transfer of power in 1947 on Dominion status basis to one or two successor authorities according to the decision taken under the plan. This will be without prejudice to the right of the Constituent Assemblies to decide in due course whether the parts of India which they represent will remain within the British Commonwealth.' The congress accepted the plan with some objections. Jawaharlal Nehru in his broadcast speech commended the Mountbatten proposal. He said:

'For generations we have dreamt and struggled for a full independent and united India. The proposal to allow certain parts to secede if they so will, is painful for any of us to contemplate. Nevertheless, I am convinced that our present decision is the right one even from the larger view point.'

The India Independence Act was law in the third week of July. The Act stated that as of 15 August 1947 the British no longer owned India. The two territories – India and Pakistan – would each have a governor general or a single governor-general could serve both. The governor general would not be appointed by the British government because Britain no longer ruled. The King could officially appoint as head of the Commonwealth. Historically important, the governor general would no longer be called viceroy and the British monarch would no longer be called Emperor or Empress of India. Of course, there was more to it than Mountbatten packing his pusser's grip and he and Edwina being at Bombay for the Friday sailing. In his final dispatch to King George VI, Attlee and the India–Burma Cabinet Committee there was a realistic foretaste of the demons already at work on the futures of the two states. An edited version of Mountbatten's final report is at the end. In some ways it says why it was always going to be difficult from the first attempts to find a way to independence and why success would bring conflict.

There was at the time among Indians but less among those in Whitehall an interest in how it was that Mountbatten, with all his setbacks and having been in India for just a few weeks, managed to get agreement, especially through Nehru. Thoughtful observers said, probably correctly, that no one other than Mountbatten with his quarterdeck genius could have done it – especially if he had people who could make the impossible happen, people like Edwina Mountbatten and Pandit Nehru.

The consequence of what had happened, the closing down of more than 300 years of British history, was not simply an exclusive matter between the British and the Indians although the typefaces in India and England were much stretched. The

Times of India's splash *Birth of India's Freedom* was followed in
the *Hindustan Times* with a common enough blandness, *India
Independent: British Rule Ends*. The *Statesman* was thought-
provoking: *Two Dominions Are Born*. The *Civil & Military
Gazette* launched that morning with *Murder and Arson Reach
New Peak – Walled City Veritable Sea of Flame*. Then the *New
York Times*, the most famous paper in the land that was the first
to break away from Britain, the United States of America,
skipped the celebrations and on its front page: *India & Pakistan
Become Nations: Clashes Continue*. Walter Lippmann writing
in the *Washington Post* did not forget his manners to an old
friend:

> 'Perhaps Britain's finest hour is not in the past. Certainly this
> performance is not the work of a decadent people. This on the
> contrary is the work of political genius requiring the ripest
> wisdom and the freshest vigour and it is done with all the
> elegance and style that will compel and will receive an instinct-
> ive respect throughout the civilized world. Attlee and
> Mountbatten have done a service to all mankind by showing
> what statesmen can do not with force and money but with
> lucidity, resolution and sincerity.'

Mountbatten would have thought so. The role and seals of
office of viceroy were boxed away on the night of 14–15 August
1947. But that was not the end of the story and certainly not
Mountbatten's. Mountbatten was immediately sworn in as the
first governor general of independent India and remained in
India until June 1948[9]. This was no quiet period of handover
of power. The centre of Mountbatten's immediate concern
was Kashmir. He had handed over Kashmir to the wrong man.
Partition of the Indian subcontinent was an act of religious

separation. Muslims would have the new state of Pakistan. Hindus would have India. Among that partition were the 650 plus small states owned and run by the princes, the native states. This system would not do for the provision of democracy. On the death of a prince, the state would come under the rule of his family successor. So there had to be agreement to join India and Pakistan and the rule of the small state would be from either of those democracies. When it came to Kashmir, the constitutional succession seemed simple. It was not. Kashmir's prince was Maharaja Hari Singh. He was Hindu. His people, Kashmiris, were mostly Muslim. In theory, Kashmir should be part of Pakistan. The Maharaja being a Hindu would have none of that. Mountbatten allowed him his way and instead of joining the new states, Hari Singh said Kashmir would be a neutral state. It was never going to work. Pakistan and India went to war to claim Kashmir and still do. Mountbatten had ordered British troops into the Kashmir Valley against the Muslims. Nehru was determined to get Kashmir firmly into India and Churchill was calling him an enemy of Britain and telling Mountbatten that he, Mountbatten, was very wrong to have sent in his troops. The Muslims were Britain's allies.

The Mountbattens went on 10 November 1947 to England for the marriage of the then Princess Elizabeth and Prince Philip. As soon as they had gone, Nehru went to Kashmir and promised that Kashmir was Indian and the two would 'ever remain together.' In the middle of this crisis, the Mountbattens were hardly speaking. Back in England, Edwina Mountbatten was openly seeing her former lover, the conductor Malcolm Sargent, and Mountbatten seeing something of his former mistress Yola Letellier. Back in India, Mountbatten found that the Pakistanis planned to refer the matter of Kashmir to the relatively new United Nations. Significantly the UN was in the process of partitioning Palestine between Arabs and Jews. The Jews were preparing for independence. Nehru did not want the UN anywhere near Kashmir. Referring the problem to the UN would be an admittance that Kashmir was at war. Pakistanis were accused of incitement in Kashmir. To cap it all, Afghan tribesmen, armed by the Soviet Union, had moved into Kashmir. On 12 December 1947 there was some relief when Pakistan and India announced they had reached agreement on the assets each would take from Partition. It made no real difference. If there could be revolution in Kashmir, then it could spread to Punjab and from there to Delhi. In London, Attlee was accepting that Mountbatten was the failure that caused the catastrophe. He threatened to have him replaced. Mountbatten would see that as the greatest insult. Attlee started to give him military orders, including one not to move into Pakistan even as a perceived defensive manoeuvre. Major Attlee had no doubt that he was rightly advised in London. There were mass demonstrations and industrial strikes and student protests. Mountbatten, now a mere governor general, was helpless. Kashmir, about which most in Europe had never heard, was on the verge of becoming another front line in the emerging Cold War, which was exacerbated by Pakistan's annoyance that while America was about to officially recognise the newly created state of Israel, the US made no attempt to recognise Kashmir – and never did so. The Russians believed that the British had a pact with Pakistan and that the Americans were ready to push the Russian involvement to a public accusation at the UN. How to resolve the chaos? There was always the Gandhi factor.

The riots continued. No city was safe. Gandhi declared a fast. His view was typically simple and even obscure. He said that India would become a prison and perhaps it would be better that he continued his fast until his end when 'He will call me.' His fast restored to some extent Gandhi's popularity, which had suffered through the means of independence and Partition. There was, as he said daily and public prayers, an attempt on his life by a bomb thrower. Gandhi escaped. Not the next time. He lived in Birla House and, after sharing goat's milk with his grandnieces, Gandhi, supported by his grand-nieces, walked in the colonnaded gardens to the stand where he prayed with the crowds every day. From the crowd, Nathuram Godse, a Brahmin, stepped in his way and shot him three times in the chest with a small Italian handgun. The old man was dead. The irony? Gandhi the greatest pacifist of them all was carried to his funeral pyre on an army gun carriage. It was time for the British to finally go. So they did.

CHAPTER XV

THE BRITISH IDENTITY

The first viceroy, Canning, was installed in 1858 during the bloodied Indian Mutiny. As Mountbatten was packing his bags in 1948 more people were being killed than during the whole eighty-nine[1] years of the British raj.

The Sepoy Rebellion, or the Indian Mutiny, took place because the British never understood the people they ruled. The tragedy of Midnight's Children came because the British still did not understand the people they had ruled.

Imperialism had its own arrogance and demanded brilliance among those Christian kings, princes and governors who would rule and quietly govern and indifferently minister justice. None was that brilliant and India was ruled but not governed. Dalhousie was right again.

The viceroys ruled with the authority they had been given under the Crown of Victoria and right to the end viewed their subjects with the same nineteenth-century paternalism verging on nuisance. There were twenty viceroys between 1858 and 1947. Fifteen English (mostly Eton and Oxford – there were few options), three Scottish and two Irish. None was Welsh[2]. Most were aristocrats, a couple were strapped for cash and all married well. Their vicereines (an affected title) were often bored, were style leaders, did good works, had monuments built in their memory. One died on the way home, one died in India and was buried there. Not a few wasted away and died shortly after returning to England. The term of office was typically four to five years and most viceroys had good careers afterwards. Some left India mortally wounded by the stresses and the climate. One was described as arriving as a young man and five years later seen hobbling away on sticks and dead not long after. Another assumed he ruled by God's command. Another's hand shook with fatigue, another's with alcohol. Two were shot at. One of them died there and then; the assassin was said to be a madman. Some of it was about dressing up, durbars and elephant rides but certainly not all of it. The viceroys might have ruled Versailles. They were grander than the monarch they represented. They dressed exquisitely in exotic surroundings and tossed aside rough and sweaty clothing for unnoticed servants to gather and, in fresh linen, carried on ruling distinctively clean.

Apart from Edward VIII, British monarchs from Victoria onwards looked middle class, like retirees and unnecessarily small. When seen, they were usually sitting down so most thought they were smaller. They were dull because they were not Stuarts, whom the British had preferred and about whom they made up songs when at war. Their dress sense came from what they wore to protect them from British weather and a belief that they would get closer to stags. They came out and visited in public but, not being clever, were never shown anything for more than four or five minutes, which was enough to be good at pretending that they knew what they were being shown. Then, they carried a worried look in the eyes that suggested that they did not know their subjects and what they were saying – nor did they.

The viceroys on the other hand always looked the part even if they were quite small, even round. Most of all, unlike royalty, viceroys were usually clever and aristocrats and, also unlike royalty, were invariably at home with the people. There was no telling if the monarchs liked their viceroys although Victoria had a few of their wives as ladies of the bedchamber and wrote to them in the middle of mutinies about interesting visits from third cousin grand dukes from small places in Europe. Victoria, who, after Melbourne was no longer her mentor, kept herself wrapped up and was one to inquire after the health of viceregal families and sent warnings that India was no place for people of their sort. On one occasion she persuaded the prime minister not to send a family prone to sneezing to Calcutta but to send the father out to govern New South Wales. He lived into his eighties and died a marquess. There was a son whose life was taken in the Great War.

Within the cliché, born to rule, was the viceroy. It was a title aristocrats were mostly indifferent to other than that there was no question of the level of their authority. Even the well-educated aide de camp, the senior clerk, the intellectual Indian activist was aware that beyond the title and the trappings of the residence, the man who walked two paces in front of the whole of India had one thing they would never have: background. Even the seediest had background. Moreover, the viceroy's lady came with quarterings. In short, the viceroy was used to being quite apart from other men and their wives quite aware of social positions and families that mattered. Yet, if the raj had a single image that contrasted completely with that of the silk-cloaked viceroy it was the man in the loin cloth and dhoti he had spun himself: never at any time less than saintly. Gandhi was the single person who saw through the dressing-up box of the raj's hero.

The British were good at imperialism because they never believed in equality and liberty and did not know what was meant by fraternity. The viceroy emerged from the mystery (especially to the Indians) of the London appointment system which owed more to the power of the appointer than the significance of the appointment. Thus the viceroy was by distinctive appointment treated like royalty. Was this so extraordinary in a state that had more than 650 princes and once had more than twice that number?

The story about inequality has many shades. Not all is rags to riches, certainly not the other way. It is more about circumstance. The depth of inequality is longer in the telling because one side develops at an uncompetitive rate and so the story takes longer to tell. So it was with the raj and its viceroys – almost nine decades of imperialism that the British struggled to end because mostly they did not want to and that the Indians struggled to end because until they did, they did not own their own country. Moreover, does the platform for the debate set itself up because the debate is obvious or because none is listening and therefore the orator shouts until they give him a rostrum and his authority is visible?

The most powerful authority in the debate of independence for India was not the government in London, certainly not the viceroy, and there was no government in India, that of course, the whole point of the debate. The focal point after the Great War and the point when independence was never a euphemism was Gandhi. Jinnah sadly never encouraged the way in which a minority leader should have been. And the authority of Gandhi lay not in his mysticism and his own mystery nor even the intellectual dishevelment that when whispered appeared as wisdom. The eight viceroys who knew Gandhi, and all who hung to their imperial tails, feared him. They did so not as they might have imagined fearing a tiger – which not one of them would – but because they did not understand him. They did not easily know what he was. In the way that a monarch represents the identity of the nation, so the instinct of the viceroy was that Gandhi must be the nation. There were too many of his own people, people who had his ear, who were as uncertain as British India as to the identity of this loin-clothed man dressed for effect for he had no other status to appear as a spectral guru. To know what they feared tells us something of who they were. The Inner Temple lawyer who had worked the streets and late courts of South Africa was not the lawyer disguised as a scrawny figure from central casting. Lord Irwin, from a letter Gandhi sent him on 2 March 1930, had the clue set anyone would need. In it is what he wanted Irwin to think he was like and what he wanted of the British. In short, Gandhi, never motiveless, would, when he had finished the letter, know a little more of himself. Most of all, Gandhi came to represent an image that could demonstrate if not the weakness of the raj, then certainly its inability to step outside its set-piece way of the superior caste of them all, the British, dealing with a simple, logical manner of telling them that soon, just within his lifetime, all would change. They would during those dragged-out discussions resort to the thought that if Gandhi had not been so Gandhi about it all, then independence would have come sooner. The only image taken away from the post-Second World War to the end the raj, was that of Gandhi. His remains the only surviving universal image of that period. It is doubtful that many, including the British and in spite of Hollywood's best efforts, will remember Mountbatten's part as much as they do Gandhi's. As for the other nineteen viceroys, it is a pretty sure bet that not one of them is remembered by name and certainly there is no public record of anything that happened while they were in India. Yet they were exceptional men.

Canning seemingly stopped work only to bury his wife. Elgin lasted a year. Lawrence was brave. Mayo was the only one to be murdered. Northbrook was hard to please. Lytton – *hoc virtutis opus?* Almost. Ripon. Admired the Indians and hated child labour. Dufferin. Knew where it would end but ahead of his time. Lansdowne redrew the map of India. Who lives where but not who runs what. Elgin. An ancestor bought the Marbles. Curzon. Divinely appointed. Kitchener thought not. Hardinge. Wasted opportunities. A bomb all but killed him. Brave. Chelmsford. India should have had more like him. Reading. This, the 1920s. Needed a brilliant man. He was that. Irwin. Later Halifax. Triumphant (Delhi Pact 1931) and at 6'5" looked it. Willingdon. Good cricketer. Linlithgow. Did not deserve so much criticism, especially from Churchill. Wavell. They should have believed him about his military plans and the inevitability of chaos at Partition. Mountbatten. None could have done what he did better. Except Wavell. Yes, they were exceptional if only because they ruled in exceptional circumstances.

No other nation had such a single tapestry that centred its empire so far in other climates, other religions and languages. Sent to India was no Coventry. How the British behaved in India through the nineteenth and early twentieth centuries was noted round the globe. The monarch was a reflection of the British identity and each rule gave the British and the rest of the world a chapter heading: the Georgians, Victorians, the Edwardians. Then it stopped. After the Great War the world decade by decade abandoned separate identities as

Communism, Naziism, Superpowerdom etc. identified a period without human character, only ideology. There was an exception: how the world saw the British. Because of the biggest and widest-spread empire of all and particularly because of the British India of the raj, how others saw the British was frozen. Was the perception of the British in, say, the twenty-first century, based on what others saw as colonial history of the British and the image of sometimes misguided, certainly assumed importance among the lower British castes, of a right to rule. The preservation of an active aristocracy in the United Kingdom with its exclusive St James's clubs, pecking order of titles, right to rule taken for granted and a significance of schooling – among the lower classes as well as the upper caste – was all part of a tableau that insiders as well as outsiders thought would be found in British colonial, especially Victorian history. Even in modern literature and movies including television series, the relevance and reality of British rule over more than 400 million people in more than 50 states is rarely more than stereotypical. Paul Scott's *The Raj Quartet* is a distinguished literary exception to this proposition. Two final thoughts present themselves: should the raj in the instinctively counter-colonial mood of the twenty-first century, the Raj, mainly from 1858 to 1947, be condemned as a tragedy for its peoples and a shame on the British? Secondly, is the twenty-first-century image of the British that emerged from their colonial occupation of the subcontinent. Even, do many outside the United Kingdom see the British as a nation moulded by the raj and comfortable still in that image?

The first part of the debate on colonial heritage is hard to fathom the further we move on from that period of the raj. There is of course the uneasy assumption that the white British of today do not find the subject of much interest. The argument is simplified here in the view that it was a long time ago,

the attitudes, realities of politics, international relations and the
history of acquisition in India was not an invasion for territory
but commerce and it developed in the world that was then,
then and not now, during five centuries. During the monarch's
rule through her viceroy, we have the images of what we see as
the British in India. As remarkable as are the reputation of Lord
Clive and certainly the misfortunes of the governor general
Hastings, most of the imperial history is rarely approachable
and loses what is to be touched in a muddle of names, places
and history not easily understood by modern British generations. The raj, led in India by easily learned and remembered
characters such as Canning, Curzon, Gandhi and Jinnah
together with incidents imagined and truthfully recorded such
as the Black Hole, the Mutiny and almost anything put to paper
and script by Kipling and onwards. Even the moment in the
1920s when the monkeys in Jakho were all shot dead by the
staff of the Bevan-Petmans after one monkey savaged Mrs.
Bevan-Petman's new petticoat (that had been left on a table). It
was the act of outrage that could have been ordered by Robin
Hood's sheriff of Nottingham 600 years earlier. Authority over a
monkey in the twentieth century promised a social as well as a
political debate and the sacking of a colony of a different kind.
Those were the times. ('The vengeance against attacking
seagulls in modern times might have a place in that debate –
these too were the times). Honed to the colonial bone, the
seemingly irresolvable debate in a simple form comes down to
one question: did the way the British ruled India in the seventeenth, eighteenth, nineteenth and finally the twentieth century
(each century produced different debate content) divide and
then subdivide India society, or was it 'compelled to adapt to
native styles, and merely preside in glorified manner over the
more subterranean movements of Indian history?'[3] Khilnani

makes the fundamental point that whatever and however we think through the economic and social state of India at any time during the British occupation, the British 'intrusion' was 'unambiguous and resounding'. There is the main response to what we might mean by occupation and rule. Firstly, the British arranged India as best they could on the subdivision of the land by sections and administrative ties and means – almost a huge subdivision of counties and councils to be found in the changing United Kingdom. The British also drew the boundaries of nations in the subcontinent and the state itself. It is not a surprise that the state boundary had not been decided for centuries. We might remember that continental Europe was not distinctly drawn until the twentieth century and the Middle East until the 1920s and 1930s. British rule in India changed directions and purpose not because there was military, political and commercial advantage but because of ambitions for the state's purpose. Part of the British function was to protect India from the destructive powers within its own societies. Thus the raj had a mediaeval role. In the European Middle Ages the ruling of the people by recognised boundaries, and the principle of ruling demarcations, allowed those ruled to understand who they were and the obligations and consequences of defending boundaries; without direct reference to times past, the British were in the late nineteenth century ruling in a form based in this manner. India presented its own cultural, religious, regal and geographic opposition to rule of this manner and not entirely incidentally, because its own leaders, although not always recognised by its own people, were members of the new elite – the age of political understanding of hitherto unthought-of ideas. By the formation in 1885, for example, of the Indian Nation Congress Party, India was filling with ideas that were not simply a radical or rebellious dialogue among the seekers of change in the country. Congress was founded by Dinshaw Edji, Dadabhai Naoroji and, importantly, Allan Hume. Here was a moment that would ring true in the twenty-first century. Congress asked that privileges the British expected should also be given to Indians who lived within and kept the laws of the land. The debate that followed over Good or Bad Colonial Rule deserves more space than available here. It should begin with the observation that the formation of Congress in the 19th century was encouraged by the viceregal system and challenges the idea that the British were simply out to rule for their own good. The major British problem to find an integral way in which India could be governed (if not ruled) by the Indians. There was no reliable agreement nor proposal among Indians themselves. In the modern debate over democracy in India and the British rule, it could be remembered that the reform in the British Isles was also limited. The parliamentary reform that followed the 1932 Act was hardly a transposable example to set in India. It took more than a hundred years for the British to get universal suffrage after the 1832 Reform Act. The British in India could never have done anything but reflect, if at all, reform in Britain. That did not happen although the viceroy et al worked during the post-Mutiny period to reach the first stage of reform and self-government – and failed.

From the beginning, in the 1860s, an influential and often caring part of the British ruling classes in India understood that India would be better self-governed, but failed to find a structure in such a complex society to bring that about. As the raj moved from that politically developing late nineteenth century into the radically open thinking of the new century the debate among influential British was not suppression but between those who saw the future as self-government and those who not simply accepted, but promoted the idea of future independence. India itself was split between the ideas of how to govern itself; the difference was on religious grounds and certainly by the beliefs and actions of the leading personalities. Some saw and others feared that ridding India of the British would produce a colonialism of another kind and one even less trustworthy to be in charge of care of the nation that was not and could hardly be imagined as one nation. There was too the single widest uncrossable width between the British Empire and in particular, the raj – language.

The most influential non-British English-speaking community was in India. The English-speaking Indians, especially those sent 'back' to the London and Oxbridge houses and those given places at the Indian university and college system that followed the 1835 Education Minute of Thomas Babington Macaulay, became the truly significant servants of the British raj. The rest of India was the servants of the servants. The English speakers were essential to the raj. The English language gave the Indians who had it position and therefore power in the raj and therefore they preserved the raj in order to preserve their own power and, of course, the power of the hordes whose numbers and reliance on patronage strengthened their own positions. Khilnani points out that these same anglophiles had their own Marathis, Bengali or Hindustani milieu and this was the quality that made them useful porters to the British. Here again that suggestion that because of the times and not simply the chance, Indians with exceptional talents and opportunities helped create part of the raj still misunderstood and certainly regretted. If that sounds as if it could not have been different, the answer is that the British did go to establish a raj but when they came to govern as a raj for 200 years or so, through them India had become a different subcontinent with a structure of its society, real and not imagined enemies without and within and for the first time an attempt at one ruling structure and, just as the rule of the princes had produced often terrible ways of government and living far worse than the British rule, so an intermediary Indian bureaucracy had in itself produced a significant moment in the history of rule in India that found itself in the school of imperial criticism.

From 1885 there was a constant debate on India's future. Before that formation of Congress, there had been no debate. Truly the weakness of that debate was the division between Muslim and Hindu and the hopeless misunderstanding that during the twentieth century when India, so often an intellectual hothouse, rarely included democracy in the opportunities of idealism until independence itself arrived. Like so much political, there comes a point when democracy is possibly the only hope when all fails.

The image of the viceregal British continued while the rest of the world was gathering a speeding identity of technologies, personalities and even fractious ideologies. But British India carried on. While others were confirming their identities, the raj still had its regalia, its durbars and elephants ridden in ceremonial loyalties, its stiff upper lips, its display of aristocracy envied as well derided and all supported by monarchs who still behaved like royalty and above all its language with phrases and tales from the raj scattered at will and without question, nor hope, copied by most of the world. In short (and not without discussion) the identity of the British was created by the images of the British and her viceroys in India.

When the raj was over, the British themselves prolonged the image. Partly thanks to the new BBC where cultured pronunciation was standard in broadcasting to the people, the adoption of something approaching, but more perfect than, an aristocratic drawl could be heard from castles to bus stops.

Privilege, knowing one's social place and arrogance was everyday class distinction of either aspiration of condition. The
people mimicked plain tales of the raj and quietly mocked
those who did not understand or those who did, and hated it.
The final irony is that the British went to India to better their
positions and live a style they would never have afforded in
England and with a manner with which they would soon have
been found out as social climbers and ordinary people, trade
even, trying to play above their station in life.

Long after the British left India, the style, the Received
Pronunciation and the perfect understanding and place of the
British who had never even been to India was part of the British
identity. Moreover, long into the twentieth century, the one
social aspect the British failed to accept in India, the caste
system, had its place firmly in the United Kingdom. So from
the raj came the international recognition of what was British
(and largely exists still) and how the British wanted others to
see them. Long after Mountbatten packed his pusser's grip, the
raj lived on in suburban England. Its image does still.

NOTES

Introduction

1. The Dutch built their first forts on the West African coast in 1598 in what is now Ghana, West Africa. The Dutch East India Company was formed in 1652 and established itself in both the East Indies and the West Indies. The French empire was late Napoleonic, but covered much territory that was relinquished quickly yet survived in Africa. There are some French who would mention Quebec. In the second century BC the borders of an imperial China emerged, when Qin Shi Huang conquered and brought together the dynasties and kingdom that would form the beginnings of the Chinese empire and eventually the state itself.
2. 1394–1460.
3. 1577–1580.

I   In the Beginning

1. Elisabeth I, *Proclamations*, British Library.

II   The Retreat to India

1. Strachan, Michael, *Sir Thomas Roe 1581–1644. A Life*, Salisbury, 1989.
2. 1556–1605.
3. Kaye, John William, *The Administration of the East India Company*, 306, Richard Bentley, London, 1853.
4. Charles II had gone into exile and constitutionally his late brother's

Therefore the throne was restored and the King returned never having been anything other than Charles II even during the Commonwealth.

5. Aurangzeb (1618–1707), third son of Shah Jahan, Emperor of India. His unremarkable grave is to be seen in the mausoleum at Khuldabad.

IV Cornwallis and Shore

1. Smith became the first Lord Carrington, whose successors included Margaret Thatcher's foreign secretary between 1979 and 1982.
2. *The Asiatic Journal and Monthly Register for British and Foreign India, China and Australasia* Vol. 10 January–April 1833.
3. For a breakdown of social and military structures of the army in the poor recruiting areas, see *India Office Records, Military Department Records 1708-1959* and *Haileybury Archives 1749-1857*
4. Hastings, Francis Rawdon-Hastings, First Marquess of (1754–1826).
5. The Marchioness of Bute, ed. *The Private Journal of the Marquess of Hastings KG, Governor-General and Commander-in-Chief in India.*
6. 1839.
7. Macnaghten, William Hay (1793–1841).
8. Pollock, Sir George (1786–1872).
9. Durand, Sir Henry Marion (1812–1871).
10. Napier, Sir Charles James (1782–1853).
11. See Cohen, Stephen, *The Indian Army, its Contribution to the Development of a Nation*, Berkeley, Ca., University of California Press, 1971. Also, Barat, Amiya, *The Bengal Native Infantry, its Organization and Discipline, 1796–1852*, Calcutta, K.L. Mukhopadhyay, 1962.

V Dalhousie and Land Grabbing

1. Warner, W.L., *The Life of the Marquess of Dalhousie*, 1904, Vol.1, p24.
2. Dalhousie, James Andrew Broun-Ramsay, Knight of the Thistle and Marquess of Dalhousie(1812–1860).
3. Prasad, S.N., *Paramountcy under Dalhousie*, 1946, 106.
4. Canning, Charles John, 1st Earl (1812–1862), third son of the British statesman, George Canning (1770–1827).

VI Why the Sepoys Rebelled

1. Hunter, W.W., *The Indian Empire: Its People, History and Products*, Trubner, London, 1886.
2. Lawrence, Sir Henry Montgomery (1806–1857).
3. For more on this see, Dr Saul David, *The Indian Mutiny 1857*, Viking, London 2002.

4. Dalrymple, William, *The Last Mughal – the Fall of Delhi, 1857*, Bloomsbury, London 2006.

VII   The Mutiny

1. Barnard, Major General Sir Henry, 1799–1857.
2. Anson, The Hon. George, 1797–1857.
3. Reed, Major General Thomas, 1796–1883.
4. Havelock, Brigadier-General Sir Henry, 1795–1857.
5. After independence the British monarch continued to appoint the governor general, on the advice of the Indian government, and this continued until India became a republic. Thus the last governor general was not Earl Mountbatten of Burma but Chakravarti Rajagopalachari, who took his place in the Viceroy's House, was styled His Excellency and served as governor general from 21 June 1948 to 26 January 1950.

VIII   Canning and the First First Lady

1. Government House or Governor's Palace and today the official address of the 37 state governors of India.
2. Harewood Collection, Lady Canning's papers, Leeds District Archives.
3. *Lord Canning's Diary*, 29 February 1856, at The British Library, family correspondence, MS47469.
4. Benson, Arthur C., ed., & Viscount Esher, ed., *The Letters of Queen Victoria, 1837–61*, John Murray, London, 1907.
5. In, *The Tears of the Rajas*, Ferdinand Mount, Simon & Schuster, London, 2015.
6. Low, General Sir John, 1788–1880. Was back in India at time of Mutiny and, with Canning, advocated leniency.
7. Edwards, M., *British India 1772–1947*, Sidgwick & Jackson, London, 1967, 231.
8. Cunning, H.S., *Canning, Earl*, Clarendon Press, Oxford, 1891, 250.

IX   Elgin, Lawrence and Mayo

1. Bruce, James, *Letters and Journals of James, Eighth Earl of Elgin*, With Foreword by Arther P. Stanley, Dean of Westminster, March 4, 1872.
2. First Viscount Halifax and in 1862 secretary of state at the India Office.
3. ibid. 498.
4. ibid. 499.
5. Ibid.
6. Schweinitz Jr., Karl de, *The Rise & Fall of British India*, Methuen, New York, 1983, 175.
7. Ibid.
8. S. Gopal, *British policy in India, 1858–1905* (1965) · D. Pal, *Administration*

of Sir John Lawrence in India, 1864–1869 (1952) · H. Tinker, The founda-
tions of local self-government in India, Pakistan and Burma (1954) · Barclay
Fox's journal, ed. R. L. Brett (1979), 229–30 · BL OIOC, Lord Lawrence
MSS · BL, Iddesleigh MSS, Add. MSS 50023, 50024.

9. For more see Chandra, Sudhir, 'The Income Tax (1860–1872): A Study in
   Basic Contradictions.' The Indian Economic & Social History Review, 1966.

10. Strachey, Sir John, India, its Administration and Progress, Macmillan,
    London, 1903, 192.

X   Queen Empress and Northbrook

1. Hunt, G.W. By Jingo was publicly acceptable swearing and meant By Jesus.

2. Northbrook, Letter to Bessborough, 25 January 1875, Northbrook MSS, MS
   Eur. C.144/23.

3. Northbrook to Mallet, 2 Oct, 29 Oct 1874, Northbrook MSS, MS Eur. C.
   144/23.

4. Northbrook to Dufferin, 5 Feb, 30 July 1886, Northbrook MSS, MS Eur. C.
   144/5; Hansard 3, 317, 6 July 1887, 902.

5. Fowler, Marian, Below the Peacock Fan, Penguin Books, Canada, 213.

6. Edwardes, M., British India 1772–1947, Sidgwick & Jackson, London, 1967, 182.

7. Northbrook to Salisbury, 26 Feb, 12 Sept 1875, Salisbury MSS, HHM/3M/
   E12.

8. Lytton, Earl of, Wilfrid Scawen Blunt, Macdonald, London, 1961.

9. Judd, Denis, The Lion and the Tiger. The Rise and Fall of the British Raj,
   Oxford University Press, 2004, 93.

10. Denholm, 161.

11. Dufferin to Sir William Gregory, 1 January 1888, India Office, Eur. F130/29.

12. Bengal Tenancy Act 1885, Oudh Rent Act 1886, Punjab Tenures Act 1887.

13. Dufferin to Sir Harry Verney, 6 January, 1888, BL OIOC, Eur. F 130/29A.

14. For a fuller insight into Dufferin see Richard Davenport-Hines, entry for
    Blackwood in Oxford Dictionary of National Biography.

15. Forrest, George W., The Administration of the Marquis of Lansdowne as
    Viceroy and Governor-General of India, 1888–1894, Office of the
    Superintendent of Government Printing, India, 1894, 2.

16. The Administration of the Marquis of Lansdowne as Viceroy and Governor-
    General of India, Leopold Classic.

17. ibid.

18. ibid.

XI   Curzon

1. Curzon, George Nathaniel, 1st Marquess, 1859–1925.

2. David Gilmour, 'Curzon, George Nathaniel, Marquess Curzon of Kedleston

(1859–1925)', *Oxford Dictionary of National Biography*, Oxford University Press, 2004; online edn, Jan 2011 [http://www.oxforddnb.com/view/article/32680, accessed 4 April 2017.

3. Bradley, John, ed. *Lady Curzon's India*, Beaufort Books, New York, 1985, 21.
4. ibid., 25.
5. The Indian capital was moved from Calcutta to Delhi in December 1911. In 1927 it was renamed New Delhi and inauguration took place in 1931 when Lutyens' city of homes and government buildings were opened. In August 1947 as part of independence celebrations, New Delhi was named as the capital of independent India.
6. Broderick, St. John, TO COME
7. This partition was revoked in 1912. In 1947 Bengal was split between India and the new state of Pakistan.
8. Kitchener of Khartoum and of Broome, Horatia Herbert Kitchener, 1st Earl, 1850–1916.
9. Mosley, Leonard, *Curzon: The End of an Epoch*, Longmans, Green & Co. Ltd.

XII Minto–Morley Reforms

1. Minto, Gilbert John Elliot-Murray-Kynynmound, 4th Earl of, 1845–1914.
2. Morley, Viscount, 1838–1923.
Ripon, George Frederick Samuel Robinson, Marquess of, 1827–1909. His father, the Earl of Ripon, (1782–1859), is remembered as Viscount Goderich, sometime chancellor of the exchequer; very briefly in 1827, prime minister and colonial secretary. Ripon became viceroy in 1880 and, like his father, colonial secretary (1892–1895).
3. Macaulay, Thomas Babington, 1st Baron, 1800–1859.
4. Since 2001 Kolkata and the capital of West Bengal and the centre of East India's commerce and university education. In 1690 the Nawab of Bengal granted the East India Company a trading licence and the Company developed the region and in 1793 established the city as the British capital of all that it ruled on the subcontinent.
5. Delhi became New Delhi in 1927 and then capital of India in 1931 as New Delhi and capital of the Union of India in 1947.
6. Mahatma, Sanskrit: venerable or high-souled.
7. Named after Judge Sir Sidney Rowlatt, the president of the Delhi committee that sat to protect India during wartime from sedition.
8. Tunzelmann, Alex von, *Indian Summer, The Secret History of the end of an Empire*, Pocket Books, London, 2007, 46
9. Fischer, Louis, *Life of Mahatma Gandhi*, Vintage, London, 2015, 202.
10. February 1922 Members of Congress and Kalifists attacked Chauri Chaura police station. 22 officers were killed.

XIII   The Last Grandees

1. British Library, Asia, India, Indian Independence. Gandhi No. 77.
2. Birkenhead, Earl of, *Halifax: the Life of Lord Halifax*, Hamish Hamilton, London, 1965.
3. Gandhi studied at the Inner Temple.
4. Roberts, Andrew, *The Holy Fox*, Phoenix, London, 1991, 42.
5. Dawson to Irwin, 2 January, 1931, (C152/19/1/199b).
6. I Zingari, founded in 1845, is the most exclusive cricket club in the world. The name comes from Spanish, gypsies. The side wanders, it has no clubhouse nor a ground of its own and wears its colours upside down in the year that an English monarch dies – or so is said.
7. Nehru, Jawaharlal, *Autobiography*, Bodley Head, London, 1936, 294.
8. In *The Viceroy at Bay*, Collins, London, 1971, 21.
9. Trench, Charles Chenevix, *Viceroy's Agent*, Jonathan Cape, London, 1987, 204.

XIV   In the End – the general and the admiral

1. Fort, Adrian, *Archibald Wavell: The Life and Times of an Imperial Servant*, Jonathan Cape, London, 2009.
2. 3 January 1947.
3. King George V was monarch when the royal family changed its name from Saxe-Coburg and Gotha (arrived at through Prince Albert of Saxe-Coburg and Gotha to Windsor.
4. Jinnah, Mohammed Ali, 1876–1948, the first leader and architect of Pakistan.
5. Gokhale, Gopal Krishna, 1866–1915.
6. Cripps, Sir Richard Stafford, 1889–1952.
7. 30 April 1947. See Jinnah Papers, Vol. 1., Pt. 1.
8. Viceroy's Report No. 1 31 March 1947.
9. The second governor general of the Dominion of India was Chakravarti Rajagopalachari 1948–1950.

XV   The British Identity

1. The raj ended in 1947. Mountbatten became first governor general of independent India and left in 1948.
2. Canning was Anglo-Irish, Elgin Scottish, Lawrence Anglo-Ulster, Mayo Irish, Northbrook English, Ripon English, Dufferin English, Lansdowne English, Elgin Scottish, Curzon English, Minto Scottish, Hardinge English, Chelmsford English, Reading English, Irwin English, Willingdon English, Linlithgow Scottish, Wavell English, Mountbatten English.
3. Khilnani, Sunil, *The Idea of India*, Hamish Hamilton, 1997, London, 21.

A SHORT BIBLIOGRAPHY

The bibliography, to reflect even a short record of Indian publishing and splendid authors, would run to hundreds of pages. Below is a useful and short selection that will bring further and enjoyable reading. A longer list I leave to readers.

Oriental and India Office Collection, including Chelmsford and Montagu *Summary of Constitutional Reforms of India*, British Library.

Allen, Charles, *A Glimpse of the Burning Plain*, Michael Joseph, London, 1986.

Bhasin, Raaja, *Simla, The Summer Capital of British India*, Rupa, New Delhi, 2011.

Ball, Charles, *History of the Indian Mutiny*, London 1858–9, London Library.

Ball, Stuart (ed) *Conservative Politics in National and Imperial Crisis, Letters from Britain to the Viceroy of India 1926–31*, Ashgate, 2014.

Bayley, Emily, *The Golden Calm: An English Lady's Life in Moghul Delhi*, London, 1980.

Bayly, C.A., *Imperial Meridian: the British Empire and the World 1780–1830*, London, 1948.

Beaumont, Penny & Roger, *Imperial Divas*, Haus, London, 2010.

Bence-Jones, Mark, *Clive of India*, Constable, London, 1974.

Bernier, Francois, *Travels in the Moghul Empire, 1656–68*, Oxford, 1934.

Bradley, John (ed) *Lady Curzon's India, Letters of a Vicereine*, Beaufort, New York, 1985.

Bruce, James (ed) *Letters and Journals of James, Eighth Early of Elgin*, Alex Struik, London, 2012.

Butler, Iris, *The Viceroy's Wife, Letters of Alice, Countess of Reading from India, 1921–1925*, Hodder & Stoughton, London, 1969.

Chakravarty, Gautam, *The Indian Mutiny and the British Imagination*, CUP, 2005.

Chawla, Muhammad Iqbal, *Wavell and the Dying Days of the Raj*, OUP, 2011.

Chenevix Trench, Charles, *Viceroy's Agent*, Jonathan Cape, London, 1987.

Dalrymple, William, *The Last Mughal, The Fall of Delhi,1857*, Bloomsbury, London, 2006.

David, Saul, *The Indian Mutiny*, Viking, London, 2002.

Edwardes, Michael, *A Season in Hell*, Hamish Hamilton, London, 1973.

Fowler, Marian, *Below the Peacock Throne, First Ladies of the Raj*, Viking, London, 1987.

Glendevon, John, *The Viceroy at Bay*, Collins, London, 1971.

Guha, Ramchandra, *India After Gandhi*, Macmillan, London, 2007.

Holmes, Richard, *Sahib: British Soldier in India*, Harper Collins, London, 2005.

Judd, Denis, *The Lion and the Tiger, the Rise and Fall of the British Raj*, Oxford University Press, 2004.

Kaye, J.W., *A History of the Sepoy War in India, 1857–8*, London, 1877.

Kahn, Yasmin, *The Great Partition*, Yale, New Haven, 2008.

King, Peter, *The Viceroy's Fall, How Kitchener Destroyed Curzon*, Sidgwick & Jackson, 1986.

Lee, Christopher, *This Sceptred Isle, Empire*, BBC Books, London, 2005.

Longford, Elizabeth, *A Viceroy's India, Leaves from Lord Curzon's Notebook*, Sidgwick & Jackson, London, 1984.

Maclagan, Michael, *Clemency Canning*, Macmillan, London, 1962.

Malaviya, Madan Mohan, *Pandit M.M. Malaviya's Letter to the Viceroy and Governor General of India on the Indian Situation*, Bombay, 1932.

Mersey, Viscount, *The Viceroys and Governors-General of India 1757–1947*, John Murray, London, 1949.

Mill, James, *The History of British India*, Baldwin, Craddock and Joy, London, 1917.

Montgomery Hyde, H., *Lord Reading*, Farrar, Straus and Giroux, New York, 1967.

Mosley, Leonard, *Curzon: The End of an Epoch*, Longmans, London, 1960.

Mount, Ferdinand, *The Tears of the Rajas*, Simon & Schuster, London, 2015.

Mowbray, Patricia, *Florence Nightingale and the Viceroys*, Haus, London, 2008.

Nicolson, Nigel, *Mary Curzon*, Harper & Row, San Francisco,1977.

Nugent, Lady Maria, *Journal of a Residence in India 1811–15*, Oxford University Press, Oxford, 2014.

Roberts, Andrew, *The Holy Fox*, Weidenfeld & Nicolson, London, 1991.

Roberts, of Kandahar Lord, *Forty One Years in India*, Richard Bently and Son, London, 1897.

Rose, Kenneth, *Superior Person*, Weidenfeld & Nicolson, London, 1969.

Rudolph, Lloyd I and Susanne Hoeber (eds) with Kanota, Mohan Singh (Commentary), *Reversing the Gaze*, Westview Press, Boulder Colorado, 2002.

Russell, W.H., *My Diary in India*, Routledge, Warne, and Routledge London, 1860.

Schweinitz, Karl de Jr., *The Rise & Fall of British India, Imperialism as Inequality*, Methuen, New York, 1983.

Surtees, Virginia, *Charlotte Canning*, John Murray, London, 1975.

Tharoor, Shashi, *Inglorious Empire: What the British Did to India*, C Hurst, London, 2017.

Tharoor, Shashi, *An Era of Darkness*, Aleph, New Delhi, 2016.

Thesiger, Frederic John Napier, *Speeches by Lord Chelmsford*, Government Monotype Press, Simla, 1919.

Tytler, Harriet, *An Englishwoman in India: the Memoirs of Harriet Tytler 1828–1858*, Oxford University Press, Oxford, 1986.

Walker-Smith, Derek, *Lord Reading and His Cases*, Chapman and Hall, London, 1934.

Ziegler, Philip, *Mountbatten*, Collins, London, 1985.

INDEX